Mastering Social Studies Skills

GERARD J. PELISSON

Third Edition

AMSCO SCHOOL PUBLICATIONS, INC.
315 Hudson Street   New York, N.Y. 10013

For my wife, Margaret

About the Author

GERARD J. PELISSON taught social studies in New York City high schools for more than 20 years. In addition, he coordinated teacher training and student development programs for the High School Division of the New York City Board of Education. Mr. Pelisson is also the author of *Mastering United States History Skills* (Amsco).

Cover Design: Merrill Haber
Cover Photo: John W. Serafin
Composition by: Sierra Graphics, Inc.

Please visit our Web site at: www.amscopub.com

When ordering this book, please specify:
R 757 W or MASTERING SOCIAL STUDIES SKILLS, SOFTBOUND
or
R 757 H or MASTERING SOCIAL STUDIES SKILLS, HARDBOUND

ISBN 1-56765-651-X (Softbound edition)
ISBN 1-56765-652-8 (Hardbound edition)

TABLE OF CONTENTS

PREFACE

Mastering Social Studies Skills offers in one volume a comprehensive approach to the most important skills needed in Social Studies. This workbook combines traditional Social Studies skills with skills that were once taught only in an English class or a Mathematics class, but which are also very important for successful work in Social Studies.

The seven units of the book are organized as follows:

In **Unit One,** the reading skills most important to Social Studies are taught.

In **Unit Two,** the long-neglected, but important skill of writing is developed.

In **Unit Three,** students are taught how to use textbooks and reference books, as well as the resources of the library and the Internet. Unit Three also gives useful hints on how to study for and take tests.

In **Unit Four,** students are taught how to read tables, charts, and graphs and how to interpret photographs, drawings, and cartoons.

In **Unit Five,** students are taught how to read maps, how to recognize land and water forms on a map, and how to use directions to locate places on a map.

In **Unit Six,** students are taught latitude and longitude to find the exact location of places on a map. Latitude is also used to teach climate zones, and longitude is used to teach time zones.

In **Unit Seven,** population, relief, rainfall, climate, natural vegetation, land use, and product maps are taught. Knowing how to interpret these different types of maps is an essential Social Studies skill.

All reading selections, writing exercises, maps, and illustrations reflect as closely as possible the kinds of material students are likely to encounter in their Social Studies classes and textbooks. While the contents of this workbook are directly related to topics taught in Regional Studies courses, the skills are applicable to work in any Social Studies course.

Each chapter of this book:

• assumes that students are starting with very little knowledge of the skill to be taught.

• is written to be understood by students who usually have difficulty comprehending what they read.

• begins with a simple example and leads to a more complex example and understanding of the skill.

• asks questions throughout the chapter so that students can see if they are understanding a skill as it develops. (Answers and their explanations are given in each chapter. Through checking their answers with the ones given, students can see immediately if they are learning the skill.)

• contains numerous exercises, giving students a chance to demonstrate their understanding of each skill.

Mastering Social Studies Skills can be used at the beginning of a term to teach all the skills at once, or it can be used to supplement any standard textbook throughout the term. The 31 chapters in the workbook can be used as full class lessons taught by the teacher or as self-study lessons that enable students to work independently at their own pace.

The book can also help prepare students for standardized tests and minimum competency examinations in Social Studies. Students who master the skills in this book will have a much greater chance of doing well in all their Social Studies classes.

For their advice and assistance in developing one or more of the editions of this book, the author wishes to thank:

Sidney Langsam, Irwin Pfeffer, and Angelo Purcigliotti, former Assistant Principals, Social Studies; Sara Goodblatt and Edward F. Schwartz, former Social Studies teachers; all of New York City High Schools; Barry Berk, Assistant Principal, Social Studies, Adlai Stevenson High School, New York City; and James A. Garvey and Joseph Straus, Social Studies teachers, DeWitt Clinton High School, New York City.

GERARD J. PELISSON

1/12/22

CHAPTER 1
Finding the Main Idea

The ability to do something well means that you have a skill. One of the most important Social Studies skills is reading. In this chapter, you will learn how to become a better reader by developing the skill of picking out the most important idea in a selection, or story.

After you have finished reading a selection, you should be able to tell what it is all about. In other words, you should be able to find the main idea.

A selection may contain one or more paragraphs. Each paragraph is a group of sentences that tells you about one main idea. The main idea of a paragraph is usually found in the first sentence of the paragraph. But this is not always true. Any sentence in the paragraph may contain the main idea. Or it may not be found in any one of the sentences in the paragraph. When this is the case, you have to think about what all the sentences in the paragraph mean together to find the main idea. If a selection consists of more than one paragraph, the main idea of each paragraph adds up to the main idea of the entire selection.

Read the following selection. After you have finished reading, look for the main idea of each paragraph. Then decide what the main idea of the entire selection is.

Paragraph 1

Japan is a land of steep hills and mountains. The <u>rugged</u> landscape makes it difficult to find good farmland. Crops can be grown on only 15% of the land. Yet Japan has to feed about 130 million people. So it is important to use every piece of land that is good for farming.

Paragraph 2

The most important crop in Japan is rice. But large fields of potatoes, soybeans, and grains such as wheat and barley can also be seen throughout Japan. On hillsides in some parts of the country, tea plants are a common sight. Some types of fruit are also grown.

Paragraph 3

Because Japanese farmers need most of their land for growing crops, not enough land is left over for raising large herds of cattle, sheep, and pigs. As a result, meat is rarely found on most Japanese

1

dinner tables. Some food is <u>imported</u>, but it is not enough to meet Japan's needs. To get more food, the Japanese look to the sea that surrounds their island nation. The many kinds of fish living in the sea provide Japan with a large supply of food. Without this food from the sea, the Japanese would not have enough to eat.

<u>rugged</u>: rough, uneven
<u>imported</u>: brought into a country

Place a check mark (✓) next to the correct answers to the questions.

1. The main idea of Paragraph 1 is

_____ (a) Japan has plenty of land on which to grow food.

_____ (b) The rugged landscape of Japan makes it difficult to find good farmland.

_____ (c) The Japanese do not eat very much.

What did you choose? In Paragraph 1, you read that it is difficult to find good farmland in Japan. Is there a sentence in Paragraph 1 that tells you that idea? Yes, the idea is included in the second sentence "The rugged landscape makes it difficult to find good farmland." This sentence states the main idea of Paragraph 1. Therefore, the answer to question 1 is (b).

2. The main idea of Paragraph 2 is

_____ (a) Rice is the most important crop in Japan.

_____ (b) Most farmers in Japan raise tea plants.

_____ (c) Japanese farmers grow many different kinds of crops.

Which answer did you choose? Is there any sentence in Paragraph 2 that tells you the main idea of the entire paragraph? No, each sentence tells you only about the different kinds of crops grown in Japan. The main idea of the entire paragraph is that many crops are grown in Japan. Therefore, the answer to question 2 is (c).

3. The main idea of Paragraph 3 is

_____ (a) The Japanese do not like to eat meat.

_____ (b) Meat is rarely found on most Japanese dinner tables.

_____ (c) The Japanese would not have enough food for everyone if they did not have fish to eat.

Which answer did you choose this time? Choice (a) states that the Japanese do not like to eat meat. This idea is not even contained in Paragraph 3, so choice (a) cannot be the correct answer. Choice (b) states that meat is rarely found on most Japanese dinner tables. This statement is part of the second sentence of Paragraph 3. But it contains only one piece of information, not the main idea of the entire paragraph. Choice (c) states that the Japanese would not have enough food for everyone if they did not have fish to eat. Most of the sentences in Paragraph 3 lead to the idea stated in choice (c). Therefore, the answer to question 3 is (c).

4. You have read all three paragraphs of the selection on Japan. Which one of the following groups of words states the main idea of the entire reading selection?

_____ (a) How the Japanese catch fish

_____ (b) How the Japanese provide food for themselves

_____ (c) How the Japanese farm their land

Which answer did you choose? Is there any one idea contained in all three paragraphs? Yes, all three paragraphs in the selection tell about providing food for the Japanese people. Therefore, the best answer to question 4 is (b).

No one is born knowing how to read or how to pick out important ideas in a selection. All of us have to learn these skills through much practice. The following exercises will give you more practice in finding the main ideas in what you read.

USING WHAT YOU HAVE LEARNED

A. Place a check mark next to the correct answers to questions 1 to 5.

1. Reading skill is the ability to read

    _____ (*a*) fast.

    _____ (*b*) well.

    _____ (*c*) slowly.

2. When you have finished reading a selection, you should be able to give

    _____ (*a*) every fact of the selection.

    _____ (*b*) every date in the selection.

    _____ (*c*) the main idea of the selection.

3. A paragraph is a

    _____ (*a*) group of sentences that tells you about one main idea.

    _____ (*b*) phrase.

    _____ (*c*) main idea.

4. The main idea of a paragraph

    _____ (*a*) is always stated in the first sentence.

    _____ (*b*) is never stated in the paragraph.

    _____ (*c*) may be stated anywhere in the paragraph or not at all.

5. The main idea of a selection is

    _____ (*a*) what the selection is all about.

    _____ (*b*) always contained in the first paragraph.

    _____ (*c*) never stated in the selection.

B. Read the following selection, which is made up of three paragraphs. After you have finished reading, look for the main idea of each paragraph and of the entire selection.

Paragraph 1

Many people think of Africa as a poor continent that has only deserts, jungles, and rain forests. It is true that many parts of Africa have land too poor to be farmed. But it is also true that Africa is a continent with great wealth. Africa contains some of the largest supplies of minerals in the world.

Paragraph 2

All over the world, diamonds and gold are considered to be two of the most valuable minerals. Nearly all of the world's diamonds and more than half of the world's gold are mined in Africa. Africa also provides large amounts of cobalt, copper, manganese, phosphate, uranium, and petroleum.

Paragraph 3

Most of the minerals mined in Africa are sold to other areas of the world. Countries all over the world need the minerals found in Africa. In fact, many factories in the United States and Europe would have to shut down if they could not buy Africa's minerals. Indeed, the minerals of Africa <u>benefit</u> the whole world.

<u>benefit</u>: help

Place a check mark next to the correct answers to questions 1 to 4.

1. The main idea of Paragraph 1 is

____ (a) Africa has more minerals than any other area of the world.

____ (b) Africa has much good farmland.

____ (c) Africa's great wealth lies in its minerals.

2. The main idea of Paragraph 2 is

____ (a) More than half of the world's gold is mined in Africa.

____ (b) Africa is an area of the world rich in diamonds.

____ (c) Africa produces large amounts of many valuable minerals.

3. The main idea of Paragraph 3 is

____ (a) Europeans have dug many mines in Africa.

____ (b) The minerals of Africa are used to benefit the whole world.

____ (c) Nearly all the minerals found in Africa are sold to the United States and Europe.

4. The main idea of the entire reading selection is

____ (a) Africa is an area of the world rich in minerals.

____ (b) Nearly all of the world's diamonds are mined in Africa.

____ (c) Nearly all the minerals found in Africa are sold to other countries.

5. Make up a title that will help you remember the main idea of this reading selection.

_____

_____

C. Read the following selection, which is made up of three paragraphs. After you have finished reading, look for the main idea of each paragraph and of the entire selection.

Paragraph 1

<u>Transportation</u> is important to the people of South America. <u>Modern</u> ways of traveling can be seen in every country of this large continent. Modern boats move up and down the rivers. Railroads and

airlines connect <u>major</u> cities. In fact, more than 50 airlines now fly to and from the major cities of South America. Land travel is almost impossible in the large sections of South America that are covered with rain forests and high mountains. The coming of the airplane has made traveling easier over these rugged areas.

Paragraph 2

The automobile is probably the fastest growing way of traveling in South America. South Americans want automobiles for the same reasons that the people of the United States want them. Automobiles are easy to use. They allow people to live far from where they work, and they make it easier for people to take trips. Throughout the continent, there are more than 2,708,000 miles of roads. Of these, only 350,200 are paved. But more roads are being paved every year to meet the growing use of automobiles.

Paragraph 3

Even though there are many modern ways of traveling in South America, not everyone can use them. For many people there, the most common way of traveling is by foot or by boat. Travel by train, bus, or automobile is almost impossible in the high mountains and in many areas of the rain forests. Some areas of South America have no roads at all. In these areas, pack animals and oxcarts are used to carry people and goods. The old ways of traveling are still useful in this rugged land.

<u>transportation</u>: way of traveling
<u>modern</u>: new, up-to-date
<u>major</u>: important, great

Place a check mark next to the correct answers to questions 1 to 4.

1. The main idea of Paragraph 1 is

____ (*a*) South America has many rain forests and high mountains.

____ (*b*) South America has many railroads that connect the major cities.

____ (*c*) South America has many modern ways of traveling.

2. The main idea of Paragraph 2 is

____ (*a*) Automobiles are easy to use.

____ (*b*) The automobile is the fastest growing way of traveling in South America.

____ (*c*) South America has more than 2,708,000 miles of roads.

3. The main idea of Paragraph 3 is

____ (*a*) Some areas of South America have no roads at all.

____ (*b*) It is difficult to use trains, buses, and automobiles in the high mountains.

____ (*c*) The old ways of traveling—by foot, pack animals, and oxcarts—are still useful.

4. The main idea of the entire reading selection is

 _____ (a) The automobile is the fastest growing way of traveling in South America.

 _____ (b) The most common way of traveling in South America is by foot.

 _____ (c) South America has many modern ways of traveling, but it also has many old ones.

5. Make up a title that will help you remember the main idea of this reading selection.

_____

_____

D. Read the following selection, which is made up of three paragraphs. After you have finished reading, look for the main idea of each paragraph and of the entire selection.

Paragraph 1

My name is Victor Orlovsky. When I first went to school in the late 1970's, the Soviet Union was still in existence. My teachers would tell stories of how the Soviet Union was the most important country in the world. I was very proud to learn so many wonderful things about my country. We were a <u>military</u> power the equal of the United States, and our space program had put the first human being in space. Every four years, our athletes were among the top medal winners at the Winter and Summer Olympics. Russian music and <u>literature</u> were admired around the world. The list of accomplishments seemed endless.

Paragraph 2

By the late 1980's, I was old enough to understand that my country had many problems. The Soviet system was based on the Communist idea that the government should own and control farms, businesses, and industries. But under this system, the people never really <u>prospered</u>. Stores always had shortages of food and long lines. Families lived in small apartments, often sharing them with other families. Another serious problem was that many of the <u>ethnic</u> people living under the Soviet flag wanted their freedom. Little by little, I came to understand that the Soviet Union was not only a country. It was also an empire, forcibly controlling other countries that had their own history and way of life. All these problems finally led the people, including me, to demand an end to communism—indeed, an end to the Soviet Union itself.

Paragraph 3

I am still proud of my country, but today this means that I am proud to be Russian. Russia had been one of the 15 <u>republics</u> of the Soviet Union. It became an <u>independent</u> republic with the collapse of the Soviet Union in 1991. Like most Russians, I yearn for the day when Russia will be a truly modern and truly <u>democratic</u> country. We need better-paying jobs and better living conditions. Trade with other countries must improve. The more than 100 ethnic groups living in the country must learn to live in peace. Religious freedom and equality must be guaranteed. Above all, we need to make sure that our problems do not lead us back to communism. If we succeed in making Russia a truly modern and democratic country, I will have much to be proud of, and my country will again be one of the most important in the world.

<u>military</u>: having to do with soldiers, weapons, or war
<u>literature</u>: the writings of respected authors
<u>prospered</u>: became successful; had enough money
<u>ethnic</u>: having to do with a religious, racial, or national group
<u>republics</u>: forms of government in which the people elect representatives to run the government
<u>independent</u>: free, on one's own
<u>democratic</u>: having free elections of government leaders and/or representatives

Place a check mark next to the correct answers to questions 1 to 4.

1. The main idea of Paragraph 1 is that

   _____ (a) the Soviet Union still exists.

   _____ (b) in his youth, Victor was proud of the Soviet Union.

   _____ (c) Russian music and literature are admired around the world.

2. The main idea of Paragraph 2 is that

   _____ (a) there were always food shortages in the Soviet Union.

   _____ (b) many unresolved problems finally brought an end to the Soviet Union.

   _____ (c) Communist ideas needed more time to see if they could improve the lives of the people in the Soviet Union.

3. The main idea of Paragraph 3 is that

   _____ (a) Russia today is one of the most important countries in the world.

   _____ (b) the breakup of the Soviet Union caused more problems than it solved.

   _____ (c) Russia has many problems to solve before it is a truly modern and truly democratic country.

4. The main idea of the entire reading selection is that

   _____ (a) Victor did not support the end of Communist rule in the Soviet Union.

   _____ (b) Victor is proud to be Russian.

   _____ (c) Victor's pride in his country has not stopped him from seeing its many problems.

5. Make up a title that will help you remember the main idea of this reading selection.

CHAPTER 2
Finding Facts

As you have seen in Chapter 1, being able to pick out the main idea of a reading selection is an important Social Studies skill. Another important skill is the ability to find facts about people, places, and events that give more information about the main idea of a selection. A *fact* is true information or something that really happened.

The following reading selection contains many facts. Some of them are the date 1869, the number 5,000 miles, and the names of places such as South-West Asia/Africa and South Asia. Other facts in the selection can be found in complete sentences rather than in one or two words or numbers. For example, you will find this fact in the reading selection: "Ships carrying oil, rubber, and other goods pass through the canal almost every day." Look for these and other facts as you read the selection.

South-West Asia/Africa (South-West Asia also known as the Middle East) contains some of the busiest trade routes in the world. For this reason, South-West Asia/Africa is often called the "Crossroads of the World." One of the most important trade routes in South-West Asia/Africa is the Suez Canal, a human-made waterway connecting the Mediterranean Sea and the Red Sea. Since the Suez Canal opened in 1869, ships from many parts of the world have passed through it. By using the Suez Canal, ships sailing between South Asia and Western Europe shorten the trip by as much as 5,000 miles. Without the canal, ships would have to sail all the way around Africa.

Ships carrying oil, rubber, and other goods pass through the canal almost every day. Many of the ships bring these raw materials to the United States. The United States also uses the Suez Canal to send its products to many countries in Africa and Asia. Truly, the Suez Canal is one of the busiest trade routes in the world.

trade route: course of travel used to transport goods

---

1. South-West Asia/Africa is called the "Crossroads of the World" because it

   _____ (a) is in the middle of the world.

   _____ (b) has a lot of good highways.

   _____ (c) contains some of the busiest trade routes in the world.

Which answer did you choose? Is the answer to question 1 stated anywhere in the selection? Yes, the first two sentences state that South-West Asia/Africa is called the "Crossroads of the World" because it contains some of the busiest trade routes in the world. Therefore, the answer to question 1 is (c).

2. The Suez Canal is a human-made waterway connecting

   _____ (a) the United States and Europe.

   _____ (b) the Mediterranean Sea and the Red Sea.

   _____ (c) Africa and Asia.

8

Which answer did you choose? Is the answer to question 2 stated in the selection? Yes, the third sentence states that the Suez Canal connects the Mediterranean Sea and the Red Sea. Therefore, the answer to question 2 is (b).

3. The United States uses the Suez Canal

_____ (a) to send its products to countries in Africa and Asia.

_____ (b) to catch fish.

_____ (c) to get to Africa and Asia because there is no other way to go.

Which answer did you choose? Where in the selection does it state why the United States uses the Suez Canal? The next-to-the-last sentence says that the United States uses the Suez Canal to send its products to many countries in Africa and Asia. Therefore, the answer to question 3 is (a).

Now let us see some of the facts you have learned from this section.

1. South-West Asia/Africa is called the "Crossroads of the World" because it contains some of the busiest trade routes in the world.

2. The Suez Canal is a human-made waterway connecting the Mediterranean Sea and the Red Sea.

3. The United States uses the Suez Canal to send its products to countries in Africa and Asia.

These facts give you important information about South-West Asia/Africa and the Suez Canal. Use this information to answer question 4.

4. Which one of the following sentences states the main idea of the entire reading selection?

_____ (a) The Suez Canal connects the Mediterranean Sea and the Red Sea.

_____ (b) The United States uses the Suez Canal.

_____ (c) The Suez Canal is one of the most important trade routes in South-West Asia/Africa and in the entire world.

Which answer did you choose? The main idea is not just an important fact. The main idea is what the entire reading selection is about. Choices (a) and (b) state certain facts found in the selection. Only choice (c) tells you what the entire selection is about. Every fact in the selection points to the idea that the Suez Canal is a very important trade route. Therefore, the answer to question 4 is (c).

The following exercises will give you more practice in finding facts that support the main idea of a selection.

USING WHAT YOU HAVE LEARNED

A. Read the following selection. Then look for the many facts it contains and decide what the main idea of the entire selection is.

Millions of years ago, a great change took place in the surface of the earth in East Africa. The earth collapsed, leaving a long, deep ditch known today as the Great Rift Valley of East Africa.

The Great Rift Valley is really divided into two long valleys. The Eastern Rift, the larger of the two valleys, is about 4,000 miles long and 2,000 feet deep. In some places, it is more than 30 miles wide. The Eastern Rift runs through the countries of Ethiopia, Kenya, Tanzania, and Mozambique. The Western Rift starts in southern Sudan and runs through the countries of Uganda, Rwanda, Burundi, Zambia, and Malawi.

Most of the lakes of East Africa were formed when the Great Rift Valley came into being. As the earth cracked, water flooded many areas. Lakes Rudolf, Manyara, Nyasa, and Tanganyika are a few of the large lakes in the Great Rift Valley. The most important body of water in the Rift Valley is Lake Nyanza, the second largest fresh-water lake in the world.

Some of Africa's tallest mountains and volcanoes are found near the Great Rift Valley. One is Mount Kilimanjaro, the highest mountain in Africa. This 19,340-foot high mountain is located in Tanzania. The second tallest mountain in Africa is Mount Kenya, located in Kenya.

The tops of many of the inactive volcanoes near the Great Rift Valley contain wide, deep craters, or holes. The largest one in East Africa is the Ngorongoro Crater. About 2,000 feet below its top is the floor of this huge crater. The area of the crater floor is about 100 square miles. Today the craters, as well as other areas in the Great Rift Valley, are home to thousands of wild animals.

surface: the top layer or outside of something
collapse: to cave in, to fall apart

rift: a split, a crack
inactive: not in use, showing no sign of life or movement

Place a check mark next to the correct answers to questions 1 to 10.

1. The long, deep ditch in East Africa is called the

   ____ (a) Grand Canyon.

   ____ (b) Ngorongoro Crater.

   ____ (c) Great Rift Valley.

2. The collapse of the earth's surface in East Africa happened

   ____ (a) 20 years ago.

   ____ (b) 4,000 years ago.

   ____ (c) millions of years ago.

3. The Great Rift Valley is really divided into

   ____ (a) two valleys.

   ____ (b) five valleys.

   ____ (c) seven valleys.

4. The Eastern Rift is about

   ____ (a) 2,000 miles long and 2,000 feet deep.

   ____ (b) 4,000 miles long and 2,000 feet deep.

   ____ (c) 4,000 miles long and 4,000 feet deep.

5. The Eastern Rift can be seen in

   ____ (a) the Sudan.

   ____ (b) Zaire.

   ____ (c) Kenya.

6. Most of the lakes of the Great Rift Valley

   ____ (a) were there before the valley was formed.

   ____ (b) were formed when the valley came into being.

   ____ (c) have been empty for millions of years.

7. The second largest lake in the world is

___ (a) Lake Nyanza.

___ (b) Lake Manyara.

___ (c) Lake Tanganyika.

8. The tallest mountain in Africa is

___ (a) Mount Kenya.

___ (b) the Ngorongoro Crater.

___ (c) Mount Kilimanjaro.

9. The floor of the Ngorongoro Crater is

___ (a) empty.

___ (b) home to millions of people.

___ (c) home to thousands of wild animals.

10. Which one of the following sentences states the main idea of this selection?

___ (a) Thousands of wild animals live in the Great Rift Valley.

___ (b) East Africa contains many mountains and lakes.

___ (c) The Great Rift Valley and the mountains and lakes near it are important land and water features in East Africa.

B. Read the following selection. Then look for the many facts it contains and decide what the main idea of the entire selection is.

Before the 1970's, few American teenagers had ever heard of soccer. This is strange because soccer is one of the oldest and most popular sports in the world. In many countries in Europe, South America, Africa, and Asia, soccer is the national sport. It is so popular in some countries that huge soccer stadiums have been built to hold as many as 200,000 fans.

No one knows for sure where or when the game of soccer started. The Chinese played a game like it 2,500 years ago, and so did the Romans almost 2,000 years ago. But the modern game of soccer seems to have started in England. From there the game spread to other countries in Europe. In the late 1800's, European traders and sailors spread the sport all over the world.

Today, soccer is truly an <u>international</u> game. Every four years, teams from more than 100 countries compete in the World Cup championships. Hundreds of millions of people watch these championship matches on television, making them the most popular sporting event in the world.

Soccer did not begin to become popular in the United States until the mid-1970's. Since then, it has become the fastest-growing college and high school sport. In the United States today, more than 14 million boys and girls under the age of 18 play soccer. One of the oldest and most popular sports in the world has finally found a place in American life.

<u>international</u>: involving two or more nations

Place a check mark next to the correct answers to questions 1 to 5.

1. It is possible that a game like soccer was played

____ (a) 2,500 years ago.

____ (b) 5,200 years ago.

____ (c) 12,500 years ago.

2. Soccer as we know it started in

____ (a) England.

____ (b) Brazil.

____ (c) China.

3. The World Cup championships are held

____ (a) every year.

____ (b) every two years.

____ (c) every four years.

4. How many boys and girls in the United States under the age of 18 play soccer?

____ (a) Almost 10 million

____ (b) 12 million

____ (c) More than 14 million

5. Which one of the following sentences states the main idea of the selection?

____ (a) European traders and sailors spread the sport of soccer all over the world.

____ (b) Teams from more than 100 countries compete in the World Cup championships.

____ (c) One of the oldest and most popular sports in the world has finally found a place in American life.

C. Read the following selection. Then look for the many facts it contains and decide what the main idea of the entire selection is.

> High in the Andes Mountains of South America, the Quechua, or Incas, once ruled over a large <u>empire</u>. At the height of its power in the early 1500's, the Incan Empire stretched more than 2,500 miles north to south along the Andes. Perhaps as many as 16 million people were under its control.
>
> We do not know the full history of the Incas. We do not know who they were or where they came from. We do not even know their <u>original</u> name. The Spanish conquerors in the 1500's first called them Incas. The word Inca means king or prince in the Quechuan language, which was the language spoken by the Incas.
>
> What we do know is that the Incan Empire, at its height, was better organized than any other Native American nation in North or South America. The government was ruled by "The Inca," who was considered a god. His sons and other nobles enforced "The Inca's" will throughout the empire. Though the empire did grow through war, it also got neighboring peoples to accept Incan rule peacefully.

The Incas built great temples and palaces that still stand today. They built roads that connected all parts of the empire. Where there were rivers and canyons, they built suspension bridges (some nearly 328 ft. in length). They were skilled farmers, the first to cultivate the potato. They tamed the guanaco, alpaca, and llama—three animals related to the camel.

The Incas believed in many gods and goddesses, who ruled over the stars, the earth, and the sea. To assure good crops and keep illnesses away, the Incas offered sacrifices to the gods. Usually they sacrificed food and animals, but sometimes they sacrificed human beings.

Between 1527 and 1532, civil war weakened the Incas. As a result, the arriving Spanish conquerors had little trouble gaining control of the land that had once been the Incan Empire.

empire: a group of lands or countries controlled by a single authority
original: going back to the beginning
cultivate: raise or produce crops
goddesses: female gods
civil war: a war between people living in the same country

Place a check mark next to the correct answers to questions 1 to 10.

1. The Incan Empire stretched for more than 2,500 miles along the

____ (a) Andes Mountains of South America.

____ (b) Rocky Mountains of North America.

____ (c) Himalaya Mountains of Asia.

2. The Incan Empire was at the height of its power in the early

____ (a) 1400's.

____ (b) 1500's.

____ (c) 1600's.

3. The word "Inca" means

____ (a) Indian.

____ (b) language.

____ (c) prince.

4. The Incas built their empire

____ (a) only through war.

____ (b) through war, but also through peaceful means.

____ (c) only through peaceful means.

5. "The Inca" was considered

____ (a) a god.

____ (b) a goddess.

____ (c) only a human being.

6. Which one of the following statements is supported by the reading selection?

    ____ (a) Roads built by the Incas still exist today.

    ____ (b) Suspension bridges built by the Incas still exist today.

    ____ (c) Temples built by the Incas still exist today.

7. The Incas were the first to cultivate

    ____ (a) rice.

    ____ (b) oranges.

    ____ (c) the potato.

8. To assure good crops and keep illnesses away, the Incas

    ____ (a) offered sacrifices to the gods.

    ____ (b) did not work on rainy days.

    ____ (c) developed indoor farming.

9. According to the selection, the main reason for the collapse of the Incan Empire was

    ____ (a) climate changes.

    ____ (b) insect-carried disease.

    ____ (c) civil war.

10. Which one of the following sentences states the main idea of the entire reading selection?

    ____ (a) By the early 1500's, the Incas had produced an important and powerful empire.

    ____ (b) At its height, the Incan Empire was more powerful than any other empire in the world.

    ____ (c) The Incas were famous as great builders and farmers.

CHAPTER 3
Arranging Events in Sequence

A Social Studies reading selection often tells about many events, or things that happened. If these events are not described in the correct order in the selection, you might have difficulty understanding what the selection is about. The following example shows how strange a story seems when the events are not in the correct order.

"At 8 o'clock I left the house. I woke up at 7 o'clock this morning. I got dressed and arrived at class at 9 o'clock. Soon the bus to go to school came along, and I got on."

Confusing, isn't it? Most of the events are in the wrong order. For a story or a reading selection to make sense, the events described have to be placed in the order in which they happened. The first event usually comes at the beginning. Then the second event follows. This continues all the way to the last event, which usually appears at or near the end of the selection. Putting events into their correct order is also called "arranging events in the proper sequence."

In the following selection about the Dutch and British in South Africa, all the events are in the correct order. As you read the selection, watch for words like "first," "in the early 1800's," "later on," "soon," and "in the end." These "time" words and phrases will help you follow the sequence of events.

The first settlers from Europe, the Dutch, arrived in South Africa in 1652. They established a small trading post at the southern tip of the African continent. This settlement came to be called Capetown. In the early 1800's, the British also became interested in South Africa. They took control of Capetown and forced the Dutch to move farther north. Later on in the 1800's, gold and diamonds were discovered in the new territory where the Dutch had settled. When the British heard about these discoveries, they pushed north into the Dutch territory. The British now wanted to control this area because it was rich in gold and diamonds. Soon a war started between the British and the Dutch. In the end, the British defeated the Dutch, and South Africa became a British possession.

establish: to set up
territory: an area of land
possession: land or territory owned by another country

Did you follow the sequence of the story? To see how well you remember the order of events in the selection, answer the following questions.

1. Which words in the selection indicate, or point to, the start of the first event?

_____ (a) The first settlers

_____ (b) In 1652

_____ (c) The Dutch

Which answer did you choose? In a selection, you may see words such as "in the beginning," "at the start," or "first." These words are often used to indicate the first event in a sequence. The first event in the above selection is stated in sentence one, "The first settlers from Europe, the Dutch, arrived in South Africa in 1652." The words "the first settlers" suggest the first event or beginning of the sequence. Therefore, the answer to question 1 is (a).

2. Which words indicate the start of the second event?

_____ (a) Soon

_____ (b) Later on

_____ (c) In the early 1800's

Which answer did you choose? The second event in the sequence is that the British became interested in South Africa. Are there any words in the selection that indicate the start of the second event? Yes, the words "in the early 1800's" in the fourth sentence introduce this event. Dates are often used to introduce an event in a selection. Therefore, the answer to question 2 is (c).

3. Which words show the start of the third event in the sequence?

_____ (a) In the early 1800's

_____ (b) Later on in the 1800's

_____ (c) Soon a war started

Which answer did you choose? The third event in the sequence is that gold and diamonds were discovered in the Dutch territory. The words "later on in the 1800's" in the sixth sentence show the start of the third event. Therefore, the answer to question 3 is (b).

4. When the British heard about the discovery of gold and diamonds, they pushed north into the Dutch territory. Which word is used to show the start of the next event?

_____ (a) Later

_____ (b) Soon

_____ (c) After

Which answer did you choose this time? The next event is that a war started between the British and the Dutch. This event is introduced by the word "soon" in the ninth sentence. Therefore, the answer to question 4 is (b).

The word "soon" is important for two reasons. First, it tells you that another event is about to happen. Second, the word "soon" tells you that the coming event happened only a short time after the event you just read about.

5. Which word or words indicate the start of the last event in the sequence?

_____ (a) Later

_____ (b) Soon

_____ (c) In the end

Which answer did you choose? In a selection, you may see the words such as "at last," "finally," or "in the end." These words are often used to indicate the last event in a sequence. The last event in the above selection is stated in the tenth sentence, "In the end, the British defeated the Dutch, and South Africa became a British possession." The words "in the end" tell you that you are about to read the final event in the sequence. Therefore, the answer to question 5 is (c).

So far in this chapter, you have seen that events can be arranged in sequence to tell a story. How well do you remember the sequence of the selection about the Dutch and British in South Africa? The main events of the selection are stated below, but this time they are in the wrong order. Read the five statements carefully. Then read how to put them into the proper sequence.

_____ In the early 1800's, the British took control of Capetown and forced the Dutch to move north.

_____ The first settlers from Europe to arrive in South Africa were the Dutch.

_____ The British defeated the Dutch in a war and made South Africa a British possession.

_____ Later on in the 1800's, gold and diamonds were discovered in the new territory where the Dutch had settled.

_____ When the British heard about the discovery of gold and diamonds in the Dutch territory, they moved into the territory.

How can you arrange these five events in their proper sequence? After each event, write the numbers of the sentences in which it appears in the selection. For example:

____ In the early 1800's, the British took control of Capetown and forced the Dutch to move north. **4, 5**

__1__ The first settlers from Europe to arrive in South Africa were the Dutch.   1

__5__ The British defeated the Dutch in a war and made South Africa a British possession.   **9, 10**

__3__ Later on in the 1800's, gold and diamonds were discovered in the new territory where the Dutch had settled.   **6**

__4__ When the British heard about the discovery of gold and diamonds in the Dutch territory, they moved into the territory.   **7**

Do this for each event. After you have found the sentences in which each of these events appears, look for the event with the lowest numbers after it. The event with the lowest numbers came first in the selection and in the sequence. Put the number 1 in front of that statement. The statement with the second lowest numbers after it should have the number 2 placed in front of it. This continues all the way to the statement with the highest numbers after it. That statement came last in the selection and in the sequence. It should be given the number 5.

When you have finished, your answer should look like this.

__2__ In the early 1800's, the British took control of Capetown and forced the Dutch to move north.   **4, 5**

In this chapter, you have learned to arrange events in their proper sequence. The following exercises will give you more practice in using this important Social Studies skill.

USING WHAT YOU HAVE LEARNED

A. Read the following selection about India. Try to remember the proper sequence of the events it tells about.

> The British first became interested in India in the 1600's, establishing trading posts as early as 1612. By the late 1800's, most of India was under British rule. Shortly thereafter, trouble broke out when the Indian people began to demand the right to govern themselves.
>
> In time, the British allowed the Indians to have a small role in the government. But the Indians were not pleased with this because they wanted to be completely <u>independent</u>.
>
> Not all Indians agreed on how independence should be achieved. Many followed Mohandas Gandhi, who led a peaceful struggle for freedom. Others thought only violence and force would end British rule. There was also the question of how to deal with religious differences. While most Indians were Hindus, there was a large <u>minority</u> of Muslims. The Muslims did not want to be controlled by the Hindus. As a result of all of this, fighting erupted as different <u>political</u> and religious groups tried to achieve independence in their own way.
>
> At last, the British gave up, and India was given its independence in 1947. To avoid further fighting, India was divided into two independent countries—India, controlled by Hindus, and Pakistan, controlled by Muslims.
>
> <u>independent</u>: free, on one's own
> <u>minority</u>: a part that is less than half of the whole
> <u>political</u>: having to do with government

A-1. Place a check mark next to the correct answers to questions 1 to 5.

1. Which word indicates the start of the sequence of events in the reading selection?

   _____ (a) First

   _____ (b) After

   _____ (c) Then

2. Which words indicate the start of the second event in the sequence?

   _____ (a) Shortly thereafter

   _____ (b) In time

   _____ (c) By the late 1800's

3. What happened shortly after the British took over India?

   _____ (a) The Indian people welcomed the British.

   _____ (b) Trouble broke out.

   _____ (c) India got its independence.

4. The Indian people were not happy with their small role in the government. What did they do?

   _____ (a) They all turned to violence and killed the British.

   _____ (b) They all left India to live in other countries.

   _____ (c) Different groups tried to achieve independence in their own way.

5. The British gave India its independence in 1947. This is the last event of the sequence. Which words indicate the start of the last event?

   _____ (a) In time

   _____ (b) By the late 1800's

   _____ (c) At last

A-2. Write the number 1, 2, 3, 4, or 5 next to each of the following statements to show its proper sequence in the selection.

_____ By the late 1800's, most of India was under British rule.

_____ Different political and religious groups tried to achieve independence in their own way.

_____ The British first became interested in India in the 1600's.

_____ The British allowed the Indians to have a small role in the government.

_____ India became an independent country in 1947.

B. Read the following selection about Russia. Try to remember the proper sequence of the events discussed.

> At the start of World War I, in 1914, the Russian people expected their army to win battles easily. And early in the war, the army did well against Germany and the other Central Powers. But as the war

continued, defeats on the battlefield began to outnumber victories. By 1917, almost 2 million Russian soldiers had been killed, and over 4 million had been wounded. Food had become scarce for the soldiers as well as for the people back home.

The Russian people turned against the war and against their ruler, Czar Nicholas II. They blamed him for food shortages and other problems Russia faced. On March 8, 1917, riots erupted in St. Petersburg. A week later, on March 15, the Czar was forced to give up his throne.

A new government, first led by Prince Lvov and then by Alexander Kerensky, was determined to keep Russia in the war. But most Russians were no less determined to take their country out of the war.

Vladimir Lenin, the leader of a group called the Bolsheviks, promised peace. In November 1917, with the support of angry mobs, Lenin and the Bolsheviks seized control of the government. Four months later, Russia signed a separate peace treaty with Germany. For Russia, the war may have been over, but new hardships were on the way.

B-1. Place a check mark next to the correct answers to questions 1 to 5.

1. Which phrase indicates the beginning of the sequence of events in the selection?

_____ (a) And early in the war

_____ (b) At the start of World War I

_____ (c) A week later

2. At the beginning of World War I, the Russian army did well on the battlefield. What words signal that defeats on the battlefield began to outnumber victories?

_____ (a) But as the war continued

_____ (b) By 1917

_____ (c) On March 8, 1917

3. What event happened a week after riots broke out in St. Petersburg on March 8, 1917?

_____ (a) World War I ended.

_____ (b) The Bolsheviks came to power in Russia.

_____ (c) The Czar was forced to give up his power.

4. The use of "first" and "then" in the third paragraph tells the reader that

_____ (a) Prince Lvov and Alexander Kerensky shared power in the new government.

_____ (b) Prince Lvov led the new government before Alexander Kerensky did.

_____ (c) Prince Lvov's government was overthrown by Alexander Kerensky.

5. Which word or phrase indicates the start of the last sequence of events in the selection?

_____ (a) With the support of angry mobs

_____ (b) In November 1917

_____ (c) Four months later

B-2. Make a list of the words found in the reading selection that are used to indicate the start of different events in the selection. One is already listed for you.

At the start _____ _____

_____ _____

_____ _____

_____

B-3. Write the number 1, 2, 3, 4, or 5 next to each of the following statements to create a sequence of events that matches the sequence in the selection.

_____ Alexander Kerensky became the leader of the new Russian government.

_____ Czar Nicholas II was forced to give up power.

_____ Rising numbers of dead and wounded turned the Russian people against the war.

_____ Russia signed a separate peace treaty with Germany.

_____ Lenin and the Bolsheviks seized control of the government.

CHAPTER 4
Time Lines and Dates

When you study history, it is important to take notice of dates. Dates tell you when events took place and help you keep track of the sequence of events. Knowing the order in which events happened makes it easier to understand how one event may have influenced another.

Look at the following important events in Japanese history.

In 1638 the Japanese government closed Japan to most visitors from other countries.

In 1853 Commodore Matthew Perry of the United States visited Japan with many warships. As a result of this visit, Japanese leaders turned to making Japan a great military power.

In 1895 Japan moved toward becoming a world power by defeating China in a war.

Knowing the dates of these three events and their correct order is important. Remembering the proper order will help you understand better how each event influenced the one that followed.

Time Lines

One of the ways to remember the correct order of events is to use a *time line*. The time line at the bottom of the page starts with the year 1600 and ends with the year 1900. The three events you just read about took place between these years.

Read the statements that follow. In the space at the left of each statement, place the letter that represents, or stands for, the period of the time in which the event took place.

_____ 1. Japan defeated China in a war.

_____ 2. The Japanese government closed Japan to most visitors from other countries.

_____ 3. Commodore Matthew Perry of the United States visited Japan.

If you put a **C** next to number 1, you are correct. Japan defeated China in 1895. The letter **C** represents the years between 1870 and 1900. The year 1895 is in this time period.

If you put an **A** next to number 2, you are correct. The Japanese government closed Japan to most visitors in 1638. The letter **A** represents the years between 1600 and 1810. The year 1638 is in this time period.

If you put a **B** next to number 3, you are again correct. Commodore Perry visited Japan in 1853. The letter **B** represents the years between 1810 and 1870. The year 1853 is in this time period.

As you saw in Chapter 3, dates make it easier to arrange events in sequence. Time lines help you see which events came first. Knowing how to use a time line will help you remember the correct sequence of events.

B.C. and A.D.

In a reading selection about history, you might see such dates as 300 B.C. or A.D. 300. These dates contain the same number, but

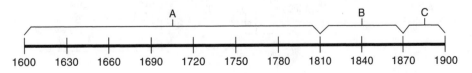

the letters B.C. and A.D. tell us that the two dates stand for different times.

B.C. means BEFORE CHRIST.

A.D. means ANNO DOMINI. ANNO DOMINI are Latin words that mean "in the year of the Lord."

This way of writing dates was started hundreds of years ago. At that time, the Christian Church decided to change the calendar to show that it regarded the birth of its founder, Jesus Christ, as the most important event in the history of the world. So the year of Christ's birth became A.D. 1, or "in the year of the Lord 1." (Historians now believe that Jesus Christ was born four to six years earlier, but changing the calendar would cause many problems.)

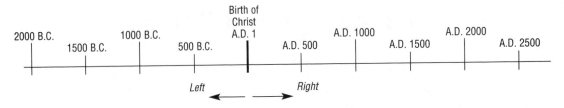

All dates that come after A.D. 1 are marked with the letters A.D., as you can see on the above time line. A.D. dates become higher as they go forward in history (to the right on the time line). Therefore, the year A.D. 1000 happened *after* the year A.D. 500.

All dates that come before A.D. 1 are marked with the letters B.C.—also shown on the above time line. B.C. dates become higher as they go backward in history (to the left on the time line). Therefore, the year 1000 B.C. happened *before* the year 500 B.C.

Now you know the difference between 300 B.C. and A.D. 300. By tradition, the letters B.C. come after the number in a date, while the letters A.D. come before the number in a date.

B.C.E. and C.E.

While the terms B.C. and A.D. are still used in much of the world, a growing number of people prefer to use the terms B.C.E. and C.E.

B.C.E. means Before the Common Era.

C.E. means Common Era.

The date 300 B.C.E. is 300 years before the start of the Common Era. It is the same year as 300 B.C. The date 300 C.E. is 300 years after the start of the Common Era. It is the same as A.D. 300.

Just like B.C., the letters B.C.E. and C.E. always appear after the number in a date.

Most of the time, the dates you see do not have letters before or after them. When there are no letters, the date is always A.D. (or C.E.). This means that 2000 is the same year as A.D. 2000 (or 2000 C.E.). A date showing B.C. or B.C.E. time will always use the letters B.C. or B.C.E.

The following rules will help you use B.C. and A.D. (or B.C.E. and C.E.) correctly.

1. To find out how long ago a B.C. (B.C.E.) date was, add the date to the present year.

2. To find out how long ago an A.D. (C.E.) date was, subtract the date from the present year.

Let us see if you can follow these rules.

1. Imagine that this is the year A.D. 2100. How many years ago was A.D. 1500?

_____ (a) 600 years

_____ (b) 1,500 years

_____ (c) 3,500 years

Which answer did you choose? You want to find out how many years ago an A.D. date was? To do this you must follow rule 2 and subtract 1500 from 2100. (Look at the time line below.) Therefore, the answer to question 1 is (a).

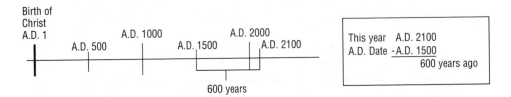

Let us try another example. The Suez Canal in Egypt opened in 1869. How many years ago was that? There are no letters before or after 1869, so it is an A.D. (or C.E.) date. Follow rule 2.

2. Imagine that this is the year 2100 C.E. How many years ago was 500 B.C.E.?

_____ (a) 600 years ago

_____ (b) 2,100 years ago

_____ (c) 2,600 years ago

Which answer did you choose? You want to find out how many years ago a B.C.E. date was. To do this, you must follow rule 1 and add the B.C.E. date to the C.E. date. (Look at the time line below.) Therefore the answer to question 2 is (c).

Let us try another example. How many years ago was 1000 B.C.E.? This is a B.C.E date, so follow rule 1.

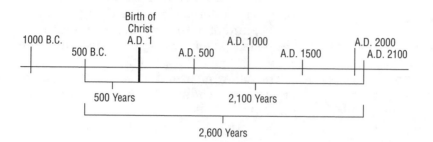

This year	2100 C.E.
B.C.E. Date	+500 B.C.E.
	2,600 years ago

Centuries

You now know the meaning of dates such as 1400 B.C. or A.D. 1400 (1400 B.C.E or 1400 C.E.). But what if you see this date: fifteenth century? Would you know what period of time this date represents?

There are no letters after the date fifteenth century. Therefore, the date is A.D. (C.E.). But when did the fifteenth century take place? To find out, look at the chart on the right.

This chart is divided into *centuries,* which are periods of 100 years. The 100 years from 1 through 100 are called the first century. If an event happened any time between 1 and 100, we say it happened in the first century. For example, if an event happened in the year 25, we say it happened in the first century.

The 100 years between 101 and 200 are called the second century. If an event happened in the year 150, we say it happened in the second century.

This sequence of centuries continues from the years 201 to 300 (third century) all the way to the years 2001 to 2100 (the twenty-first century). Though not shown in the chart, the sequence could also run backward with centuries for B.C. (B.C.E.) years.

So what years does the fifteenth century represent? The chart on page 23 shows that the fifteenth century includes the years 1401 to 1500.

| Centuries Since A.D. 1 (1 C.E.) ||
Century	Years
First	A.D. 1 to A.D. 100
Second	A.D. 101 to A.D. 200
Third	A.D. 201 to A.D. 300
Fourth	A.D. 301 to A.D. 400
Fifth	A.D. 401 to A.D. 500
Sixth	A.D. 501 to A.D. 600
Seventh	A.D. 601 to A.D. 700
Eighth	A.D. 701 to A.D. 800
Ninth	A.D. 801 to A.D. 900
Tenth	A.D. 901 to A.D. 1000
Eleventh	A.D. 1001 to A.D. 1100
Twelfth	A.D. 1101 to A.D. 1200
Thirteenth	A.D. 1201 to A.D. 1300
Fourteenth	A.D. 1301 to A.D. 1400
Fifteenth	A.D. 1401 to A.D. 1500
Sixteenth	A.D. 1501 to A.D. 1600
Seventeenth	A.D. 1601 to A.D. 1700
Eighteenth	A.D. 1701 to A.D. 1800
Nineteenth	A.D. 1801 to A.D. 1900
Twentieth	A.D. 1901 to A.D. 2000
Twenty-first	A.D. 2001 to A.D. 2100

Answer the following questions about centuries.

1. If an event happened in A.D. 639 (639 C.E.), in what century did it occur?

_____ (a) The sixth century

_____ (b) The seventh century

_____ (c) The eighth century

Which answer did you choose? Look at the chart. It shows that any event between the years 601 and 700 happened in the seventh century. Therefore, the answer to question 1 is (*b*).

2. If an event happened at the beginning of the seventeenth century, how many years ago did it happen?

_____ (*a*) About 17 years ago

_____ (*b*) About 300 years ago

_____ (*c*) About 400 years ago

Which answer did you choose? First of all, look at the chart on page 23 to see that the seventeenth century covers 1601 to 1700. Next, the same chart shows that we are now in the twenty-first century, which covers 2001 to 2100. The question does not give exact years, so your answer cannot be an exact year. This explains why all the choices start with "About." Because the event happened at the *beginning* of the seventeenth century and we are at the *beginning* of the twenty-first century, you can pick any year from the beginning of each century and subtract the earlier year from the later year. It is easier to subtract years that end in the same number, so let us pick 1602 and subtract it from 2002 to get 400 years. Therefore, if an event happened at the beginning of the seventeenth century, it happened about 400 years ago and the answer to question 2 is (*c*).

The following exercises will give you more practice in reading dates and using time lines.

USING WHAT YOU HAVE LEARNED

A. Read the following selection about Japanese history from 1894 to 1945. Pay careful attention to the dates when events occurred.

Japan Becomes a Powerful Country

By the 1890's, Japan was on the way to becoming one of the most powerful countries in the world. But first it had to solve a serious problem. Japan needed natural resources. Because there are few such useful materials in the island nation, Japan had to look to other countries for the resources it needed.

Japan first looked to nearby China. In 1894, the two countries went to war. The following year, China was defeated by Japan and had to pay Japan 165 million dollars. The money could buy resources. Other nations of the world now realized that Japan was gaining power.

Nine years later, Japan went to war again. This time it turned against Russia in a war called the Russo-Japanese War. At the end of this war, in 1905, Japan received land from Russia. Five years later, in 1910, Japan seized control of Korea.

When World War I ended in 1918, Japan was on the winning side. As a result, Japan was given in 1920 a number of islands that had belonged to Germany, one of the losers in the war.

The population of Japan grew rapidly during the 1920's. By 1930, there were 64 million people crowded onto the small islands of Japan. Once again Japan looked for countries that could provide it with natural resources.

In 1931, Japanese soldiers invaded Manchuria, which is part of northern China. The Japanese took control of this area and renamed it Manchukuo. But Japan was not finished underlying expanding, and in 1937 it attacked several other areas of China.

The United States tried to stop this expansion by Japan. Starting in 1940, the United States refused to sell scrap iron and oil to Japan because it believed that Japan was using these materials to prepare for future wars. Japan became angry with the United States. On December 7, 1941, the Japanese attacked the U.S. naval base at Pearl Harbor in the Hawaiian Islands.

This was the beginning of World War II for the United States. For four years, it fought hard against Japan (and the other Axis powers). Then, in 1945, the United States dropped two atomic bombs on Japan. Soon afterward, Japan gave up.

<table>
<tr><td>natural resources: materials found on or in the earth that are used to benefit humans. Some examples are water, trees, animals, gold, iron ore, oil.</td><td>seized: took by force
population: the number of people living in a place
rapidly: quickly, with great speed
expanding: growing larger</td></tr>
</table>

Use this time line to answer the questions.

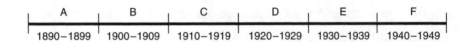

A	B	C	D	E	F
1890–1899	1900–1909	1910–1919	1920–1929	1930–1939	1940–1949

Look back at the reading selection to find out what year each of the following events took place. Then in the space at the left of each sentence, put the letter from the time line that represents the period of time when each event occurred. The first one is done for you.

__C__ 1. World War I ended.

_____ 2. Japan seized control of Korea.

_____ 3. China paid Japan 165 million dollars.

_____ 4. Japan fought Russia in the Russo-Japanese War.

_____ 5. Japan attacked Pearl Harbor in the Hawaiian Islands.

_____ 6. Japanese soldiers invaded Manchuria.

_____ 7. The United States refused to sell oil to Japan.

_____ 8. Japan was given islands that had belonged to Germany.

_____ 9. Japan attacked China a second time.

_____ 10. Atomic bombs were dropped on Japan.

B. Place a check mark next to the correct answers to questions 1 to 10.

1. The letters B.C. after a date mean

    ____ (a) Before Christ.

    ____ (b) Before the Common Era.

    ____ (c) Before the Christian Era.

2. The Latin letters A.D. before a date translate to

    ____ (a) After Death.

    ____ (b) Any Date in the Common Era.

    ____ (c) Anno Domini (in the year of the Lord).

3. The year 700 B.C. can also be written

    ____ (a) 700 C.E.

    ____ (b) A.D. 700

    ____ (c) 700 B.C.E.

4. The year 500 B.C.E. happened

    ____ (a) before 300 B.C.E.

    ____ (b) after 300 B.C.E.

    ____ (c) at the same time as 300 B.C.E.

5. How long ago was 200 B.C.? You find the answer by

    ____ (a) subtracting 200 B.C. from the present year.

    ____ (b) adding 200 B.C. to the present year.

    ____ (c) adding 200 B.C. and A.D. 200 together.

6. The year 1222 can also be written

    ____ (a) 1222 B.C. or 1222 B.C.E.

    ____ (b) A.D. 1222 or 1222 C.E.

    ____ (c) the twelfth century.

7. How long ago was 1000 C.E.? You find the answer by

    ____ (a) subtracting 1000 C.E. from the present year.

    ____ (b) adding 1000 C.E. to the present year.

    ____ (c) adding 1000 B.C.E. and 1000 C.E. together.

8. The fourteenth century covers the years

    ____ (a) 401 to 500.

    ____ (b) 1301 to 1400.

    ____ (c) 1401 to 1500.

9. The first century A.D. covers the years

    ____ (a) A.D. 101 to A.D. 200

    ____ (b) A.D. 1 to A.D. 100

    ____ (c) 1 B.C. to A.D. 1

10. How long ago was the beginning of the twelfth century?

____ (a) About 12 years ago

____ (b) About 800 years ago

____ (c) About 900 years ago

C. Time Line

C-1. Completing a Time Line. Complete the dates on the time line below and on the list of events that follow. For each date, you decide whether the letters B.C. and A.D. or the letters B.C.E. and C.E. should be used. Put the letters you choose in the correct place, either before or after the number in the date.

(The letters **A** to **G** on the above time line show where the events listed **A** through **G** below fit on the time line.)

List of Events

A. Growing of corn began in eastern North America, ____ 800 ____

B. First section of the Great Wall of China completed, ____ 214 ____

C. Gupta ruler united northern India, ____ 320 ____

D. Muhammad fled from Mecca to Medina, ____ 622 ____

E. Rule of Mansa Musa over the Mali Empire began, ____ 1312 ____

F. Catherine the Great became Czarina of Russia, ____ 1762 ____

G. The United Nations began the International Decade for a Culture of Peace and Non-Violence for the Children of the World, ____ 2001 ____

C-2. Using a Time Line. Place a check mark next to the correct answers to questions 1 to 4 and write the answer to question 5 on the line provided.

1. Each letter (**A** to **G**) along the bottom of the time line represents

____ (a) 100 years.

____ (b) 500 years.

____ (c) 1,000 years.

2. How many years passed between the flight of Muhammad from Mecca to Medina and the beginning of the rule of Mansa Musa of Mali?

____ (a) 622 years

____ (b) 690 years

____ (c) 1,312 years

3. How many years passed between the completion of the first section of the Great Wall of China and the uniting of northern India by the Gupta ruler?

____ (a) 106 years

____ (b) 214 years

____ (c) 534 years

4. Mansa Musa could not have known of

____ (a) Catherine the Great.

____ (b) the Great Wall of China.

____ (c) Muhammad.

5. How many years ago was corn first grown in eastern North America?

_____

CHAPTER 5
Separating Fact From Opinion

Some of the things that you read in books, newspapers, or magazines or on the Internet are facts, while others are opinions. How can you tell the difference?

A *fact* is something that is true or something that really happened. A fact can be proved to be true.

An *opinion* is something that a person believes to be true or is how a person feels about something. An opinion cannot be proved to be true.

Here are two statements that may be fact or opinion. Place an **F** next to the one that is a fact and an **0** next to the one that is an opinion.

_____ 1. There are more people in China than in any other country.

_____ 2. The Chinese are the hardest working people in the world.

If you put an **F** next to the first statement, you are correct. By counting people, it can be proved that China has the largest population in the world. This makes the first statement a fact.

If you put an **0** next to the second statement, you are also correct. Some people may believe that the Chinese are the hardest working people in the world, but this would be very hard, if not impossible, to prove. Therefore, the second statement is an opinion.

Not everything you read or hear is fact.

Just because things are printed as facts in books, newspapers, or magazines or are spoken about on radio or television programs, they are not necessarily true. Writers and speakers sometimes make mistakes or fail to tell the truth. In such cases, things presented as facts are not facts at all. It is important to learn to separate the facts from the opinions so that you don't confuse the two.

Very often several people use the same facts to form different opinions. This is known as "interpreting facts." Different people may interpret facts in different ways.

Let us imagine that the students in a Social Studies class were asked to write reports on imperialism in Africa. Their teacher told them that during the nineteenth century, the powerful countries of Europe took over and settled land in Africa. This was known as European imperialism in Africa. The students were directed to report on the good or bad effects of that imperialism.

The reports all contained many of the same facts and events. But the students were divided in their opinions about the effects of imperialism in Africa. Some students wrote that imperialism helped Africa. Others wrote that imperialism hurt Africa.

The following reports were written by two students in the Social Studies class. Read each one carefully to see how these two students used the same facts to form different opinions.

Student A

Many of the Europeans who went to Africa in the late nineteenth century were selfish. They were mainly interested in becoming rich. But the Europeans also introduced many new ways of doing things. These changes helped Africa more than they hurt it.

Many Africans welcomed European culture. For the first time, modern medicine was used in Africa. Modern machines were put to work on farms and in factories. Some Africans were taught to read and write. When the African nations received their independence, many educated Africans became the leaders of their new nations. As a result of European imperialism, Africa was introduced to the modern world.

Student B

The Europeans who went to Africa in the late nineteenth century were selfish. They were concerned only with making themselves rich. As a result, they robbed Africa of great amounts of natural resources.

The people in Africa had been happy, but the Europeans upset their lives. Many Africans were killed, and many others were forced to work for the Europeans. The Europeans claimed that they introduced modern medicine, but they also brought diseases that the Africans had not known before. Even though the Europeans educated some Africans, they also did much to destroy African culture. The Africans were forced to see the world through European eyes. The Europeans changed Africa forever.

culture: the common way of life of a large group of people or a nation

As you read, you should have seen that each student agreed on certain facts. Here are some of the facts on which they agreed.

1. Europeans went to Africa in the late nineteenth century.
2. The Europeans changed Africa.
3. The Europeans educated some of the Africans.

Go back and underline these three facts in each report.

You also should have seen in the reports that each student interpreted facts and events differently. Let us see how well you picked up these different interpretations.

Answer the following questions:

_____ 1. Which student said that the Europeans were concerned only with making themselves rich?

Which report did you choose? If you look over both of them, you will see that the answer is Student B. The second sentence of B's report states that the Europeans were concerned only with making themselves rich.

_____ 2. Which student said that many Africans welcomed European culture?

Which report did you choose? This time the answer can be found in Student A's report. Sentence five in A's report states that many Africans welcomed European culture.

_____ 3. Which student said that imperialism helped Africa?

Which report did you choose? Student A used all the facts to show that European imperialism helped Africa. Student A even stated this in the fourth sentence of the report.

These two reports show clearly how the same facts can be used to support different opinions. The following exercises will give you more practice in separating fact from opinion.

USING WHAT YOU HAVE LEARNED

A. The following selection is about going to school in China. After you have read the selection, try to separate the facts from the opinions.

Going to School in China

Before the Communists took control of China in 1949, few Chinese people went to school. Today most Chinese young people have the chance to receive a formal education.

Schooling for Chinese boys and girls begins at the age of three. They go to kindergarten until they are seven years old. Starting school at such a young age is a good idea. It helps the children learn how to act with other children in an orderly way.

Primary education begins at the age of seven and lasts for five years. In the primary schools, students work very hard in their study of mathematics, science, music, art, and the Chinese language. Primary schools in China are much better than primary schools in the United States.

Secondary education consists of three years of junior middle school followed by two to three years of senior middle school. The subjects in the middle schools include politics, the Chinese language, mathematics, history, geography, farming, biology, chemistry, physical education, music, and art. Unfortunately, formal education for most Chinese ends with graduation from the junior middle school.

Some students who graduate from the junior middle school attend secondary technical schools. There they receive training for three or four years in such fields as farming, forestry, medicine, or fine arts.

Universities and colleges admit students who have graduated from senior middle school and who have passed a national entrance examination. The students do not have to pay to attend a university or college. This is a wise policy because deserving students are not deprived of higher education just because they are poor. Universities offer study in many subjects, but the colleges provide courses in one field or a few closely related fields.

Chinese students appreciate the opportunity to go to school. They realize that a good education will help them and their country as well. It can be said that the Chinese value their education more than any other people on earth.

Each of the following statements is based on the selection you just read. If the statement is a fact, put an **F** in front of it. If the statement is an opinion, put an **0** in front of it. It is important to remember the meanings of fact and opinion. Not everything you read will be a fact.

_____ 1. Before 1949, few Chinese went to school.

_____ 2. Today most Chinese young people have a chance to receive a formal education.

_____ 3. It is a good idea for children to start school at the age of three.

_____ 4. Chinese students start primary school when they are seven years old.

_____ 5. Primary schools in China are much better than primary schools in the United States.

_____ 6. Secondary education consists of junior middle schools and senior middle schools.

_____ 7. Unfortunately, formal education ends for most Chinese with graduation from junior middle school.

_____ 8. Students must pass a national entrance examination before they are admitted to a university or college.

_____ 9. It is a wise policy that deserving students do not have to pay to go to college.

_____ 10. The Chinese value their education more than any other people on earth.

B. In the spaces below, write two new statements that are facts and two new statements that are opinions. These statements can deal with anything you wish, but *not* with the selection you just read in Exercise A.

FACTS:

1. _____

_____

2. _____

_____

OPINIONS:

1. _____

_____

2. _____

_____

C. The following two selections deal with cutting down the rain forest in Brazil. The persons who wrote the selections used the same facts, but they reached different conclusions. Read each selection carefully.

Selection 1

Brazil is a large country with a land area of 3,286,470 square miles. Yet most of Brazil's population of 175 million live near the <u>coast</u>. The <u>vast</u> inland areas of the country are covered by rain <u>forest</u> and <u>inhabited</u> mainly by <u>indigenous</u> peoples, animals, and insects. The

---

government has already cleared some of the rain forest and built cities in its place. More of the rain forest should be cleared and more cities built. Large numbers of Brazilians who now crowd the coastal cities, such as São Paulo and Rio de Janeiro, can move into these new cities. The rain forest should not be left just to indigenous groups, animals, and insects.

Selection 2

Destroying the rain forest of Brazil will do more harm than good. It is true that most of Brazil's 175 million people live near the coast and that in some cities, such as São Paulo and Rio de Janeiro, conditions are very crowded. But the answer to this problem is not to cut down the rain forest. The rain forest affects weather all over the world, especially in North America. Forests cool the earth. If the rain forest is destroyed, the earth will become warmer. The destruction of the rain forest will also mean the end of a way of life for the indigenous peoples who live in it. Such great changes may even kill the indigenous peoples. Let us not help some people while doing harm to others.

coast: land next to the sea   vast: large, covering a great area
inhabited: lived in   indigenous: original, first
destruction: the act of destroying or damaging something

C-1. As you read each selection, you should have seen that both writers agreed on certain facts. In the spaces below, list two facts on which both writers agreed.

1. _____

_____

2. _____

_____

C-2. Can you remember the different opinions reached by the two writers? Place the number of the correct selection on the answer line at the left of each question.

_____ 1. Which selection stated that destroying the rain forest will do more harm than good?

_____ 2. Which selection stated that the rain forest should not be left to indigenous groups, animals, and insects?

_____ 3. Which selection stated that more of the rain forest should be cleared and more cities built?

_____ 4. Which selection stated that clearing away the rain forest might kill the indigenous peoples?

_____ 5. Which selection stated that the answer to overcrowded cities is not to cut down the rain forest?

C-3. Place a check mark next to the correct answers.

1. Which statement best describes the opinion of the person who wrote Selection 1?

_____ (*a*) Brazil has a land area of 3,286,470 square miles.

_____ (b) The destruction of the rain forest will mean an end to the way of life of the indigenous peoples who live there.

_____ (c) The clearing of the rain forest will solve the problems of over-crowding in Brazil's cities.

2. Which statement best describes the opinion of the person who wrote Selection 2?

_____ (a) Most of Brazil's 175 million people live near the coast.

_____ (b) The destruction of the rain forest will have no effect on weather conditions around the world.

_____ (c) The rain forest should not be cleared to benefit some people while harming others.

D. When World War II began in 1939, the United States was not involved. Not until December 8, 1941, did the United States enter the war. This was one day after Japan attacked the U.S. naval base at Pearl Harbor in Hawaii. In August of 1945, after nearly four years of fighting, the United States dropped two atomic bombs on Japan. Several days later, Japan surrendered, and World War II was over. The following two selections deal with the dropping of the two atomic bombs on Japan.

Ms. Ruiz

In August of 1945, the United States dropped two atomic bombs on Japan. President Harry Truman gave the order to drop the bombs on the cities of Hiroshima and Nagasaki.

This was the worst thing that the United States ever did. In war, soldiers are supposed to fight only soldiers. Only <u>military</u> targets are supposed to be attacked, but these Japanese cities were not military targets. Thousands of <u>civilians</u> were killed without reason.

This was a foolish attack by a nation that should have known better. There was no reason for the United States to kill innocent people because our soldiers were defeating the Japanese soldiers. It would have been only a matter of time before Japan surrendered. Dropping the atomic bombs was not needed to win the war.

Mr. Vesey

President Harry Truman ordered the atomic bombs dropped on the Japanese cities of Hiroshima and Nagasaki in August of 1945. He believed that this would stop the fighting.

World War II had dragged on for four years. Many lives had been lost on both sides, and there was no sign that Japan was ready to surrender. President Truman believed that if the war continued, many more lives would be lost.

To drop the atomic bombs was not an easy decision for President Truman to make. He knew that thousands of civilians would be killed, but he thought that he would be saving lives by ending the war quickly.

No one is happy that the United States took this action, but it was something that had to be done.

<u>military</u>: having to do with soldiers, weapons, or war
<u>civilians</u>: people not in the military

D-1. As you read each selection, you should have seen that both writers agreed on certain facts. The following are two facts on which they agreed:

1. The atomic bombs were dropped on Hiroshima and Nagasaki.
2. Thousands of civilians were killed.

In the following spaces, list two other facts on which Ms. Ruiz and Mr. Vesey agreed:

1. _____

_____

2. _____

_____

D-2. Can you remember the different opinions reached by Ms. Ruiz and Mr. Vesey? Place an **R** in front of the opinions expressed by Ms. Ruiz. Place a **V** in front of the opinions expressed by Mr. Vesey.

____ 1. Which person called the dropping of the bombs a foolish attack?

____ 2. Which person said that in war only military targets are to be attacked?

____ 3. Which person probably supported Truman's belief that in the long run, more lives would be saved by dropping the bomb?

____ 4. Which person said that our soldiers were already defeating the Japanese soldiers?

____ 5. Which person said there was no sign that the Japanese would surrender?

D-3. Place a check mark next to the correct answers.

1. Which statement best describes the opinion of Ms. Ruiz?

____ (*a*) Hiroshima and Nagasaki were not military targets.

____ (*b*) Dropping atomic bombs on Japan was wrong and unnecessary.

____ (*c*) Soldiers should be allowed to kill civilians during a war.

2. Which statement best describes the opinion of Mr. Vesey?

____ (*a*) Many lives had been lost in World War II by 1945.

____ (*b*) President Truman made a difficult decision.

____ (*c*) The United States had to drop the atomic bombs on Japan to end the war.

CHAPTER 6
Writing Sentences and Paragraphs

In Unit One, you learned how to improve your reading skills. Just as it is important to read well, it is also important to write well. Your success in taking tests, taking notes, or writing reports depends on the quality of your writing. Being able to express yourself clearly and correctly is a necessary Social Studies skill.

In this chapter, you will learn how to answer a question in sentence and paragraph form. (A paragraph is a group of sentences that express one main idea.)

Study the following questions and sample answers. You will see that a single-sentence answer doesn't tell the reader very much. But a three- or four-sentence paragraph both informs and interests the reader.

One way to write a one-sentence answer is to repeat part of the question in your answer. Then add one or two facts to finish the sentence. Here is an example of a possible one-sentence answer.

Why do few people live in the Sahara, a desert in Africa?

One-Sentence Answer

Few people live in the Sahara, a desert, because of the lack of water and the heat.

You could also have answered the same question in more than one sentence. The more information you give, the more your reader will know about living in the Sahara. Here is the question again. This time it has been answered in a paragraph.

Why do few people live in the Sahara, a desert in Africa?

Paragraph Answer

Few people live in the Sahara, a desert, because of the lack of water and the heat. Without rain, it is difficult to grow food. The burning heat makes living in the desert very uncomfortable.

The paragraph you just read contains three sentences. Each gives a reason why few people live in the Sahara. Now the reader knows more than he or she would if the answer were only one sentence.

Look at the next example of a question that has been answered in one sentence and in a paragraph.

Why do the people of the island nation of Japan look to the sea for food?

One-Sentence Answer

The people of Japan look to the sea for food because it contains a great supply of fish.

Paragraph Answer

Japan is an island nation. It cannot grow enough food to feed its people.

So Japan turns to the sea to find food. The waters around Japan provide the country with a great supply of fish.

Once again, a question has been answered in two different ways. The one-sentence answer is correct. But it is the paragraph answer that shows the reader you have a greater knowledge of Japan. The more you know, the longer your paragraph can be.

Being able to write good sentences and paragraphs is an important Social Studies skill. The following exercises will give you more practice in developing this skill.

USING WHAT YOU HAVE LEARNED

A. Read the following selection. Then answer each question in one sentence. The first question has been answered as an example.

Cows Are Sacred in India

Most of the people in India practice the Hindu religion. This religion teaches that killing cows is wrong. To the Hindus of India, therefore, the cow is a sacred animal.

More than 200 million cows live in India, and many of them move freely through the countryside and the city streets. Sometimes they eat food that the people need, and some of them carry diseases. But the Hindus are still opposed to killing them.

Despite these problems, cows are useful to the Indians. Cows serve as work animals on farms. Food is made from their milk, and their dung (manure) is used as fuel. Cows in India help the people and, at the same time, cause harm.

sacred: holy

---

1. What religion do most Indians practice?

Most Indians practice the Hindu religion.

2. Why don't the Hindus kill cows?

_____

_____

3. How many cows are there in India?

_____

_____

4. What harm do the cows in India cause?

_____

_____

5. How are cows useful to the Indians?

_____

_____

_____

B. Read the following selection. Answer the question after the selection in both a single sentence and a paragraph.

Rivers Are Important to the Growth of Cities

What do St. Louis in the United States, Cairo in Egypt, Manaus in Brazil, and Nanjing in China all have in common? All of them are cities built near rivers.

Since very early times, people have realized the importance of rivers. Early humans settled near rivers to be sure of having fish for food and water to drink. Rivers were used for washing clothes and for bathing. When people learned to farm, rivers were used to <u>irrigate</u> the land. The same rivers were then used to send crops quickly and easily to other places.

As more and more people settled in one place along a river, a town would develop. Some towns became stopping places for those who carried products up and down the river. These places grew larger and turned into cities.

Today rivers continue to be important to many cities. They provide food and drinking water and carry away dirt and garbage. Rivers are still used to send goods from one place to another. The next time you look at a map of the world, notice how many important cities have been built near rivers.

<u>irrigate</u>: to bring water to

---

1. Why have rivers been important to the growth of cities?

ONE-SENTENCE ANSWER

_____

_____

_____

_____

PARAGRAPH ANSWER (three sentences)

_____

_____

_____

_____

_____

_____

_____

_____

_____

_____

C. Read the following selection. Then answer the question in a paragraph.

Operations Without Pain

Imagine sticking a needle into your body to stop pain. You would think that the needle would cause pain. But thousands of years ago, the Chinese developed a method of killing pain by using needles. This method is called acupuncture. Needles are stuck into the body at certain places to numb the part of the body that hurts. Doctors can operate freely without causing any pain to their patients.

Doctors from many parts of the world have traveled to China to see the use of acupuncture in operations. They watched many operations, including open-heart surgery, during which the patients remained awake but felt no pain. Some patients who had minor operations were able to walk out of the operating room right after their operations.

No one knows why acupuncture is successful. But it does seem to work. People all over the world are becoming more interested in this very old Chinese method of killing pain.

method: a way of doing something
acupuncture: using needles to stop pain or cure disease
numb: to cause to have no feeling or pain
minor: less important, less serious

1. How does acupuncture help patients?

PARAGRAPH ANSWER (three sentences)

_____

_____

_____

_____

_____

_____

_____

_____

_____

D. Read the following selection. Then answer the question in a paragraph.

Religion in South-West Asia

South-West Asia is the birthplace of three major religions—Judaism, Christianity, and Islam. For centuries, their presence in the region has been a source of inspiration, but it has also resulted in distrust and, sometimes, war.

Judaism is the oldest of the three religions, dating back more than 5,000 years. It is the religion of most of the people of Israel. Christianity dates back 2,000 years. Today in the region, only Lebanon has a large Christian population. Islam dates back nearly 1,400 years. It is the major religion of nearly all the countries of South-West Asia.

Religion has greatly influenced all aspects of life in South-West Asia. Laws are based on the Bible, the holy book of Judaism and Christianity, and on the Koran, the holy book of Islam. Religious ceremonies mark the important events in a person's life. For example, Jews celebrate their 13th birthday with a religious ceremony known as a Bar Mitzvah for a man and a Bat Mitzvah for a woman. The style of dress and the foods people eat often reflect religious teachings. Art, too, reflects religious teachings. For example, strict Islamic teachings do not allow artworks to show a human form. Many Christian churches, on the other hand, encourage paintings and statues of Jesus Christ and other religious figures.

The shame is that members of these three religions have not always been able to live in peace with one another. Over the centuries, so-called "religious" wars have brought death and destruction. The hope is that the children of today and tomorrow will be inspired by their religion to love their neighbor.

region: area of land marked by some common geographic features
aspects: parts, areas, sides

1. How has religion played an important part in the development of South-West Asia?

PARAGRAPH ANSWER (five sentences)

_____

_____

_____

_____

_____

_____

_____

_____

_____

CHAPTER 7
Expressing an Opinion

One important part of Social Studies is the discussion of current, or present-day, problems in the world. These problems may include dirty air or water (pollution), war, too little money (poverty), crime, and poorly run government. You may be asked in your Social Studies class to write your opinion about one of these problems in a paragraph.

In Chapter 6, the paragraphs you wrote were concerned mainly with giving correct information. This information was often supplied by a reading selection that contained someone else's ideas.

In writing an opinion, you are giving your own ideas about a current problem. You may gather ideas and facts from various sources, but your paragraph should contain your own thoughts and opinions. A paragraph written to present a personal point of view is called an *essay*.

One major problem facing the United States and the world today is air pollution. The boxed paragraph at the bottom of the page is an essay about air pollution. It expresses, or states, the opinion of one person about how to deal with this problem.

This short essay is one person's opinion about the problem of air pollution. Do you agree or disagree with this opinion? Write your own essay to tell how you would deal with the problem of air pollution.

Your essay should contain two basic parts:

1. Information learned from other sources— books, television, radio, the Internet, newspapers, parents, friends, teachers.
2. Your own ideas and opinions about the information learned.

It is a good idea to think out your essay before you write it. After all, an essay starts in the mind, so let it stay in the mind for a while. Then begin to write.

How I Would Deal With Air Pollution

I hope that someday we will be able to put an end to the terrible problem of air pollution. But we have to be careful not to destroy America while trying to clean it up. I know that cars, buses, and factories are major causes of pollution. But we can't stop making cars and buses or close down all the factories in America. Right now giving Americans jobs is more important than clean air. Let's build America today. We can worry about air pollution tomorrow.

How I Would Deal With Air Pollution

_____
_____
_____
_____
_____
_____
_____
_____
_____
_____
_____
_____
_____
_____

What you have written is your opinion about how to deal with the problem of air pollution. Some persons may agree with you, and some may disagree. Some may even argue that you are wrong. Can we really say that a person's opinion is wrong? Of course! An essay must be based on logical thinking and correct information.

Imagine that your essay on air pollution contained this wild sentence: "I would deal with air pollution by sending everyone to live on the moon." Such an idea may be your opinion, but it is not a logical answer to the problem because sending everyone to the moon would be impossible.

Suppose you had written this sentence: "All air pollution is caused by factories." This may be your opinion, but you could not support this statement with facts. Auto-

mobiles, buses, airplanes, and many other things also cause air pollution.

You might have included this opinion: "Automobile companies can cut down on air pollution by providing cleaner burning engines. They would put less dirty exhaust into the air." This opinion can be supported by facts. Automobile companies have been working for years to develop cleaner burning engines. Of course, automobiles are only one part of the problem of air pollution. But this opinion is based on a realistic answer to part of the problem of air pollution.

We all have a right to our opinions. But in an essay, we must present a logical point of view that is based on facts. The following exercises will give you practice in expressing your own ideas in essays.

A. Read the following selection.

Tigers in Danger

Most people only get to see tigers in a zoo. Someday it may be the only place to see them. It is becoming harder and harder to find tigers in their natural surroundings, where they live naturally. Why are they disappearing? The answer is simple. They are being killed off rapidly, mostly for their fur.

All tigers are endangered <u>species</u>. This means that they are in danger of becoming <u>extinct</u>—that is, of dying out entirely. Two of the most endangered species are the Siberian and Sumatran tigers. Only 150–430 of the Siberian tigers and 400–500 of the Sumatran tigers exist in the wild.

Governments, wildlife groups, and individual citizens are trying to save endangered species in various ways. One method is to raise them in zoos. Another is to keep hunters out of the animals' natural surroundings. Another is to make it <u>illegal</u> to kill an endangered species. But more must be done—because once a species is gone, it is gone forever.

<u>species</u>: a class of living things having common qualities
<u>extinct</u>: a species that no longer exists
<u>illegal</u>: against the law

Do you think that more should be done to save the tigers from extinction? Write an essay expressing your opinion on this issue.

PARAGRAPH ANSWER (three sentences)

B. Read the following selection.

---

*Should English Be the Official Language
of the United States?*

It might come as a surprise to many Americans that English is not the official language of the United States. It is not the language required by law to be used in this country. Nevertheless, English is the most widely used language in the United States. This is true in every area of the society, from television and publishing to the operation of schools and the running of the government. More than 200 years ago, when the United States came into existence, most Americans spoke English. Thereafter, nearly all immigrants who came to this country, or their children, learned to speak English. As more states were added to the Union, English became the most widely used language in those states too.

Today, some Americans fear that the United States is slowly dividing into a country with different language regions. They want English to be made the official language. They argue that there are areas of large cities where Spanish is heard more often than English. In cities such as Miami, some Americans have difficulty getting jobs because they do not speak Spanish. The largest numbers of new immigrants now coming into the United States are from Asia. The supporters of English want to know if these groups from Asia will demand that their languages be accepted in place of English.

English supporters believe that this country has been successful because the millions of people who came from Europe, Africa, Asia, and Latin America in years past learned to speak English. They believe that by encouraging the use of any language other than English, we will see problems arising similar to those faced by Canada. There English-speaking and French-speaking Canadians are at odds with each other. A worse situation exists in India, where 14 different main languages are used.

There are, however, many Americans who want to encourage the ethnic differences in the United States. Concerning Spanish, they remind us that great parts of the American Southwest and Florida heard the Spanish language long before English was ever heard. Those who speak languages other than English fear that their cultures will be lost. They believe that American society would be enriched by allowing people to maintain their original languages. The many-languages supporters remind us that other ethnic groups, such as the Italians, have come to this country and lived in communities in which their native language was widely spoken. The people who oppose making English the official language are concerned that those who do not speak English might be denied their rights, such as the right to vote. Finally, this group argues that no harm will be done if the various ethnic groups use their native languages, for nearly all of them will also eventually learn to speak English.

official language: one that a government must use
immigrants: people who come to live in a country that is not their original
   home

Do you think English should be made the official language of the United States? Write an essay expressing your opinion about this question.

YOUR OPINION (four or five sentences)

_____

_____

_____

_____

_____

_____

_____

_____

C. Pick any current problem facing the United States or the world. You may have read about this problem in a book or a magazine or have seen a television program about it. Write an essay expressing your opinion about how to deal with this problem.

YOUR OPINION (four or five sentences)

_____

_____

_____

_____

_____

_____

_____

_____

CHAPTER 8
Writing a Summary

Have you ever read something and just a short time later forgotten what it was all about? It is not possible to remember everything you read. But what if you were to take notes while you were reading? What if you were to write down the highlights—the important points? If you did this, you could remember what you had read by going over your notes.

When you take notes on what you read, you are *summarizing*. You are reducing many sentences to one or two sentences or a few phrases. The sentences or phrases you write down will help you recall the entire selection.

In Chapter 1, you learned how to find the main idea of a reading selection. The main idea is what the selection is all about. A good summary states the main idea of a selection, but usually adds more information. If you can find the main idea, you have the start of a good summary.

Read Selection A about the importance of oil in the world. Then see how the selection is summarized in one sentence.

Summary A states the main idea of Selection A. One sentence summarizes a reading selection containing six sentences. But Selection A contains many facts that you may need to remember. To include them, another sentence or a few phrases are needed. A more complete summary might look like this:

Summary A

The world depends on the oil of South-West Asia for many uses:
- —fuel for cars, trucks, planes, buses, and ships
- —plastic goods, electrical power, and heat

Now you have a better idea of what information is contained in Selection A. A few phrases added to the summary sentence make it easier to remember what is in the entire selection.

Notice that this summary contains the same opinion that is found in the selection.

Selection A

South-West Asia is the world's leading producer of oil. The United States, Western Europe, Japan, and other parts of the world need the oil found in South-West Asia. Oil is used for fuel in cars, trucks, buses, airplanes, and ships. It is also used to make plastic and to produce electrical power to run factories. Homes and office buildings are heated by oil. Much of the world depends on the oil produced in South-West Asia.

Summary A

The world depends on the oil of South-West Asia for many uses.

You should not add your own opinion to a summary. It should contain only the opinion of the person who wrote the selection.

Notice also that this summary was not copied word for word from the reading selection. You should write a summary in your own words. Then you can be sure you understand the main idea and the facts of the selection.

Here is another reading selection about oil in South-West Asia. Read the selection and the one-sentence summary that appears after it. This time add to the summary phrases that will help you remember the entire selection.

Selection B

The first large deposits of oil in South-West Asia were discovered in Iran in 1908. At that time, the countries of South-West Asia did not have the money or the skill needed to take the oil out of the ground. So they allowed American and European companies to drill for the oil. These companies decided how much oil would be produced and how much to charge for the oil. The countries of South-West Asia received only a small amount of money for the oil found on their land. In the 1950's, these countries began to demand more money for their oil. Within a short time, the countries of South-West Asia gained control of their oil resources. Now they decide how much oil to produce and how much to charge for it.

Summary B

Control of South-West Asian oil resources has passed from American and European companies to the countries of South-West Asia.

_____

_____

_____

_____

_____

_____

_____

_____

_____

_____

If the phrases you have written help you remember more information from Selection B, you have written a good summary. Here is an example of what you could have written.

Summary B

Control of South-West Asian oil resources has passed from American and European companies to the countries of South-West Asia.

—*after oil discovered in 1908, South-West Asian countries allowed foreign companies to take it out of the ground*

—*small amount of money paid to South-West*

Asian countries by foreign companies

—South-West Asian countries demanded more money, and after the 1950's, took control of oil production and pricing

Sometimes the reading selection you are asked to summarize may contain more than one paragraph. When this is the case, it may be impossible to summarize the entire selection in just one sentence or a few phrases. You may need several sentences or phrases to summarize each paragraph.

The following reading selection contains three paragraphs. You have already read the first two paragraphs in Selections A and B. Now read all three paragraphs. Notice that Paragraphs 1 and 2 have been summarized. For Paragraph 3 write a summary that includes one sentence stating the main idea and at least two phrases. Use the information in Paragraph 3 to help you.

Oil Changes the World

Paragraph 1

South-West Asia is the world's leading producer of oil. The United States, Western Europe, Japan, and other parts of the world need the oil found in South-West Asia. Oil is used for fuel in cars, trucks, buses, airplanes, and ships. It is also used to make plastic and to produce electrical power to run factories. Homes and office buildings are heated by oil. Much of the world depends on the oil produced in South-West Asia.

Paragraph 2

The first large deposits of oil in South-West Asia were discovered in Iran in 1908. At that time, the countries of South-West Asia did not have the money or the skill needed to take the oil out of the ground. So they allowed American and European companies to drill for the oil. These companies decided how much oil would be produced and how much to charge for the oil. The countries of South-West Asia received only a small amount of money for the oil found on their land. In the 1950's, these countries began to demand more money for their oil. Within a short time, the countries of South-West Asia gained control of their oil resources. Now they decide how much oil to produce and how much to charge for it.

Paragraph 3

By raising the price of their oil, the South-West Asian oil-producing countries have become very wealthy. Some of this wealth has been spent by the rulers, who replaced their camels and tents with fancy, large cars and air-conditioned palaces. Recently, the rulers have begun to spend more money for the good of their people. Many of the countries now provide their people with free health care and free education. Large cities with modern housing have been built. For years, the oil of South-West Asia brought changes to the rest of the world. Now the money made from oil is changing the lives of the people of South-West Asia.

Summary of Paragraph 1

The world depends on the oil of South-West Asia for many uses:
—fuel for cars, trucks, planes, buses, and ships
—plastic goods, electrical power, and heat

Summary of Paragraph 2

Control of South-West Asian oil resources has passed from American and European companies to the countries of South-West Asia.
—after oil discovered in 1908, South-West Asian countries allowed foreign companies to take it out of the ground
—small amounts of money paid to South-West Asian countries by foreign companies
—South-West Asian countries demanded more money, and after 1950's, took control of oil production and pricing

Summary of Paragraph 3

_____

_____

_____

_____

_____

_____

_____

How you finished this summary was up to you. All that matters is that your summary helps you remember the main ideas and important facts contained in a longer reading selection.

Here are a few important points to remember when you are writing a summary:

1. Your summary should be much shorter than the reading selection.
2. Your summary should contain the main ideas of the reading selection.
3. Your summary should not contain your opinion. It should contain only the opinion of the person who wrote the selection.
4. Your summary sentences and phrases should not be copied word for word from the selection. Write a summary in your own words. Then you can be sure you understand the main ideas of the selection.

The next time you are reading something for school, make a summary of what you read. It will help you do better in school. The following exercises will give you practice in writing good summaries.

USING WHAT YOU HAVE LEARNED

A. Read the following selection. Then complete the summary that has been started. Use the information in the selection to help you.

A Great City With a Big Problem

All my life I have lived in Mexico City, the capital and largest city of Mexico. It is a city of beautiful avenues and fine buildings, a city alive with music and sports. Schools, museums, and libraries of every kind enrich the lives of the people. It is a city where people of different racial and ethnic backgrounds have learned to live in peace.

There is, however, one major problem. The city is too crowded. Believe me, I love my neighbors—but there are just too many of them. Nearly 9 million people live in Mexico City proper. When you add in the surrounding areas, the population jumps to nearly 16 million. The city's rapid growth has resulted in serious air pollution, water shortages, and major traffic jams.

You are, of course, invited to visit my great city—as long as you promise not to stay too long.

According to the writer, Mexico City is a great city with a big problem.

— capital and largest city of Mexico

— beautiful avenues and fine buildings

_____

_____

_____

_____

_____

_____

_____

_____

B. Read the following selection. Then write your own summary.

Asian Goods Have a Big Market in the United States

If you own a television set, a radio, a VCR, a tape recorder, or a DVD or CD player, look to see where it was made. There is a good chance that it was made in Asia. If your family owns a car, a computer, or a camera, it may also have been made in Asia. It is even likely that some of your clothes were made there. Asia is one of the major <u>industrial</u> areas of the world today, and the United States is one of <u>its</u> biggest customers.

Japan leads all other countries in Asia in selling goods to the United States. Its imports are valued at nearly $200 billion. One-third of this amount comes from the sale of automobiles, vans, and trucks. It is no wonder that Japanese companies such as Toyota, Honda, Sony, and Panasonic are as familiar to Americans as any U.S. company.

China is the second-largest Asian seller of goods to the United States. Its imports are valued at nearly $100 billion. Then comes Taiwan with imports valued at $55 billion. The list contains: South Korea $54 billion, Singapore $35 billion, Malaysia $30 billion, Thailand $20 billion, the Philippines $20 billion, India $13 billion, and Indonesia $7 billion.

Years ago, Americans bought Asian goods because they were cheaper than goods made in the United States. Today, this is still true for some products. But today, Americans buy Asian goods because they are made well. It seems that Americans cannot get enough of them.

<u>Industrial:</u> having to do with factories and machines; manufacturing

---

_____

_____

_____

_____

_____

_____

_____

_____

_____

C. Read the following selection. Then write your own summary.

An African Kingdom of the Past

Far into the twentieth century, Africa south of the Sahara was still a mystery to most Americans. In most U.S. schools, studying the history of the area was limited to European imperialism in Africa. It was as if Africa south of the Sahara had no history of its own.

Only in the 1960's did American schools begin to teach about the great civilizations that once existed in Africa south of the Sahara. One of those civilizations, located in West Africa, was Songhai. It extended both east and west of the Niger River and covered an area some 2,000 miles wide.

From the mid-1400's to the late 1500's was the time of Songhai's greatest strength. Its power and wealth came from trade. Every year large groups of traders from Songhai rode on camels across the Sahara carrying gold and ivory. They returned with salt, jewelry, and cloth. Iron weapons helped the rulers of Songhai control the people of their very large territory.

One of Songhai's most important cities was Timbuktu, noted for its university. A visitor from North Africa wrote about the city in 1526: "Here are a great many doctors, judges, priests, and learned men." Although Songhai was taken over by invaders in the late sixteenth century, Timbuktu has continued to be famous.

civilization: a high level of culture, science, industry and government

---

_____

_____

_____

_____

_____

_____

_____

_____

_____

_____

TEXTBOOK, REFERENCE, AND TEST SKILLS

CHAPTER 9
Using a Textbook

Imagine what it would be like if you knew everything. If you were asked any question, you could come up with the answer immediately.

The truth is that no one knows everything or is born with a knowledge of every subject. You know about things because you learn about them. School is the place where you learn about many important and interesting subjects that will help you throughout your life. In school you also learn where to find answers to questions you have.

The greatest source of knowledge is books. One of the most important books you use every day is your textbook. It can give you a lot of information if you know how to use it.

Table of Contents

Let us imagine that you are going to use a textbook entitled *Africa* in your Social Studies class. You would like to know what this book is going to teach you about Africa. To find out, you could look through every page of the book, but this would take a long time. How can you find out quickly and easily what this book on Africa is all about? You could look at the *table of contents,* which can be found within the first few pages of almost every book. A table of contents is a list of the main topics contained in a book.

In a textbook, the table of contents usually lists units and chapters. The units deal with the most important subjects covered in the book. Each unit is divided into several chapters. Each chapter covers a specific (certain) subject, which is part of the general subject of its unit. For example, a unit on United States geography might have separate chapters on each region of the country.

On page 55 is the table of contents for the textbook on Africa. Notice the number that is listed to the right of each chapter title. This number is the page on which the chapter begins. For example:

Chapter 3   Animals of Africa   12

This means that Chapter 3 begins on page 12.

In many textbooks, no page number is listed to the right of each unit title in the table of contents. This means that each unit begins on the same page as the first chapter of that unit. Thus, in the textbook on Africa, Unit One begins on page 3, Unit Two begins on page 25, and so forth.

Answer the following questions using the table of contents.

1. The table of contents of the book *Africa*

_____ (a) lists every subject covered in the book.

_____ (b) lists only ten of the most important subjects in the book.

_____ (c) lists the important subjects in the book and the pages on which they are found.

Which answer did you choose? No table of contents lists every subject in a book. The purpose of a table of contents is to list the important subjects and the pages on which they are found. The table of contents of the book *Africa* does this. Therefore, the answer to question 1 is (c).

_____ 2. True or False: The table of contents shows that this book tells the story of Africa's history.

What was your answer? Look at the table of contents. Is there any unit in the book that deals with the history of Africa? Yes,

Unit Two is entitled History and Government. Is there any chapter in Unit Two that deals only with Africa's history—its past? Yes, Africa's past is covered in Chapter 5. Now you know that the book does tell the story of Africa's history. Therefore, the answer to question 2 is True.

_____ 3. True or False: The table of contents shows that this book tells about the different kinds of clothing Africans wear.

What was your answer? Look over the table of contents carefully. There is nothing in the table of contents that deals specifically with African clothing. Therefore, the answer to question 3 is False.

Index

Because you could not find anything about African clothing in the table of contents does not mean that the topic is not mentioned in the book. Remember, the table of contents lists only the main subjects to be covered in the book. African clothing is surely discussed somewhere in the book. To find out by looking through every page for the information would take a long time. How then can you find the pages in the book where African clothing is discussed? You can answer this question by using the *index* of the book. It is usually at the back of a book. Every subject in a book is listed in the index in alphabetical order. This means that the subjects are arranged in the order of the letters of the alphabet. Next to each subject, you can find the page number or numbers where the information can be found.

Here is a part of the index from the book on Africa. This example shows only the subjects in the book that start with the letter C. Remember, however, that an index uses all the letters in the alphabet.

C

Cairo, Egypt, 95-96
Cameroon, 37,112
Cape of Good Hope, 6, 10
Capetown, South Africa, 10, 21, 54-55, 82
Caravans, 8, 26, 90. *See also* Animals.
Casablanca, Morocco, 99
Central African Empire, 55,113
Chad, 56, 92
Churchill, Winston, 41, 43
Cities, 95-103
    capital, 95-96, 98-99, 101
    change in population, 95, 100
    port, 97, 99, 103
Climate, 7-11
Clothing in Africa, 20, 83, 113-116
Colonialism, 35-49
    Belgian, 36
    British, 37-39, 43-44
    French, 39-40, 44-45
    German, 42
    Portuguese, 41, 49
    Spanish, 41
Communication, 56, 91
Congo. *See* Democratic Republic of the Congo and Republic of Congo.
Congo River, 5, 76, 92
Crops, 61, 63-65, 73

Use the index to answer the following questions.

1. Which pages in the book contain information about clothing in Africa?

    _____ (*a*) 47, 112

    _____ (*b*) 97, 99, 103

    _____ (*c*) 20, 83, 113-116

Which answer did you choose? First of all, find the word "clothing" in the index. Remember, the index is in alphabetical order. When you find the word "clothing," you will see numbers next to it. These numbers are the pages in the book that contain information about clothing in Africa. Next to the words "Clothing in Africa" in the index are the numbers 20, 83, 113-116. Therefore, the answer to question 1 is (*c*).

The information about clothing in Africa is found in three separate places in the book. The first place is on page 20. The second place is on page 83. The third place is on pages 113-116. The dash (-) between 113 and 116 stands for all the pages between 113 and 116. In this case, the dash stands for pages 114 and 115. So when you see a dash between pages in an index, you know it really stands for all of the pages between those listed.

2. Which one of the following subjects comes first in the index?

    _____ (*a*) Churchill

    _____ (*b*) Congo

    _____ (*c*) Caravans

Which answer did you choose? Remember that the index is arranged in alphabetical order. Look at the choices to the answer to question 2. Caravans starting with the letters Ca comes before Churchill (Ch) and

Congo (Co). Therefore, the answer to question 2 is (c).

Next to the word "Caravans" in the index are the numbers 8, 26, 90. You now know that these numbers stand for pages where information on caravans can be found. But there are other words on the same line as Caravans, 8, 26, 90. These words are "See also Animals." This means that by looking under Animals in the index, you can find more information about caravans.

The words "See also Animals" are called a *cross-reference* because they refer, or send, you to another part of the book to find more information on the subject.

Notice that the name "Churchill" is listed in the index like this: Churchill, Winston. The person's name was really Winston Churchill. But a person's last name is more important than her or his first name. So the last name is written first, followed by a comma (,) and then the first name.

Notice also the word "Congo" in the index. There are no pages given after the word. Instead, you read "*See* Democratic Republic of the Congo and Republic of Congo." This means that you have to look elsewhere in the index. You would look under D for Democratic Republic of the Congo or R for Republic of Congo. For both listings, you would find pages.

3. The book *Africa* tells how strong European countries controlled weaker areas of Africa. These areas were considered to be colonies, or possessions. The system of control was called colonialism. Which pages in the book contain information on Portuguese colonialism in Africa?

_____ (a) 35-37

_____ (b) 41, 49

_____ (c) 54, 59

Which answer did you choose this time? In the index, would you look under P for Portuguese or under C for colonialism? In some books, you could look under either letter. In your book on Africa, the pages are given under C for colonialism. When you find colonialism in the index, you see that the information is divided into six parts. It looks like this:

> Colonialism, 35-49
> Belgian, 36
> British, 37-39, 43-44
> French, 39-40, 44-45
> German, 42
> Portuguese, 41, 49
> Spanish, 41

The main countries that had colonies in Africa are listed in alphabetical order. The pages listed next to each country contain information about its colonialism in Africa. Look under colonialism until you find the word "Portuguese." You can see that the pages next to Portuguese are 41 and 49. On these pages you can find information on Portuguese colonialism in Africa. Therefore, the answer to question 3 is (b).

Glossary

Another important part of many textbooks is the *glossary*. It is a list of difficult terms and their meanings in alphabetical order. A glossary is usually found at the back of a book just before the index. In the textbook *Africa,* the table of contents shows that the glossary starts on page 131. When you come across a difficult word in a book, look to see whether it is in the glossary. Knowing the meaning of every word will help you understand more clearly what you are reading.

Here is a glossary with some of the Social Studies terms from this book.

Glossary of Social Studies Terms

century   period of 100 years
civilization   high level of culture, science, industry, and government
culture   the common way of life of a large group of people or a nation
endangered species   type of living thing (a species) in danger of dying out
industrial   having to do with factories and machines, manufacturing
natural resources   materials found on or in the earth used to benefit humans
population   total number of people living in a place

Answer the following questions using the glossary.

1. A glossary

    _____ (a) lists every subject covered in a book.

    _____ (b) lists difficult terms in the order in which they appear in a book.

    _____ (c) lists difficult terms in alphabetical order.

Which answer did you choose? A glossary does not list every subject. Nor does it list difficult subjects in the order in which they appear, for that would make them too hard to find. A glossary lists difficult terms in alphabetical order. Therefore, the answer to question 1 is (c).

_____ 2. True or False: The glossary on page 57 gives the page numbers on which the correct definitions appear.

What was your answer? You can see that this glossary gives the definitions themselves, not the pages where they appear. Therefore, the answer to question 2 is False.

A textbook is a useful tool. Proper use of your textbook will help you find information, do your homework, and study for tests.

The following exercises on the use of a table of contents, an index, and a glossary will help you get more out of your textbooks.

USING WHAT YOU HAVE LEARNED

A. Place a check mark next to the correct answers to questions 1 to 10.

1. The table of contents provides

    ____ (a) a list of every subject in a book.

    ____ (b) a list of important subjects in alphabetical order.

    ____ (c) an overall view of the major subjects in a book.

2. The table of contents is usually found

    ____ (a) in the first few pages of a book.

    ____ (b) in the middle of a book.

    ____ (c) in the back of a book.

3. The table of contents in a textbook is usually divided into

    ____ (a) units and chapters.

    ____ (b) books and volumes.

    ____ (c) pages.

4. Every subject in a book is listed in the

    ____ (a) table of contents.

    ____ (b) index.

    ____ (c) glossary.

5. The index of a book is arranged

    ____ (a) like the table of contents.

    ____ (b) by page order.

    ____ (c) in alphabetical order.

6. The index is usually found

  ____ (*a*) in the front of a book.

  ____ (*b*) in the middle of a book.

  ____ (*c*) in the back of a book.

7. Which one of the following subjects would be listed first in an index?

  ____ (*a*) World War II

  ____ (*b*) Woodrow Wilson

  ____ (*c*) women's rights

8. In an index example Pollution, 172-175, information on pollution can be found

  ____ (*a*) on lines 172 and 175.

  ____ (*b*) on pages 172 and 175 only.

  ____ (*c*) on pages 172, 173, 174, and 175.

9. The difficult words in a textbook are often explained in the

  ____ (*a*) index.

  ____ (*b*) glossary.

  ____ (*c*) table of contents.

10. The glossary in a book is usually found

  ____ (*a*) just after the table of contents.

  ____ (*b*) just before the index.

  ____ (*c*) in the middle of the book.

B. Study the following table of contents and index.

SOUTH-WEST ASIA/AFRICA: *Table of Contents*

SOUTH-WEST ASIA/AFRICA: *Index*

A

Place a check mark next to the correct answers to questions 1 to 10.

1. The book on South-West Asia/Africa is divided into

 _____ (*a*) two units.

 _____ (*b*) four units.

 _____ (*c*) six units.

2. Unit Two deals with

 _____ (*a*) the land and people of South-West Asia/Africa.

 _____ (*b*) South-West Asia/Africa in modern times.

 _____ (*c*) the history of South-West Asia/Africa.

3. The chapter on traveling in South-West Asia/Africa begins on

 _____ (*a*) page 53.

 _____ (*b*) page 7.

 _____ (*c*) page 75.

4. The table of contents shows that this book

 _____ (*a*) deals with the importance of oil in South-West Asia/Africa.

 _____ (*b*) contains homework assignments.

 _____ (*c*) contains many colored photographs.

5. If you come across a difficult word in this book, you can look up its meaning in the

 _____ (*a*) table of contents.

 _____ (*b*) glossary.

 _____ (*c*) index.

6. When a subject is not listed in the table of contents,

    ____ (*a*) there is no way to look it up.

    ____ (*b*) it is necessary to look through every page of the book to find it.

    ____ (*c*) you can most likely find it listed in the index.

7. The index in the book begins on

    ____ (*a*) page 3.

    ____ (*b*) page 89.

    ____ (*c*) page 93.

8. Information on the Aswan Dam can be found on

    ____ (*a*) page 6.

    ____ (*b*) page 35.

    ____ (*c*) page 40.

9. Which one of the following subjects is listed first in the index?

    ____ (*a*) Kemal Ataturk

    ____ (*b*) Alexander the Great

    ____ (*c*) Animals

10. The index lists the pages for Saudi Arabia

    ____ (*a*) under A for Arabia.

    ____ (*b*) under S for Saudi Arabia.

    ____ (*c*) under C for Countries of South-West Asia/Africa.

C. Study the following table of contents and index.

THE ASIAN WORLD: *Index*

Place a check mark next to the correct answers to questions 1 to 9.

1. The book, *The Asian World,* is divided into

    ____ (*a*) two units.

    ____ (*b*) four units.

    ____ (*c*) five units.

2. Unit Two of the book deals with

    ____ (*a*) Russia and Central Asia.

    ____ (*b*) China and its neighbors.

    ____ (*c*) Japan.

3. Unit Four begins on

    ____ (*a*) page 54.

    ____ (*b*) page 93.

    ____ (*c*) page 121.

4. The table of contents shows that this book deals with

    ____ (*a*) the early history of Russia.

    ____ (*b*) the early history of Africa.

    ____ (*c*) the early history of the United States.

5. The chapter on the people of Japan begins on

    ____ (*a*) page 98.

    ____ (*b*) page 104.

    ____ (*c*) page 110.

6. Information on Kashmir can be found on

    ____ (*a*) page 148.

    ____ (*b*) page 101.

    ____ (*c*) page 72.

7. Which one of the following subjects is mentioned on more than one page in the book?

    ____ (*a*) Lena River

    ____ (*b*) Koran

    ____ (*c*) Mao Zedong

8. The book tells about Muslims in

    ____ (a) Russia and Central Asia only.

    ____ (b) India and Southeast Asia only.

    ____ (c) South Asia, Southeast Asia, Russia, and Central Asia.

9. In the index listing for Korea, the words "*See also* Manchuria" are called a cross-reference because

    ____ (a) they refer, or send, you to another part of the book for more information on Korea.

    ____ (b) all the information in the book on Korea is found on four pages.

    ____ (c) they refer, or send, you to another part of the book for more information on Manchuria.

10. Describe in your own words the difference between a table of contents and an index. (Answer in two or three sentences.)

D. Study the following table of contents and index of the book *The Latin American World.*

THE LATIN AMERICAN WORLD: *Table of Contents*

THE LATIN AMERICAN WORLD: *Index*

D-1. Place a check mark next to the correct answers to questions 1 to 10.

1. This book, *The Latin American World,* is divided into

    ____ (*a*) four units.

    ____ (*b*) five units.

    ____ (*c*) ten units.

2. Unit Three deals with

    ____ (*a*) South America.

    ____ (*b*) Mexico and Central America.

    ____ (*c*) Mexico only.

3. The chapter on Puerto Rico begins on

_____ (*a*) page 29.

_____ (*b*) page 136.

_____ (*c*) page 182.

4. Which one of the following is found in the front of the book?

_____ (*a*) The table of contents

_____ (*b*) The glossary

_____ (*c*) The index

5. The table of contents shows that the book deals with

_____ (*a*) Napoleon III's takeover of Mexico.

_____ (*b*) the United States' interest in Latin America.

_____ (*c*) the Panama Canal.

6. If you come across a difficult word in the book, you can probably find its meaning in the

_____ (*a*) table of contents.

_____ (*b*) glossary.

_____ (*c*) index.

7. The index in the book begins on

_____ (*a*) page 4.

_____ (*b*) page 205.

_____ (*c*) page 213.

8. Which one of the following is listed first in the index?

_____ (*a*) Panama Canal

_____ (*b*) Panama

_____ (*c*) Pan-American Highway

9. If you look up oil in the index, you are told

_____ (*a*) that the information is on pages 72 and 148.

_____ (*b*) to see Natural Resources.

_____ (*c*) that no information is given in the book.

10. The index shows that information on the natural resources of South America is on pages 69-81. This means that information can be found on

_____ (*a*) two pages.   _____ (*b*) ten pages.   _____ (*c*) 13 pages.

D-2. Look at the index and then fill in the correct page or pages where the following information can be found.

1. Pampas _____

2. Bernardo O'Higgins _____

3. Natural Resources in Mexico _____

4. Patagonian Desert _____

5. Puerto Rican Nationalism _____

CHAPTER 10
Using Reference Materials

The most important source of information in your Social Studies class is your textbook. But it may not give you as much information on a certain subject, or topic, as you would like. To find more detailed information, you may need to use special reference materials.

Reference Materials in Book Form

Let us first learn about reference materials in book form. Your school or public library will have a large number of reference books in an area of the library marked REFERENCE. Because many people use these reference books, you are not allowed to take them out of the library. Reference books contain a great deal of information on many topics, so you usually do not read through them. Instead, you pick out only the information you need.

Encyclopedias

Let us suppose that you are reading about glaciers in your Social Studies class. You want to know more about them than your textbook tells you. A good place to start your research is with an *encyclopedia*. Encyclopedias give detailed information on almost every subject.

All the subjects in an encyclopedia are arranged in alphabetical order. Because an encyclopedia contains so much information, it is usually divided into several books, or volumes. In the drawing on the right, you can see an example of how an encyclopedia may be divided into volumes. Letters are printed on the spine (narrow end) of each

volume. This way you know which volume to pick up when you are looking for a certain subject. For example, the first letter in the subject glaciers is g. You will find articles on glaciers and on all other subjects beginning with g in the volume with the letter G on the binding.

You can also see in the drawing that some letters need more than one volume while other letters share a volume. Notice also the special index volume (Volume 23), which lists in alphabetical order all the subjects covered in the encyclopedia. The index gives the volume and pages where each subject can be found.

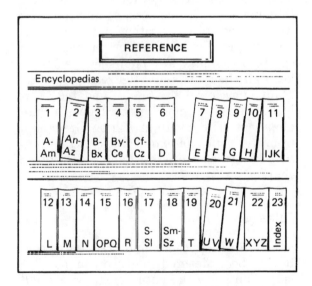

Many encyclopedia articles include maps, photographs, and useful facts and figures. Long articles are divided into sections, with each section dealing with a different aspect of the subject. In the *World Book Encyclopedia,* the article on glaciers is divided into an introduction, five smaller topics called subtopics, and a list of related articles at the end. The entire article is printed in Exercise C of this chapter on pages 74–75. The sections of the article are:

GLACIER
Kinds of Glaciers
How Glaciers Form
The Movement of Glaciers
How Glaciers Shape the Land
Famous Glaciers
Related Articles

The headings of the different sections are bold typed to make it easier to see where they begin. The headings help you find information quickly. For example if you want to know why glaciers move, you can go quickly to the subtopic "The Movement of Glaciers." If the article does not contain all the information you need, you can go to the section "Related Articles." It lists other articles relating to glaciers that are found elsewhere in the encyclopedia.

Almanac

Another helpful reference book is an *almanac*. It contains useful, up-to-date facts and figures on a large number of subjects that include art, business, countries of the world, geography, education, industry, farming, religion, science, entertainment, and sports. Almanacs are published yearly to keep all their facts and figures up to date. Many encyclopedias are also updated yearly, but they are much more expensive than almanacs. The entire article on Greenland from the *Time Almanac 2001 with Information Please* is printed in Exercise D of this chapter, on page 77.

Atlases

An *atlas* is another helpful reference book. It is a book devoted mostly to maps. The maps can show the entire earth or a small area of it, boundaries, population, rainfall, heights of land features, natural resources, products, and other subjects.

Perhaps you want to locate Malaspina Glacier on a map. First, look at the index of the atlas. Here is a small section of the index from the Hammond *Medallion World Atlas*:

Malargue, Arg. 143/C4
Malartic, Que. 174/B3
Malaspina (glac.), Alaska 196/K3
Malaspina (str.), Br. Col. 184/J2
Malatya, Turkey 59/C2
Malatya (prov.), Turkey 63/H3
Malawi, 3/L6

Malaspina Glacier is the third entry. The abbreviation (glac.) is for glacier. This glacier is located in Alaska. Notice the indication 196/K3. The first number means that you are to look at the map on page 196. "K" and "3" are guidelines for locating the glacier itself. Along the top of the map on page 196 are letters from A to Q. Along the sides are numbers from 1 to 3. Find K and follow it down to the level of 3. In the area where these two meet, you will find Malaspina Glacier.

There are other items in this sample section of an index that are worth noting. A country appears by itself—Malawi. Cities and towns are followed by the names of larger areas in which they are located—Arg. (country of Argentina) or Que. (province of Canada). A capital city is indicated by the abbreviation "cap." in parentheses. A physical feature, such as a glacier, river, lake, or strait, is also indicated in parentheses.

In Units Five, Six, and Seven, you will learn more about using maps.

Dictionaries

Another important reference book is a *dictionary,* which is an alphabetical list of the words in a language and their meanings. For each word listed, a dictionary gives the spelling, the pronunciation, the part of speech, the various meanings, and the origin (where the word comes from).

Let us take a close look at a word in a dictionary. Here is what the paperback edition of *The American Heritage Dictionary* says about the word "current":

cur•rent (kûr´ ənt) *adj.* **1.** Belonging to the time now passing; now in progress. **2.** Commonly accepted; prevalent.—*n.* **1.** A steady and smooth onward movement, as of water. **2.** The part of any body of liquid or gas that has a continuous onward movement. **3.** A general tendency. **4. a.** A flow of electric charge. **b.** The amount of electric charge flowing past a specified circuit point per unit time. [<L. *currere,* to run.]

The entry first shows that "cur•rent" is divided into two parts, or syllables. The respelling in parentheses shows how to pronounce the word. (You will see on the dictionary page a key that indicates how to say each letter.) Next comes the part of speech, *adj.* for adjective. Later comes another part of speech, *n.* for noun. There are seven meanings, or definitions, of the word. (Make sure you know which meaning you want.) The L stands for Latin, so we know that current comes from (<) a Latin word *currere,* meaning "to run."

Let us see what you have learned about reference material in book form.

1. Which reference book would be likely to give the most information on ocean currents?

   _____ (*a*) Dictionary

   _____ (*b*) Almanac

   _____ (*c*) Encyclopedia

Which answer did you choose? A dictionary will give you the meaning of ocean currents. An almanac might list different ocean currents and their locations. But an encyclopedia would be the most likely to give you detailed information on ocean currents, along with maps and drawings. Therefore, the answer to question 1 is (*c*).

2. Which reference book in a library is most likely to have the latest population figures for Alaska?

   _____ (*a*) Encyclopedia

   _____ (*b*) Almanac

   _____ (*c*) Atlas

Which answer did you choose? All these reference books could give population figures for Alaska. But your library is most likely to buy an almanac every year because it is less expensive than an encyclopedia and most atlases. Moreover, the almanac would most likely have the latest population figures for Alaska. Therefore, the answer to question 2 is (*b*).

Reference Materials on Computers

Many encyclopedias, almanacs, atlases, and dictionaries also come in CD (compact disk) form for use on a computer. The material on a CD usually looks the same as in book form.

When the computer is turned on, you will see a flashing *cursor* I on the screen. The keyboard is similar to a typewriter. As you type, what you type will appear on the screen where the cursor is. The cursor will move one space to the right for each letter, number or character you type.

You can avoid some of the typing by using the *mouse.* (The mouse is a small two-button device connected to the computer by a wire.) Notice the arrow ↖ on the screen. As you move the mouse on a flat surface, the arrow on the screen will move in the same direction. Move the mouse until the arrow on the screen touches the item you want. Then click the left button on the mouse.

Reference materials may already be installed on the computer you use. If not, they can be installed easily on a computer that has a *CD-ROM drive.* Push the button of the CD-ROM drive on the front of the computer, and a tray will open. Place the CD on the tray and press the button to close the tray. The installation may automatically start. If it does not, follow the installation instructions that come with the CD.

Card Catalog and Computer Catalog

Perhaps you could not find the information you want on glaciers in the reference materials already mentioned in this chapter.

Broaden the search by using the *card catalog* or the *computer catalog* in the library.

A card catalog is a listing on cards of every book in a library. Every book is listed on at least three cards—*subject* card, *title* card, and *author* card. Thus, you can look for a book by subject, title, or author. No matter which card you look up, the title, author, author's year of birth (and year of death), publisher, publication date, description (such as the number of pages), and subject will appear on the card.

All the cards are arranged in alphabetical order in small drawers in cabinets. When the title of a book begins with "The," "A," or "An," the next word in the title is used to determine the alphabetical order. Author cards are listed by the author's last name.

All nonfiction (true or factual) books in the card catalog have a number. Under the number is the first letter of the author's last name. The same number and letter appear on the spine of each copy of the book. Nonfiction books are arranged on shelves in the library according to their number. (Most shelves in the library are numbered.) For example, you may see a shelf numbered 500–549. You would look on that shelf if you were looking for a book marked 511.8 F.

Fiction books (untrue or made-up stories) do not have a number. They are found in the part of the library marked FICTION. Fiction books are placed on the shelves in alphabetical order by the author's last name.

In recent years, libraries have turned to computers as the main way to catalog their books and other resources.

The first screen of the computer catalog will give instructions. By following them, you will come to a screen (similar to the one below) on which you will type your request.

```
TYPE AN AUTHOR, TITLE, OR SUBJECT.
THEN PRESS "ENTER":

I

                    Enter [    ]

Erase Entry [    ]        Help [    ]
```

If you know the author of a book on glaciers, type the author's last name, comma, first name (unless there are different instructions on the screen). Each letter and character that you type will appear in the box on the screen. If you know the title of a book on glaciers, type the title. (If the title begins with "The," "A," or "An," start with the second word in the title.) Perhaps you have to search by subject. Type the word *glaciers*. Then move the mouse until the arrow on the screen touches the Enter box, then click the mouse. A new screen will appear.

You will see a listing of books on glaciers. In the example at the top of the right column on this page, the search found 117 books, and 3 out of the 117 books appear on this first screen. To see the next group of books, you would click on More Matches.

```
1   Carlin, Joseph, 1953–              2000
    Fighting the Glaciers of the North

2   Emmet, Robin, 1954–                1995
    Glaciers of the Alps              551.3 E

3   Simmonds, John, 1936–              1994
    The Major Glaciers of the World   551.3 S

    Check on list number for more information.
    3 out of 117 matches

More Matches [  ]   Go Back [  ]   Help [  ]
```

The books are listed in the order of publication, with the most recent listed first. Each listing gives the author, title, and year of publication.

3. Which of the three books listed would you find on a library shelf numbered 525–585?

___

Nonfiction books have a number, followed by the first letter of the author's last name. Book 2 on the screen list is marked 551.3 E and Book 3 is marked 551.3 S. Both numbers are between 525 and 585, so books 2 and 3 would be found on the shelf numbered 525–585. Book 1 has no shelf number because it is fiction. In a part of the library marked FICTION, fiction books are placed on shelves in alphabetical order by the author's last name.

But before you go to the shelves, you can find more information on the books by clicking the numbers to the left of the books. For example, if you click the 3 box with the mouse, you will see the following screen.

```
Title: The Major Glaciers of the World
Author: Simmonds, John, 1953–
Publisher: Chicago: Smith, 1994
Description: 384 pages, illustrated
Subject: Glaciers, location and description of
         the world's major glaciers

Status: one copy, in

Go Back [  ]   Help [  ]   New Search [  ]
```

This screen shows the same information found in the card catalog, but it also tells you if the book is in the library. If the book is checked out, you can click on Go Back and return to the previous screen to choose another book. When you finish with glaciers, you can look for a book on a different subject by clicking New Search. The first screen will reappear and you can type in a different author, title, or subject.

Resource Material on the Internet

If the computer you use is connected to the *Internet,* you have another valuable source of information available to you.

The Internet is a network of computers that uses a system known as the World Wide Web to provide information and resources on almost every subject. To gain access to the Internet, the computer you use must be connected to an Internet Service Provider (ISP).

If a computer has access to the Internet, the computer screen will display an *icon* (picture) that represents the Internet. Using the mouse, move the arrow on the screen to the icon. When you click the icon once or twice, the computer will connect to the Internet.

The appearance of the first Internet screen will vary. Near the top of the screen you may see one or more of the following ways to start your search:

Icon   Word **S̲earch**

"Search" box

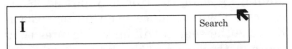

You can type your search request in the search box provided. If you click on the icon or on the S in S̲earch, a new screen will appear with a list of search programs. The list will probably include Yahoo!, Google, and Alta Vista—three popular search programs. Click on the program you want to use, and it will appear on another screen. The program you choose will also show a wide box. In the box, type a word or phrase that must appear in all your search results.

Let us say that you type in *glaciers,* as shown below. You click on the "Search" box.

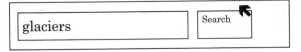

The search program will list on a new screen all the resources it has that match your request. Each resource will offer a brief description, and the word *glaciers,* if it appears in the description, will be in bold type. You can see what the screen of a search result looks like in Exercise F of this chapter on page 79.

On the first screen of results, the search program will state the total number of resources found and the number of resources that appear on that first screen. At the bottom of the screen, you will see an underlined group of words, such as <u>Next 10 Site Matches</u>. These underlined words are called a *link.* When you bring the arrow down the screen and touch the link with it, the arrow turns into a small hand. Click on the link and a new screen will appear with the next 10 listings.

Here is an example of a listing:

What are glaciers?

What are **glaciers**? . . . Go to What are the physical effects of **glaciers**?
Return to **Glaciers** and the glacial ages? . . .
www.uvm.edu/whale/GlaciersWhatAre.html - 2k

Each listing is a separate *Web site,* with its own particular way of presenting information. The real Internet address of each Web site may be on the last line of the listing and usually begins with www. But to go to this site, you click on the link (the underlined group of words) on the first line. By clicking on the link, you will be connected to the information and resources found on that Web site.

Before you choose the first Web site to visit, consider limiting (narrowing) your search. For the word *glaciers,* some search programs will list as many as 270,000 Web sites. In limiting your search, you could decide to look for photographs of the Malaspina Glacier in Alaska. At either the top or the bottom of the screen, you will see a box with your entry glaciers and next to it a "Search" box.

Place the cursor before the g in *glaciers* and hit the Delete (Del) key on the keyboard eight times to remove the eight letters in glaciers. Type in *Malaspina Glacier* and click the "Search" box.

When the next screen appears, you might see that the number of Web sites listed has been reduced to fewer than a 1,000. Those are still too many Web sites to look through. Here is a way to narrow the search even more. Place quotation marks around *Malaspina Glacier,* as shown below, and click on the "Search" box.

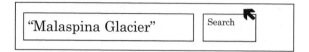

When the next screen appears, you might see that about 500 Web sites match your request. What exactly did the quotation marks do? They told the search program to list only those Web sites in which the words Malaspina and Glacier appear together and in that order.

But 500 Web sites are still too many to search through. You can further narrow your search by adding key words. You must put a plus sign (+) before each word and before any group of words in quotation marks. You are looking for photographs, so type in +photos. When your search box looks like the following, click on the "Search" box.

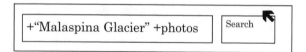

This time the screen will probably list no more than 50 Web sites. You could still narrow the search more by adding other +words or by adding −words. By placing a minus sign (−) in front of a word, you are telling the search program not to list any Web site that contains that word. For example, if you did not want any Web site that contained the word *iceberg,* you would type:

+"Malaspina Glacier" +photos −iceberg

Let us say that you decide to look down the list of 50 Web sites until you find one that seems to match your needs.

When you come to a listing that looks worthwhile, click on the underlined link. The opening screen of a Web site is called the *home page.* There may be many pages on that Web site. As you move the arrow around

a page, it will turn into a hand when it touches a link to another page or to another Web site.

When you find the photograph of Malaspina Glacier that you want, move the arrow onto the photograph and hit the right button on the mouse. Options for copying and saving the photograph will appear.

After you have visited a page you can return to the previous page by clicking the Go-Back arrow (←) on the top of the screen. After you go back to a previous page, you can click the Go-Ahead or Forward arrow (→) to return to a page in the other direction.

If you click the Go-Back arrow (←) enough times, you will go back to the home page of the Web site.

Let us see what you have learned about using the Internet for research.

4. Which one of the following entries in an Internet search program would result in the smallest number of Web sites?

_____ (*a*) North America

_____ (*b*) "North America"

_____ (*c*) "North America" +glacier

Which answer did you choose? The quotation marks around *North America* in choice (*b*) will only produce results that have the words "North America" together and in that order. Thus, choice (*b*) will produce fewer results than choice (*a*). But adding +glacier to "North America" as in choice (*c*) will produce even fewer results because the search will only give sites that contain the words "North America" and "glacier." Therefore, choice (*c*) is the answer to question 4.

5. Why are the underlined words in a listing of an Internet search called a link?

_____

_____

_____

What did you write? A good answer would contain the following idea. A link, by definition, connects two things. The underlined words are called a link because when you click on them, they connect you to a Web site.

Finally, you should remember that any source of information may contain material that is out of date or inaccurate. This is true of material in book or computer form. It is especially true of resource material on the Internet because anyone who knows how to create a Web site can put material of any kind on the Internet. It is a good idea to see if the material you find in a particular source can be found in other sources.

The following exercises will give you more practice in using reference materials.

USING WHAT YOU HAVE LEARNED

A. Which reference book would you look at first to find the following information? Mark **E** for encyclopedia, **D** for dictionary, **AL** for almanac, or **AT** for atlas.

_____ 1. The use of wood in African art

_____ 2. A listing of the five longest rivers in the world

_____ 3. Various meanings of the word "history"

_____ 4. A map showing the greatest number of cities in Algeria as possible

_____ 5. The names of the U.S. Senators from your state

_____ 6. The building of the Panama Canal

_____ 7. The most recent population figures for Thailand

_____ 8. The life of Mohandas Gandhi

_____ 9. The correct way to pronounce "Himalaya"

_____ 10. The location of the island nations of Tonga and Vanuatu and their distance from each other

B. Place a check mark next to the correct answers to questions 1 to 10.

1. An encyclopedia contains information

____ (a) on subjects usually not found in textbooks.

____ (b) on almost all subjects.

____ (c) only on special subjects.

2. The letter M on the spine of a volume of an encyclopedia means that

____ (a) the volume contains only subjects beginning with the letter M.

____ (b) M is the first letter of the last name of the author of the articles in that volume.

____ (c) the volume covers all subjects starting with the letters A to M.

3. A dictionary is a reference book that

____ (a) gives detailed information on many subjects.

____ (b) uses just pictures and no words.

____ (c) gives the pronunciation, meanings, and origin of words.

4. The most important feature of an almanac is that it

____ (a) gives complete details on every subject.

____ (b) gives up-to-date facts and figures on many subjects.

____ (c) has an index.

5. You would most likely use an atlas to find

    ____ (a) the location of different countries.

    ____ (b) the present ruler of a country.

    ____ (c) information on the military strength of a country.

6. Which of the following is an example of a resource material in book form?

    ____ (a) The Web site of *Information Please* almanacs

    ____ (b) The CD version of *Encyclopaedia Britannica*

    ____ (c) A paperback version of *The American Heritage Dictionary*

7. Which information can be found in a library's computer catalog, but not in its card catalog?

    ____ (a) The publisher of a book

    ____ (b) The library status of a book: "in" or "checked out"

    ____ (c) The number of pages in a book

8. The marking 541.6 L on a book's binding identifies the book as

    ____ (a) fiction.

    ____ (b) partly fiction.

    ____ (c) nonfiction.

9. The Internet is a worldwide network of information and resources that can be

    ____ (a) accessed by anyone using a computer with a modem that is connected to an Internet Service Provider

    ____ (b) expected to have only up-to-date and accurate material.

    ____ (c) accessed only if a search program is installed on the computer.

10. In an Internet search program, you first typed in +"South Africa" +Zulu. By adding +Boer to your first search request, you would be

    ____ (a) broadening your search.

    ____ (b) narrowing your search.

    ____ (c) expanding your search.

C. Read the following encyclopedia article on glaciers. Then answer the questions that follow based on the article and on what you have learned about encyclopedias in this chapter.

GLACIER is a huge mass of ice that flows slowly over land. Glaciers form in the cold polar regions and in high mountains. The low temperatures in these places enable large amounts of snow to build up and turn into ice. Most glaciers range in thickness from about 300 to 10,000 feet (91 to 3,000 meters).

Kinds of Glaciers. There are two main kinds of glaciers, *continental glaciers* and *valley glaciers*. They differ in shape, size, and location.

Continental Glaciers are broad, extremely thick ice sheets that cover vast areas of land near the earth's polar regions. The continental glaciers on Greenland and Antarctica, for example, bury mountains and plateaus and conceal the entire landscape except for the highest peaks. Glaciers of this type build up at the center and slope outward toward the sea in all directions.

Valley Glaciers are long, narrow bodies of ice that fill high mountain valleys. Many of them move down sloping valleys from bowl-shaped hollows located among the peaks. In mountains near the equator, such as the northern Andes of South America, valley glaciers occur at elevations of about 15,000 feet (4,570 meters) or higher. Valley glaciers occur at lower elevations in the European Alps, the Southern Alps of New Zealand, and other mountain ranges nearer the poles.

How Glaciers Form. Glaciers begin to form when more snow falls during the winter than melts and evaporates in summer. The excess snow gradually builds up in layers. Its increasing weight causes the snow crystals under the surface to become compact, grainlike pellets. At depths of 50 feet (15 meters) or more, the pellets are further compressed into dense crystals of ice. These crystals combine to form glacial ice. The ice eventually becomes so thick that it begins to move under the pressure of its own great weight.

Glaciers are affected by seasonal variations in snowfall and temperature. Most glaciers increase slightly in size during the winter because snow falls over much of their surface. The cold temperatures promote the buildup of snow. They also limit the melting of the lower parts of the glaciers as the ice masses move downslope. In areas away from the poles, the size of glaciers decreases in summer because the rising temperatures cause the lower parts to melt. In the always frigid polar regions, glaciers shrink for other reasons. When glaciers reach the sea, for example, huge chunks of ice break away from them. These chunks fall into the water and become icebergs (see ICEBERG).

Glaciers may also increase or decrease in size as a result of changes in climate that occur over long periods. For example, the ice sheet that covers much of Greenland is growing smaller because of a gradual rise in temperature in the area since the early 1900's.

The Movement of Glaciers. A glacier flows downslope because of the pull of gravity. The ice crystals deep within the glacier glide over one another as a result of the pressure of the surface layers. These small movements of the individual crystals cause the entire ice mass to move. The melting and refreezing of the ice crystals along the base of a glacier also help it slide downslope. Heat from friction and from the earth's interior melts some of the crystals of the glacier's bottom layer. The water from the dissolved crystals flows down into nearby open spaces in the layer and refreezes, forming new ice crystals.

The surface of a glacier is stiff and rigid, unlike the mass of ice below. It often fractures and forms deep cracks called *crevasses* as the glacier flows over uneven or steep terrain (see CREVASSE). Crevasses also develop because the upper layers of a glacier move faster than its lower layers.

Most glaciers flow extremely slowly and move less than a foot (30 centimeters) per day. But sometimes a glacier may travel much faster for several years. For example, some glaciers at times flow more than 50 feet (15 meters) per day. The various parts of a glacier move at different speeds. The center and upper areas of a valley glacier flow the fastest. The sides and bottom move more slowly because they rub against the walls and floor of the valley. Scientists measure a glacier's speed by driving stakes into the ice at various points and recording the changes in their position.

How Glaciers Shape the Land. As glaciers pass over an area, they help shape its features. They create a variety of land forms by means of erosion and by transporting and depositing rock debris. Glaciers greatly altered the surface of large parts of Europe and North America during the Pleistocene Ice Age, which ended from about 10,000 to 15,000 years ago (see ICE AGE).

Glacial Erosion occurs when an advancing ice mass scoops up rock fragments and drags them along its base. In doing so, the glacier grinds the *bedrock* (layer of solid rock beneath the loose rock fragments), producing a polished but often scratched surface. When a glacier decreases in size, it leaves behind broad humps of hard bedrock called *roches moutonnées.* One side of this kind of land form is smoothly rounded while the other side is rough and irregular.

A glacier in a mountain valley may produce a rounded hollow, called a *cirque,* near the peak of the mountain. A cirque forms when the upper part of a glacier removes blocks of rock from the surrounding cliffs. A glacier also can gouge out a U-shaped depression in a river valley. Such a depression that forms below sea level and is flooded by the ocean is called a *fiord* (see FIORD).

Glacial Deposits consist of clay and sand, and rocks of various sizes. Glaciers pile up these materials, forming uneven ridges called *moraines.* The ridges along the sides of a valley glacier are known as *lateral moraines.* When two valley glaciers come together, the lateral moraines between them merge to form a *medial moraine* along the center of the combined ice mass. The hilly ridge at the lower end of a valley glacier is called a *terminal moraine.* Such a moraine also develops around the edge of a continental glacier.

Other land forms associated with glacial deposits include *drumlins* and *eskers.* A drumlin is an oval-shaped hill that usually consists of rock debris. Most drumlins occur in groups. An esker is a long, narrow ridge of sand and gravel deposited by a stream of water that flowed in a tunnel beneath a melting glacier.

Famous Glaciers. Many of the world's most notable glaciers are in Europe. The best-known ones are those in the French and Swiss Alps. These glaciers include the Mer de Glace on Mont Blanc and the Aletsch Glacier near the Jungfrau. The Jostedal Glacier in Norway is the largest on the European continent. It covers about 300 square miles (780 square kilometers).

Major glaciers also cover regions of northwestern North America. The largest and most famous of these glaciers is the 840-square-mile (2,176-square-kilometer) Malaspina Glacier on Yakutat Bay in Alaska. Other glaciers include those in Banff National Park in Alberta, in Glacier National Park in Montana, and on Mount Rainier in Washington.   ROBERT H. CARPENTER

Related Articles in WORLD BOOK include:

From *The World Book Encyclopedia.* © 1979 World Book-Childcraft International, Inc.

Place a check mark next to the correct answers to questions 1 to 10.

1. The definition of glacier is found in

____ (a) the first paragraph of the article.

____ (b) the subtopic *Kinds of Glaciers.*

____ (c) every subtopic in the article.

2. Robert H. Carpenter wrote the article on glaciers. His name appears

____ (a) just below the title heading of the article.

____ (b) at the end of the article, but before *Related Articles.*

____ (c) at the end of the entire entry for *glacier.*

3. Which phrase does the article use to tell you that the article on icebergs elsewhere in the encyclopedia has information that relates to glaciers?

____ (a) (Turn to Iceberg)

____ (b) (See Related Articles)

____ (c) (See Iceberg)

4. Which related article would appear first in the encyclopedia?

____ (a) Iceberg

____ (b) Ice Age

____ (c) Iceland

5. The article states that glaciers differ in shape, size, and location in the subtopic

____ (a) Kinds of Glaciers.

____ (b) How Glaciers Form.

____ (c) How Glaciers Shape the Land.

6. The article states that glaciers greatly altered the shape of large parts of

____ (a) Africa and Asia.

____ (b) Antarctica and Australia.

____ (c) Europe and North America.

7. Which one of the following glaciers is in the United States?

____ (a) Mer de Glace

____ (b) Jostedal Glacier

____ (c) Malaspina Glacier

8. According to the article, which one of the following factors has the most influence on the size of a glacier?

____ (a) Climate

____ (b) Movement

____ (c) Sea level

9. Which one of the Related Articles would most likely discuss glaciers in Europe?

_____ (*a*) Alaska (Glaciers)

_____ (*b*) Alps (How the Alps Were Formed)

_____ (*c*) Great Lakes (How the Lakes Were Formed)

10. In which volume of an encyclopedia would you look for both the article Iceberg and the article Jostedal Glacier?

_____ (*a*) The volume marked I

_____ (*b*) The volume marked IJK

_____ (*c*) The volume marked L

D. Read the selection below from the *Time Almanac 2001 with Information Please,* then answer the questions that follow.

Greenland

Status: Autonomous part of Denmark
Chief of State: Queen Margrethe II (1972)
High Commissioner: Gunnar Martens (1995)
Premier: Jonathan Motzfeldt (1997)
Area: 840,000 sq. mi. (incl. 708,069 sq. mi. covered by ice cap) (2,175,600 sq. km)
Population (2000 est.): 56,309 (average annual growth rate: 0.93%); birth rate: 16.9/1000; infant mortality rate: 18.3/1000; density per sq. mi.: 0.07.
Capital and largest city (1995 est.): Godthaab, 12,723.
Monetary unit: Krone. **Ethnicity/race:** Greenlander 87% (Eskimo and Greenland-born whites), Danish and other 13%. **Literacy rate:** 99%

The Inuit are believed to have crossed from North America to northeast Greenland, the world's largest island, between 4000 B.C. and A.D. 1000. Greenland was colonized in A.D. 985-86 by Erik the Red. The Norse settlements declined in the 14th century, however, mainly as a result of a cooling in Greenland's climate, and in the 15th century they became extinct. In 1721, Greenland was recolonized by the Royal Greenland Trading Company of Denmark.

Greenland was under U.S. protection during World War II, but maintained Danish sovereignty. A definitive agreement for the joint defense of Greenland within the framework of NATO was signed in 1951. A large U.S. air base at Thule in the far north was completed in 1953.

Under 1953 amendments to the Danish constitution, Greenland became part of Denmark, with two representatives in the Danish Folketing. On May 1, 1979, Greenland gained home rule, with its own local Parliament (Landsting). In Feb. 1982, Greenlanders voted to withdraw from the European Union, which they had joined as part of Denmark in 1973.

From TIME Almanac 2001 with Information Please®. Copyright © 2000 by Family Education Company. Reprinted by permission of Family Education Company.

1. What is the capital of Greenland?

_____

2. What money unit is used in Greenland?

_____

3. Does the almanac article state that Greenland is the largest or the second largest island in the world?

_____

4. State at least one category (heading in bold type) in the article on Greenland that would not be found in the article on the United States in the same almanac.

_____

5. The meaning of the Status statement "Autonomous part of Denmark" may not be clear to everyone. But in this article, you can find its meaning in the last paragraph. What do you think "Autonomous part of Denmark" means?

_____

_____

_____

E. Using the Computer Catalog. Study the following screens from a library computer catalog. Then answer the questions that follow.

SCREEN A

TYPE AN AUTHOR, TITLE, OR SUBJECT.
THEN PRESS "ENTER":

Enter ☐   Help ☐

SCREEN B

1	Thubron, Colin, 1939– In Siberia	2000 957 T
2	White, Robin A., Siberian Lights	1997
3	Masi, Alfred, 1944–1995 Remembering Siberia	1988 957.1 M

Check on list number for more information.
3 out of 117 matches

☐ More Matches   ☐ Go Back   ☐ Help

SCREEN C

Title: In Siberia
Author: Thubron, Colin, 1939–
Publisher: New York: HarperCollins, 2000
Description: 286 pages, maps
Subject: Description of travel through Siberia

Status: one copy, checked out

Go Back   Help   New Search
☐   ☐   ☐

1. Do you think that the listings in Screen B were the result of typing in an author, a title, or a subject in Screen A? Explain.

_____

2. What is the total number of books that the search found?

_____

3. Is *Siberian Lights* a book of fiction or nonfiction? Based on your answer, how would you find the book on the shelves in the library?

_____

4. You are looking at Screen B. How do you get the information on Screen C to appear?

_____

5. What information on Screen C tells you that you cannot use the library's copy of *In Siberia* for your research at this time?

_____

6. If you are looking at Screen C, how can you return to Screen B?

_____

7. According to Screen B, which author is no longer alive? How do you know?

_____

8. What factor gave *In Siberia* the number 1 slot instead of *Siberian Lights* or *Remembering Siberia*?

_____

9. Would you consider *In Siberia* to be a long book? Explain.

_____

10. If you are looking at Screen C, what can you do to see if Colin Thubron has written other books that are in the library?

_____

F. Study the following results of an Internet search for Web sites dealing with Siberia. Then answer the questions that follow based on the results and on what you have learned about the Internet in this chapter.

(←) (→)

Your search has found **263,334** matches   This page shows matches **1–8**

SIBERIA: CULTURE—ECONOMICS—BUSINESS
. . . When a Westerner hears "**Siberia**", images of frozen tundra . . .
www.friends-partners.org/oldfriends/siberia/

Crossroads of Continents—Peoples of **Siberia**
. . . Peoples of **Siberia.** These cultures are represented by four groups: Chinese-influenced cultures of the Amur River region; the Even, reindeer herders living west . . .
www.mnh.si.edu/arctic/features/croads/siberia.html

Siberian photos
Pictures of **Siberia** by William Sokolenko. (click on the image to see it enlarged).
www.feht.com/wcp/ws/

Trans-**Siberian** Railway
Information, pictures and advice about travelling on the Trans-Siberian Railway . . .
www.trans-siberia.com/

American Troops in Northern Russia and **Siberia**
American Troops in Northern Russia and **Siberia.** World War I 1918–1920. by John Culloton.
www.militaria.com/8th/WW1/siberia.html

Encyclopedia.com—Results for **Siberia:** Geography
. . . Electric Library's Free Encyclopedia **Siberia** Geography
www.encyclopedia.com/articlesnew/11848Geography.html

Russian Books for Children
. . . Fairy Tales of the Peoples of **Siberia** and The Russian Far North Includes . . .
www.therussianshop.com/russhop/books/children.htm

SIBERIA—US PROSPECTS
Siberia—US Prospects. Prepared by BISNIS. June, 2000. Below are important industries and leading imports in recent years for regions of **Siberia.** This summary . . .
www.bisnis.doc.gov/bisnis/country/000612siberia-opps.htm

| Siberia | Search | Next 10 Site Matches |

---

1. What is the total number of matches that this search found for Siberia?

   _____

2. How many Web sites are shown on this screen?

   _____

3. Which Web site would you most likely visit if you were planning to travel across the length of Siberia?

   _____

4. How can you reduce the number of Web sites that a Web search finds?

   _____

5. How would you get to the Web site of the entry **Siberian** photos?

   _____

6. Which Web site would you most likely visit if you wanted to learn about the many cultures that live in Siberia?

   _____

7. What should you do to see the next 10 results on Web site listings for Siberia?

   _____

8. Why might the information on the Web site **SIBERIA—US PROSPECTS** be out of date?

   _____

9. If in the search box you typed +*Siberia –railway* and clicked on "Search," which of the eight Web sites would not appear in the new results?

   _____

10. You want to narrow your search on Siberia by adding Joseph Stalin and communism to the search box. How would you enter *Siberia, Joseph Stalin,* and *communism* in the search box?

    _____

11. The first screen that opens when you connect to a Web site is called a *home page.* How will you get from there to other pages on that Web site?

    _____

12. Clicking on the link Encyclopedia.com—Results for **Siberia**: Geography will connect you to that Web site. On the top of the home page of that Web site, you will see the real address of the Web site displayed in a box. Did the Search result give the real address of the Web site? Explain.

    _____

13. Just above the Search results, there are two arrows (←) and (→). What are these arrows used for?

_____

14. Which Web site sells fairy tales of the peoples of Siberia?

_____

15. How would you start a new search on Antarctica?

_____

CHAPTER 11
Taking a Test

In earlier chapters, you studied a number of important Social Studies skills. Did you ever stop to think that taking a test is also a kind of skill? Indeed it is!

As with any other Social Studies skill, you can improve your ability to answer questions on a test. In this chapter, you will learn how to study for a test and how to take a test and do well on it.

Studying for a Test

Start studying several days before a test, not just the night before. It is a good idea to read over the material you are to be tested on a few times each day. If you read something many times, or review it, you have a better chance of remembering it.

You will study better without a television set or radio on. If at all possible, try to study in a quiet place where you can be alone. You will probably find that you study better sitting in a chair than lying down. A bed or a sofa may be more comfortable than a chair, but how much studying can you do if you fall asleep?

The most important material you can study is the notes you took in class. If your notes are not clear or complete enough, you may also need to read over parts of your textbook.

If your teacher gives a review lesson before a test, you should pay close attention to what is said because the information will help you remember what you learned in class. Be sure to take notes of this review lesson. After all, your teacher will probably go over the important topics that she or he knows will be on the test.

Taking a Test

The best thing to do before taking a test is to have a good night's sleep. On the day of a test, arrive on time and bring a pencil and a pen. Any delay in starting a test will only hurt you.

The most important rule in taking a test is a simple one: READ THE DIRECTIONS AND THE QUESTIONS. Many students rush to answer test questions without first reading the directions and each of the questions carefully.

Several different kinds of questions are used in tests. Some questions call on you to use one or two words to fill in the answers. Other questions may ask you to match a word with its meaning or a person with a description. But the most common kinds of questions are multiple choice, true or false, and essay. Let us learn how to answer these three most common kinds of questions.

Multiple Choice Questions

In a multiple choice question, you are given two or more choices of possible answers. You have to choose the best answer. In most multiple choice questions, you can easily eliminate (get rid of) one or two choices that do not fit at all. It is also possible that two choices may seem to be correct. But the directions often read CHOOSE THE *BEST* ANSWER. Even though two of the choices seem to be correct, only one of the choices is the *BEST* answer.

Here is an example of a multiple choice question.

1. Africa is

_____ (a) an ocean.

_____ (b) a country.

_____ (c) a continent.

Which answer did you choose? First, is there any choice that can be eliminated, or left out? Certainly Africa is not an ocean. This eliminates choice (a). You know that a country and a continent are both land masses. But in your Social Studies class, you have learned that Africa is a very large land mass and that it is a continent. So the best answer to question 1 is (c).

Most multiple choice questions are like the one you just answered, but some make you think in a different way. Because of the way these questions are worded, you need to read them very carefully. Three examples of less common multiple choice questions follow.

2. Which one of the following was NOT a reason for the European takeover of Africa in the nineteenth century?

_____ (a) The desire for the mineral wealth of Africa

_____ (b) The desire to find new lands in which to live

_____ (c) The desire to become more like the Africans

_____ (d) The desire for adventure

Which answer did you choose? In this question, three of the four choices were reasons for the European takeover of Africa. But you have to pick the choice that was NOT a reason. From your studies, you should have realized that the Europeans did not go to Africa to become more like the Africans. Therefore, the answer to question 2 is (c).

Sometimes this kind of question is worded as follows.

3. All of the following were reasons for the European takeover of Africa in the nineteenth century EXCEPT

_____ (a) the desire for the mineral wealth of Africa.

_____ (b) the desire to find new lands in which to live.

_____ (c) the desire to become more like the Africans.

_____ (d) the desire for adventure.

The important word in this question is EXCEPT. This word means that one of the choices was not a reason for the European takeover of Africa. The other three choices were reasons. As you know, the correct answer is (c).

The next example points out the importance of reading all the choices.

4. The European takeover of Africa in the nineteenth century is best explained by

_____ (a) the desire for the mineral wealth of Africa.

_____ (b) the desire to find new lands in which to live.

_____ (c) the desire for adventure.

_____ (d) all of the above.

Which answer did you choose? Read the choices in order. You can see that choice (a) is one explanation for the European takeover of Africa in the nineteenth century. But is it the only explanation? Continue reading the choices. You see that choices (b) and (c) are also explanations for the takeover. Each of the choices gives a part of the explanation. Only choice (d) puts all the parts together. This makes choice (d) the BEST explanation. Notice that you had to read all the choices to see that the best answer to question 4 is (d).

The next example also requires that you think very carefully.

5. Which one of the following is caused by the other three?

_____ (a) Cars

_____ (b) Factories

_____ (c) Pollution

_____ (d) Garbage

What was your answer this time? This question is telling you that three of the choices bring about, or cause, the fourth choice. Look carefully at the choices. Does any one of them happen because of the other three? Yes, there is pollution because of cars, factories, and garbage. Choice (c) is caused by choices (a), (b), and (d). Therefore, the answer to question 5 is (c).

There are many kinds of multiple choice questions. You will have little problem answering them if you read the questions and all of the choices carefully. Remember always to give the *BEST* answer.

True or False Questions

The second most common kind of question is the true or false. There is a very simple rule for true or false questions. A statement must be *completely* true to be true. If any part of the statement is false, the whole statement is false.

Read the following example of a true or false question.

_____ Japanese planes attacked Pearl Harbor on December 7, 1941.

Every part of this statement is true. Therefore, on a test, it should be marked true.

Here is another example of a true or false question.

_____ Christopher Columbus sailed from Spain to the Americas in 1847.

It is true that Christopher Columbus did sail from Spain to the Americas, but the date 1847 is false. Since one part of the statement is false, the whole statement should be marked false.

In a true or false question, you also have to be very careful about words that can be tricky. Some of these tricky words are "some," "many," "most," "everyone," "no one," "never," "always." What may be true of something may not be true of everything.

Example:

_____ Everyone in the United States likes to watch television.

In order for this statement to be true, every single person in the United States has to like watching television. If just one person in the United States dislikes watching television, the statement is false. More than likely there is at least one person in the United States who dislikes watching television. Therefore, the statement is false. If the statement were changed to "Most people in the United States like to watch television," then the statement would undoubtedly be true.

Here is another example of a true or false question.

_____ Periods of dry weather are always followed by periods of very wet weather.

The word "always" means that this happens all the time. We know from records kept by the Weather Bureau that dry weather is not followed by very wet weather all the time. Therefore, the statement is false. If the word "always" were changed to "sometimes," the sentence would be true. But as it reads, the statement is false.

Essay Questions

The third most common kind of question is an essay. You learned how to write essays in Unit Two. Let us now think about how to follow directions for answering essay questions. Many students rush to answer such questions without first understanding the requirements.

Read these directions for answering the essay part of a test.

Directions: Answer *three* of the following questions.

1. Give the main reasons why the United States entered World War II.
2. Explain why the United States helped Japan after World War II.
3. Explain three main causes of the war in Vietnam.
4. Explain why the United States thought it was important to put a man on the moon before the Russians did.

How many questions should you answer in this essay part of a test? Many students would answer all four questions just because they saw four questions. But the directions clearly tell you to answer three questions.

Here is another example of an essay part of a test.

Directions: Answer *two* of the following questions.

1. (*a*) Give reasons why Mao Zedong was able to take control of China in 1949.
   (*b*) Describe the changes Mao Zedong brought about in China after 1949.

2. (a) Explain why the Europeans were interested in Africa in the nineteenth century.

   (b) Give reasons why so many African countries gained independence between 1960 and 1970.

3. (a) Why has the United States always had a special interest in the problems of South America?

   (b) Explain why the United States stopped trading with Cuba in the 1960's and 1970's.

How many questions should you answer? Some students would answer 1. (a) and 1. (b) and think they had answered two questions. In fact, they would have answered only two parts of the same question. If you answered 1. (a) and 1. (b), you would have answered only one question. But the directions tell you to answer two questions (both parts of two numbered questions). You must still answer either 2. (a) and 2. (b) or 3. (a) and 3. (b).

Points to Remember

You have seen in this chapter how careful you must be in answering the three most common kinds of questions on a test. Of course, there are other kinds of questions used on tests. But reading the directions and each of the questions carefully will help you to answer any kind of question more accurately.

Here is a list of things to do when you are taking a test. Try to remember them.

1. Read the directions and the questions carefully.
2. Plan your time so that you leave enough time to answer all of the questions.
3. Leave the more difficult questions to the end. Answer the questions you know first.
4. Do not leave any answer blank. An answer left blank is always wrong, but a good guess may be correct. (However, be sure that extra points are not taken off for incorrect answers.)
5. Answer exactly as many essay questions as the directions tell you to.
6. In each essay question, answer all parts unless the directions tell you differently.
7. Some essay questions start with the words "discuss," "describe," or "explain." This means that you will have to give full, complete answers, usually written in sentences.

Learning how to take a test is an important skill. Whether you are in school or looking for a job, you will be asked to take many tests during your life. The following exercises will give you more practice in using this important skill.

USING WHAT YOU HAVE LEARNED

A. Place a check mark next to the correct answers to questions 1 to 5.

1. It is important to take good notes in class because

   ____ (a) it pleases the teacher.

   ____ (b) you can show them to your parent or guardian when you get home.

   ____ (c) notes will help you remember what you learned in class.

2. A review lesson is important because

   ____ (a) it teaches you new material.

   ____ (b) it points out important things you learned in other lessons.

   ____ (c) it takes the place of studying for a test.

3. The most important rule in taking a test is to

   ____ (a) read the directions and the questions carefully.

   ____ (b) work as fast as you can.

   ____ (c) answer all the questions.

4. In answering a multiple choice question, you will find that

_____ (a) one or two choices can usually be eliminated immediately.

_____ (b) the longest choice is most likely the correct answer.

_____ (c) the first choice is most likely the correct answer.

5. When two choices are close to being correct in a multiple choice question, you

_____ (a) can pick either choice.

_____ (b) must look for another choice.

_____ (c) must pick the choice that is better.

B. Mark each statement with a **T** for *True* or an **F** for *False*. Remember the rules you learned in the chapter about answering true or false questions.

_____ 1. A true or false question is false if any part of it is false.

_____ 2. In a review lesson, you learn only new material for the next test.

_____ 3. The most important rule in taking a test is to work quickly and finish as soon as possible.

_____ 4. The first student to finish a test always gets the highest mark.

_____ 5. In a test, essay questions marked 1. (a) and 1. (b) always stand for two separate questions.

C. Place a check mark next to the correct answers to questions 1 to 3.

1. Which one of the following may be caused by the other three?

_____ (a) Failure on a test

_____ (b) Not enough studying

_____ (c) Going to bed late the night before a test

_____ (d) Taking poor notes in class

2. All of the following will help you in taking a test EXCEPT

_____ (a) arriving at the test on time.

_____ (b) a good night's sleep.

_____ (c) bringing a pen.

_____ (d) leaving your studying to the last minute.

3. Look carefully at the following essay part of a test. Then answer questions A, B, and C.

Directions: Answer two of the following questions.

1. (a) Why did the Spanish come to the Americas?
   (b) Describe the influence Spain had on the countries of South America.
2. (a) Explain how apartheid began in South Africa.
   (b) How has apartheid affected the development of South Africa?

3. (*a*) Explain this statement: "Southeast Asia is blessed with natural resources."

   (*b*) Why was Thailand the only country in Southeast Asia able to withstand European colonization?

A. How many questions do you have to answer in this essay part of a test?

   ____ (*a*) One

   ____ (*b*) Two

   ____ (*c*) Three

B. How many questions are given on the above essay part of a test?

   ____ (*a*) Three questions, each with two parts

   ____ (*b*) Two questions

   ____ (*c*) Six separate questions

C. Is the following statement true or false? "If I answer only 1. (*a*) and 1. (*b*), I have followed the directions correctly." (Explain your answer in two or three sentences.)

   _____

   _____

   _____

   _____

   _____

4. Which one of the following statements is more likely to be *false*? Explain why. "Some countries in Africa have great trouble producing food." "A country with a large population is always a poor country." (Answer in two or three sentences.)

   _____

   _____

   _____

   _____

   _____

5. List five things you should think about when you take a test.

   _____

   _____

   _____

   _____

   _____

CHAPTER 12
Charts

Have you ever wondered how many other families in the United States earn or receive the same amount of money (income) as your family? One way to find out would be to read an article about family income. But this might take more time than you have. Also, you might have a difficult time finding the exact information you want. It would be easier and quicker to look at a *chart,* an arrangement of words and numbers that shows information in a clear and simple way.

The following chart divides families in the United States into six income groups. It shows the percent (%) of families in each group in 2000. A percent is a part of a hundred or of a total number.

Example: 10% of 50 = 5
10% of 100 = 10
25% of 100 = 25
25% of 200 = 50

U.S. FAMILY INCOME GROUPS IN 2000	
Income Group	*Percent of Families*
$ 0–$19,999	15.1%
$20,000–$39,999	23.5%
$40,000–$59,999	19.6%
$60,000–$79,999	15.4%
$80,000–$99,999	9.4%
$100,000 and over	17.0%

1. What percent of families in 2000 made between $80,000 and $99,999?

_____ (a) 9.4%

_____ (b) 15.1%

_____ (c) 19.6%

Looking at the chart, you can see that on the same line as $80,000–$99,999 is 9.4%. Therefore, the answer to question 1 is (a).

2. To what income group does the largest percent of families belong?

_____ (a) $0–$19,999

_____ (b) $20,000–$39,999

_____ (c) $100,000 and over

Looking at the chart once again, you can see that the largest percent is 23.5%. On the same line as 23.5% is the income group $20,000–$39,999. Therefore, the answer to question 2 is (b).

3. What percent of families in 2000 had an income between $40,000 and $79,999?

_____ (a) 15.1%

_____ (b) 26.4%

_____ (c) 35.0%

An income between $40,000 and $79,999 can belong to one of these two groups: $40,000–$59,999 or $60,000–$79,999. Add together the percent for each group: 19.6% + 15.4% = 35.0%. Therefore, the answer to question 3 is (c).

The chart on income shows one set of information, or group of statistics, namely, what percent of families in the United States was in each of six income groups in 2000. A chart can also show different groups of statistics at the same time. The following chart compares four sets of statistics for five countries in South-West Asia/Africa.

COMPARING COUNTRIES OF SOUTH-WEST ASIA/AFRICA

Countries of South-West Asia/Africa	Land Area (Square Miles)	Population (estimated 2000)	Literacy	Average Annual Income Per Person (estimated 1999 in U.S. dollars)
Egypt	386,900	68,359,979	51%	$ 3,000
Iraq	167,920	22,675,617	58%	$ 2,700
Israel	7,992	5,842,454	96%	$18,300
Saudi Arabia	865,000	22,023,506	63%	$ 9,000
Syria	71,498	16,305,659	79%	$ 2,500

The four sets of statistics are

Land Area: the land size of the country, in square miles.

Population: how many people live in the country.

Literacy: the percent of people in the country who can read and write.

Average Annual Income Per Person: the total of all the annual, or yearly, incomes in the country divided by the total number of people in the country. Example:

$$\begin{matrix} \text{Total of} \\ \text{Annual} \\ \text{Incomes} \\ \text{People} \end{matrix} \quad \frac{\$30,000,000}{30,000} = \$1,000 \quad \left\{ \begin{matrix} \text{Average} \\ \text{Annual} \\ \text{Income} \\ \text{Per} \\ \text{Person} \end{matrix} \right.$$

(Note: The term "per capita," meaning per head, is often used in place of "per person.")

1. Which one of these South-West Asian/African countries on the chart has the largest population?

_____ (a) Egypt

_____ (b) Saudi Arabia

_____ (c) Syria

Which answer did you choose? Looking at the column marked POPULATION, you can see that the largest number (68,359,979) is on the same line as Egypt. Therefore, the answer to question 1 is (a).

2. Using the chart, make a list of the five countries in the order of their land area, placing the largest country first.

1. _____

2. _____

3. _____

4. _____

5. _____

Looking at the column marked LAND AREA, you can see that the countries should be placed in the following order: Saudi Arabia (865,000 square miles); Egypt (386,900 square miles); Iraq (167,920 square miles); Syria (71,498 square miles); Israel (7,992 square miles).

3. How does the chart show that Israel has the highest percentage of people who can read and write? (Answer in two or three sentences.)

_____

_____

_____

_____

_____

What did you write? Here is an example of a possible answer to question 3.

> *In the column marked Literacy, you can see that Israel's literacy rate of 96% is much higher than the literacy rates in the other countries. Therefore, Israel has the highest percentage of people who can read and write.*

The information you needed to answer questions 1 to 3 was shown on the chart. But what if a question asks for information that is not on the chart? Sometimes, of course, you won't be able to answer such a question. Other times you can find the answer by rearranging information on the chart or by combining two sets of' statistics. For instance, by using the land area and population statistics on the chart, you can find the population density of each of the five countries. *Population density* means the average number of people living in a certain area, usually a square mile.

You can find the population density by dividing the population of a country by its land area. For example: to find the population density of the United States in 2002, you divide its population of 286,716,131 by its land area of 3,615,122 square miles, which comes out to over 79 people per square mile.

With this information in mind, answer the following question.

4. Which of these countries has the highest population density?

_____ (a) Saudi Arabia

_____ (b) Syria

_____ (c) Iraq

Which answer did you choose? The country with the highest population density is the country that is the most crowded with people. To find out which one this is, divide the population of each of these countries by its land area. The one with the most people per square mile has the highest population density. Syria has a higher population density than Saudi Arabia or Iraq. Therefore, the answer to question 4 is (b).

5. At the time this chart was created, which word or phrase could have been eliminated if the population for 2000 and the average annual income per person for 1999 had been known?

_____ (a) Estimated

_____ (b) Square miles

_____ (c) In U.S. dollars

Which answer did you choose? Every ten years or so, most governments conduct a census, an official count of the population. The governments also collect statistics for each year between the last census and the present year. Though not as exact as a census, these statistics, known as estimated statistics, are based on the latest available information. This chart shows estimated statistics for population and average annual income per person and so it must use the word "estimated." If the chart showed "census" statistics, it would not need to use the word estimated. Therefore, the answer to question 5 is (a).

USING WHAT YOU HAVE LEARNED

A. Study the following chart on immigration to the United States.

THE CHANGING FACE OF IMMIGRATION TO THE UNITED STATES
From Where Did the Immigrants Come?
Comparing 1898 and 1998

Areas of the World	1898 (Percent of Total Immigration)	1998 (Percent of Total Immigration)
Europe	95.0%	13.7%
Asia	3.7%	33.3%
America (All countries of the Western Hemisphere except the United States)	1.0%	45.2%
Africa	0.1%	6.2%
Oceania (Australia, New Zealand, Pacific Islands)	0.1%	0.6%
All other areas of the world	0.1%	1.0%

Place a check mark next to the correct answers to questions 1 to 5.

1. The chart shows

____ (a) the number of immigrants who come to the United States in 1898 and 1998.

____ (b) what percentage of immigrants came to the United States from various countries between 1898 and 1998.

____ (c) that the percentage of immigrants coming to the United States from different areas of the world was not the same in 1998 as it was in 1898.

2. From which *one* of the following areas did the largest percentage of immigrants come in 1898?

____ (a) Europe

____ (b) Asia

____ (c) Africa

3. In 1998, the percentage of immigrants from Africa was

____ (a) 0.6%.

____ (b) 1.1%.

____ (c) 6.2%.

4. From which area did 45.2% of immigrants come in 1998?

____ (a) Asia

____ (b) America

____ (c) Europe

5. Which area had the least change in percentage from 1898 to 1998?

_____ (*a*) America

_____ (*b*) Oceania

_____ (*c*) Africa

6. For both 1898 and 1998, choose the three areas listed on the chart from which the greatest percentage of immigrants came to the United States. Place the area with the largest percentage first, the area with the second largest percentage second, the area with the third largest percentage third.

1898	1998
1. _____	1. _____
2. _____	2. _____
3. _____	3. _____

7. What do you think is meant by the title of this chart, THE CHANGING FACE OF IMMIGRATION TO THE UNITED STATES? (Answer in three or four sentences.)

_____

_____

_____

_____

_____

_____

_____

_____

B. Study the following chart on sources of information in six countries.

SOURCES OF INFORMATION IN SIX COUNTRIES IN 1998
(Per 1,000 People)

Country	Internet Hosts*	Newspaper Circulation	Radios	Telephones (main lines)	Televisions
Australia	40.09	297	1,120	512	639
Canada	36.94	159	1,078	634	715
Israel	19.15	291	530	471	318
Japan	13.34	580	957	503	707
Poland	3.37	113	523	228	413
United States	112.77	212	2,115	661	847

*An Internet host is a computer connected to the Internet.

Place a check mark next to the correct answers to questions 1 to 9.

1. The chart

_____ (a) shows how much time people in six countries spend watching television.

_____ (b) compares the numbers of various sources of information in six countries.

_____ (c) proves that people in some countries like to listen to the radio more than watch television.

_____ (d) shows all the ways people receive information.

2. The information given in the chart is for

_____ (a) 1998.

_____ (b) 1999.

_____ (c) 2000.

_____ (d) 2001.

3. Each figure on the chart represents the number of

_____ (a) items found in a country.

_____ (b) items per 1,000 people in a particular country.

_____ (c) items per 10,000 people in a particular country.

_____ (d) people in a particular country owning each item.

4. Which one of these four countries had the smallest number of Internet hosts per 1,000 people?

_____ (a) Australia

_____ (b) Canada

_____ (c) Israel

_____ (d) Japan

5. In Israel, there were

_____ (a) 318 telephones per 1,000 people.

_____ (b) 318 telephones per 10,000 people.

_____ (c) 471 telephones per 1,000 people.

_____ (d) 471 telephones per 10,000 people.

6. Poland had the lowest number for every source of information EXCEPT

_____ (a) newspaper circulation.

_____ (b) radios.

_____ (c) telephones.

_____ (d) televisions.

7. How many countries on the chart had more televisions per 1,000 people than the United States?

____ (a) None

____ (b) One

____ (c) Two

____ (d) Three

8. Which country had the fourth largest circulation in newspapers per 1,000 people?

____ (a) Japan

____ (b) Israel

____ (c) United States

____ (d) Australia

9. In Canada, there were 1,078 radios per 1,000 people. This means that

____ (a) Canada is a very crowded country.

____ (b) some people in Canada had more than one radio.

____ (c) everyone in Canada owned a radio.

____ (d) more people in Canada bought radios that did people in any other country.

10. For which source of information did the United States *not* have the highest number per 1,000 people? Why do you think that the numbers for this source of information were not as high as for the other sources of information? (Answer in two or three sentences.)

_____

_____

_____

_____

_____

_____

C. Study the following chart on the countries of Southeast Asia.

COMPARING SOUTHEAST ASIAN COUNTRIES

Countries of Southeast Asia	Population (estimated 2000)	Population Density (people per square mile)	Land Area (square miles)	Annual Income Per Capita (estimated 1999 in U.S. dollars)
Cambodia	12,212,306	175	69,884	$ 710
Indonesia	224,784,210	306	735,268	$ 2,800
Laos	5,497,459	60	91,429	$ 1,300
Malaysia	21,793,293	170	128,328	$10,700
Myanmar	41,734,853	159	261,789	$ 1,200
Philippines	81,159,644	701	115,830	$ 3,600
Singapore	4,151,720	17,444	238	$27,800
Thailand	61,230,874	309	198,455	$ 6,400
Vietnam	78,773,873	619	127,246	$ 1,850
Totals	531,338,232	2,216 (average)	1,728,467	$ 6,262 (average)

Place a check mark next to the correct answers to questions 1 to 7.

1. Which country in Southeast Asia had the largest population?

_____ (a) Indonesia

_____ (b) Malaysia

_____ (c) Vietnam

2. Which country in Southeast Asia has a land area of 198,455 square miles?

_____ (a) Philippines

_____ (b) Laos

_____ (c) Thailand

3. Which country of Southeast Asia had the lowest population density?

_____ (a) Laos

_____ (b) Cambodia

_____ (c) Malaysia

4. The three countries of Southeast Asia with the lowest annual income per capita were

_____ (a) Philippines, Cambodia, Thailand.

_____ (b) Cambodia, Laos, and Myanmar.

_____ (c) Laos, Myanmar, and Indonesia.

5. What is the total population of all the countries of Southeast Asia?

_____ (a) 318,338,232

_____ (b) 415,338,232

_____ (c) 531,338,232

6. How many countries had an annual income per capita above the average annual income per capita?

_____ (a) Two

_____ (b) Three

_____ (c) Four

7. How many countries have a land area of more than 100,000 square miles?

_____ (a) Two

_____ (b) Four

_____ (c) Six

8. Arrange the following five countries of Southeast Asia in the order of their population, placing the country with the largest population first, the next largest second, and so on. (Indonesia, Myanmar, Philippines, Thailand, Vietnam)

1. _____

2. _____

3. _____

4. _____

5. _____

9. The Philippines had a larger population than Singapore. Yet Singapore had a greater population density than the Philippines. What information in the chart will give you the reason for this? (Answer in two or three sentences.)

_____

_____

_____

_____

_____

10. What information in the chart will most likely change when the countries listed in the chart conduct their next censuses? (Answer in two or three sentences.)

_____

_____

_____

_____

_____

CHAPTER 13
Picture and Circle Graphs

Charts are not the only way to make statistics easy to understand. Another way is to show statistics in drawings called *graphs*. In this chapter, you will learn about two kinds of graphs: picture graphs, or pictographs, and circle graphs.

Picture Graphs

The *picture graph* at the bottom of the page compares the population of five cities around the world.

Because it is a picture graph, the population statistics are given in pictures, or symbols, rather than in numbers. The note at the top of the graph states that each human figure symbol stands for 1 million people. By counting the number of symbols and multiplying by 1 million, you can find the population of each city.

1. Which city on the graph has the largest population?

   _____ (a) Mumbai

   _____ (b) Shanghai

   _____ (c) Moscow

Which answer did you choose? Remember that each symbol on the graph stands for 1 million people. Because you are looking for the city with the largest population, you should be looking for the city with the greatest number of symbols. The city of Mumbai has the most symbols (15). Therefore, the answer to question 1 is (a).

2. Which city on the graph has a population of 9½ million?

   _____ (a) Kinshasa

   _____ (b) Rio de Janeiro

   _____ (c) Moscow

POPULATION OF FIVE CITIES	
(🯅 = 1 million people)	
Cities	*Population*
Kinshasa, Democratic Republic of the Congo	🯅🯅🯅🯅🯅🯅🯅
Shanghai, China	🯅🯅🯅🯅🯅🯅🯅🯅
Moscow, Russia	🯅🯅🯅🯅🯅🯅🯅🯅🯅
Rio de Janeiro, Brazil	🯅🯅🯅🯅🯅🯅
Mumbai (Bombay), India	🯅🯅🯅🯅🯅🯅🯅🯅🯅🯅🯅🯅🯅🯅🯅

Which answer did you choose? Because each symbol on the graph stands for 1 million people, a population of 9½ million has 9½ symbols. Moscow has 9½ symbols on the graph. Therefore, the answer to question 2 is (*c*).

3. Which two cities are closest in population?

_____ (*a*) Mumbai and Moscow

_____ (*b*) Kinshasa and Rio de Janeiro

_____ (*c*) Shanghai and Mumbai

Which answer did you choose? No two cities on the graph have the same population. But the two cities with the closest number of symbols are Kinshasa with 6½ symbols and Rio de Janeiro with 6 symbols. Therefore, the answer to question 3 is (*b*).

4. Arrange the cities on the graph in order of their population. Place the city with the largest population first, the next largest second, and so on.

1. _____

2. _____

3. _____

4. _____

5. _____

How did you arrange these cities? Mumbai has the largest population with 15 symbols. Moscow is second with 9½ symbols. Shanghai is third with 8 symbols. Kinshasa is fourth with 6½ symbols. Rio de Janeiro is fifth with 6 symbols.

Picture graphs can show many other things besides differences in population. To show other subjects, different symbols are used. The meaning of the symbols is always explained on the graph.

Circle Graphs

Another important kind of graph is the *circle graph,* also called a pie graph. This graph is divided into parts, or sections, that look like pieces of a pie. Each section stands for a certain percentage of the whole graph. All the sections of the graph add up to 100%.

Look at the following circle graph. It shows the percentage of land area that is contained in each continent. The graph lets you see that all the sections or continents add up to 100%. It also lets you easily compare the sections with one another.

THE SEVEN CONTINENTS' LAND AREA

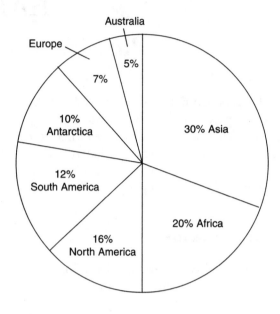

1. Which is the largest continent in land area?

_____ (*a*) Europe

_____ (*b*) Asia

_____ (*c*) Africa

Which answer did you choose? Remember that the largest continent has the highest percentage of the total land area. The highest percentage (30%) belongs to Asia. Therefore, the answer to question 1 is (*b*).

2. What percentage of the total land area is contained in South America?

_____ (*a*) 30%

_____ (*b*) 20%

_____ (*c*) 12%

Which answer did you choose? Look at the section of the graph labeled South America. You can see that South America contains 12% of the total land area. Therefore, the answer to question 2 is (*c*).

3. Which continent on the graph contains 16% of the total land area?

_____ (a) Africa

_____ (b) North America

_____ (c) Australia

What was your answer? The graph shows that North America contains 16% of the total land area. So the answer to question 3 is (b).

4. Which two continents added together contain 50% of the total land area?

_____ (a) North America and South America

_____ (b) Asia and Africa

_____ (c) Europe and Australia

What was your answer this time? The only two continents on the graph with land area that adds up to 50% are Asia with 30% and Africa with 20%. Together they contain one-half of the total land area. Therefore, the answer to question 4 is (b).

Being able to analyze picture graphs and circle graphs is another important Social Studies skill. The following exercises will give you more practice in using this skill.

USING WHAT YOU HAVE LEARNED

A. Study the following picture graph.

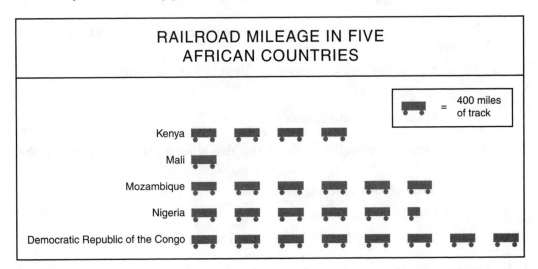

RAILROAD MILEAGE IN FIVE AFRICAN COUNTRIES

= 400 miles of track

Kenya
Mali
Mozambique
Nigeria
Democratic Republic of the Congo

Place a check mark next to the correct answers to questions 1 to 8.

1. The picture graph shows

_____ (a) the railroad mileage in five African countries.

_____ (b) the number of railroad cars in five African countries.

_____ (c) the five African countries with the longest railroad mileage.

2. The symbol used in this picture graph to represent miles of railroad is

_____ (a) a railroad station.

_____ (b) a railroad car.

_____ (c) an automobile.

3. Each symbol on the graph stands for

   ____ (a) 100 miles.

   ____ (b) 250 miles.

   ____ (c) 400 miles.

4. Which country on the graph has 3,200 miles of railroad track?

   ____ (a) Kenya

   ____ (b) Mali

   ____ (c) Democratic Republic of the Congo

5. Which country on the graph has the most miles of railroad track?

   ____ (a) Mozambique

   ____ (b) Democratic Republic of the Congo

   ____ (c) Kenya

6. How many miles of railroad track does Nigeria have?

   ____ (a) 2,000 miles

   ____ (b) 2,200 miles

   ____ (c) 2,400 miles

7. Which two countries on the graph have fewer miles of railroad track than Nigeria?

   ____ (a) Mozambique and Democratic Republic of the Congo

   ____ (b) Kenya and Mali

   ____ (c) Mozambique and Kenya

8. What does the graph tell you about the size of each country named on the graph?

   ____ (a) Mozambique is the largest.

   ____ (b) Mali is the smallest.

   ____ (c) There are no details or facts to give you the answer.

9. Arrange the five countries on the graph in the order of their railroad mileage. Place the country with the most miles of railroad track first, the next highest amount second, and so on.

   1. _____

   2. _____

   3. _____

   4. _____

   5. _____

10. Use the information on the railroad mileage graph to make a chart that has numbers and words instead of symbols.

B. Study the following circle graph on religions in India.

RELIGIONS OF INDIA

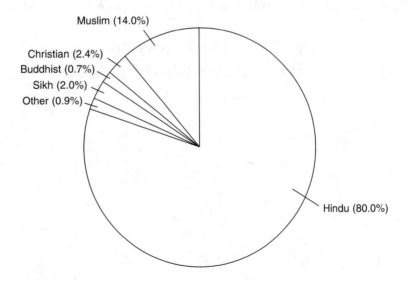

Place a check mark next to the correct answers to questions 1 to 4.

1. The circle graph shows

    ____ (*a*) how many people in India practice a religion.

    ____ (*b*) the growing importance of religion in India.

    ____ (*c*) what percentage of the Indian people practice each of the religions named on the graph.

2. What percentage of the Indian people practice the Muslim religion?

　　____ (a) 0.6%

　　____ (b) 14%

　　____ (c) 20%

3. Which religion in India is practiced by 2.4% of the people?

　　____ (a) Christian

　　____ (b) Buddhist

　　____ (c) Sikh

4. Which three religions are practiced by 96% of the Indian people?

　　____ (a) Christian, Sikh, and Hindu

　　____ (b) Muslim, Hindu, and Buddhist

　　____ (c) Hindu, Muslim, and Sikh

5. How does this circle graph show that the Hindu religion is the most widely practiced religion in India? (Answer in one or two sentences.)

　　_____

　　_____

　　_____

　　_____

C. Study the following circle graph on energy use in the United States.

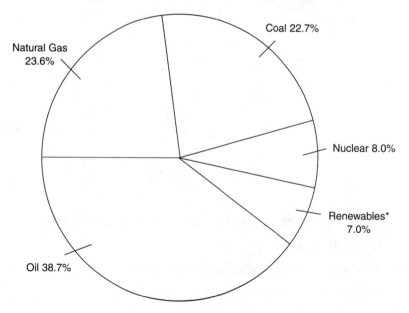

UNITED STATES ENERGY USE BY ENERGY SOURCE, 2000

Coal 22.7%

Natural Gas 23.6%

Nuclear 8.0%

Renewables* 7.0%

Oil 38.7%

*Renewable energy sources can replenish or reproduce themselves. They include wood, waste, alcohol, hydropower, solar power, and wind power.

Place a check mark next to the correct answers to questions 1 to 5.

1. The graph shows

_____ (a) the amount of energy used by the United States in 2000.

_____ (b) the importance of using different energy sources.

_____ (c) the percentage of different energy sources used by the United States in 2000.

2. Which one of the following was the leading source of energy used in the United States in 2000?

_____ (a) Coal

_____ (b) Oil

_____ (c) Natural Gas

3. Which one of the following was the third-most-used energy source in the United States in 2000?

_____ (a) Coal

_____ (b) Natural Gas

_____ (c) Nuclear

4. How much of the energy used by the United States in 2000 came from nuclear power?

_____ (a) 7.0%

_____ (b) 8.0%

_____ (c) 22.7%

5. Hydropower, a renewable energy source, accounted for 3.2% of the energy used by the United States in 2000. How much of the energy used by the United States in 2000 came from renewable sources other than hydropower?

_____ (a) 3.8%

_____ (b) 7.0%

_____ (c) 10.2%

6. How does the graph show that in 2000 the United States heavily depended on coal, natural gas, and oil for its energy needs? (Answer in one or two sentences.)

_____

_____

_____

CHAPTER 14
Bar Graphs

Another way to show information is by means of a *bar graph*. On such a graph, bars of different lengths are used to compare facts or statistics.

Simple Bar Graphs

The graph on this page uses bars to show the number of automobiles produced in 2000 by six countries. (These six countries were the leading producers of automobiles in 2000.) At the top of each bar you can see the number of automobiles produced by each country. Under the title of the graph is a note telling us that each number stands for millions of automobiles. For example, the number on top of Germany is 5.1. This means that Germany produced 5.1 million cars in 2000.

Remember to check to see if a graph has a date or year. The information on this automobile production graph is true only for 2000. Another graph with a different date or year would probably show different statistics.

Answer the following questions by referring to the automobile production graph.

1. The production of automobiles on the graph is shown in

   _____ (a) tens of thousands of automobiles.

   _____ (b) millions of automobiles.

   _____ (c) tens of millions of automobiles.

Which answer did you choose? Look at the top of the graph. It shows the words "(in millions of automobiles)." This lets you know that the number on top of each bar stands for millions of automobiles. Therefore, the answer to question 1 is (b).

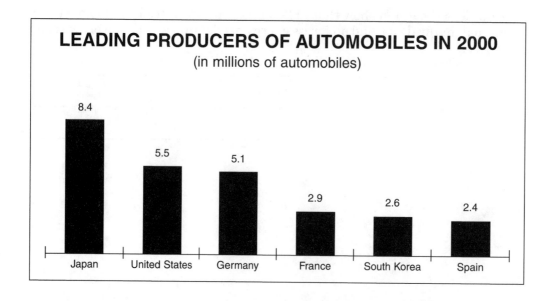

LEADING PRODUCERS OF AUTOMOBILES IN 2000
(in millions of automobiles)

8.4	5.5	5.1	2.9	2.6	2.4
Japan	United States	Germany	France	South Korea	Spain

2. Which *two* countries combined produced the same number of cars as Japan did in 2000?

_____ (*a*) United States and France

_____ (*b*) Germany and Spain

_____ (*c*) France and South Korea

Which answer did you choose? Of the three choices given, only the 5.5 million of the United States combined with the 2.9 million of France equals the 8.4 million automobiles of Japan. Therefore, the answer to question 2 is (*a*).

Double Bar Graphs

Some bar graphs can show more than one kind of information at the same time.

The bar graph at the bottom of the page compares the population of four countries. Because it has two bars for each country, it is called a *double bar graph*. The first bar ☐ stands for the population in 2000 and the second bar ▨ for the expected population in the year 2050.

Answer the following questions using this double bar population graph.

1. Which country on the graph had the largest population in 2000?

_____ (*a*) India

_____ (*b*) Brazil

_____ (*c*) China

Which answer did you choose? The white bars on the graph stand for the population in 2000. The longest white bar stands for the largest population. China has the longest white bar. Therefore, the answer to question 1 is (*c*).

2. By the year 2050, which country is expected to have a total population of 207 million?

_____ (*a*) Brazil

_____ (*b*) India

_____ (*c*) United States

What was your answer? This cross-hatched bar ▨ on the graph stands for the expected population in the year 2050. The crosshatched bar marked 207 million belongs to Brazil. Therefore, the answer to question 2 is (*a*).

3. Which country on the graph had a population nearest to that of the United States in 2000?

_____ (*a*) India

_____ (*b*) China

_____ (*c*) Brazil

Which answer did you choose this time? Look at the length of the white bar belonging to the United States. Of the remaining three white bars, which one is nearest in length to the United States? You can see that Brazil's white bar is nearer in length

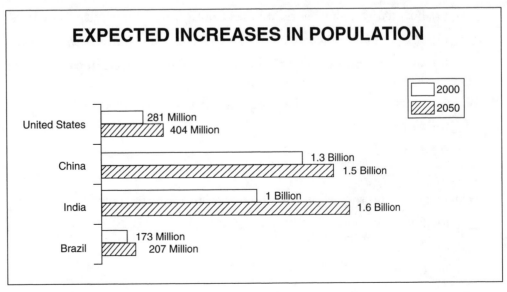

EXPECTED INCREASES IN POPULATION

☐ 2000
▨ 2050

United States — 281 Million / 404 Million
China — 1.3 Billion / 1.5 Billion
India — 1 Billion / 1.6 Billion
Brazil — 173 Million / 207 Million

than the white bars belonging to India and China. Therefore, the answer to question 3 is (c).

4. Which one of the following countries will probably have the largest increase (growth) in population by the year 2050?

_____ (a) China

_____ (b) India

_____ (c) Brazil

Which answer did you choose? Each country on the graph has two population bars. Of the three countries listed, find the one with the two population bars that are farthest in length from each other. It is the country that will probably have the largest increase in population. The bars that are farthest in length from each other belong to India. Therefore, the answer to question 4 is (b).

5. Why is this population graph called a double bar graph? (Answer in one or two sentences.)

_____

_____

_____

_____

_____

_____

_____

What did you write? Here is an example of a possible answer to question 5.

This graph is called a double bar graph because two bars are used to show statistics for each country on the graph.

You have seen in this chapter how bar graphs show facts and information clearly and quickly. The following exercises will give you more practice in analyzing bar graphs.

USING WHAT YOU HAVE LEARNED

A. Study the bar graph on page 107.

Place a check mark next to the correct answers to questions 1 to 5.

1. The bar graph shows

_____ (a) how many people worked in six South American countries in 1999.

_____ (b) the per capita income of six South American countries in 1999.

_____ (c) the per capita income of the poorest South American countries in 1999.

2. Which country on the graph had the highest per capita income?

_____ (a) Argentina

_____ (b) Brazil

_____ (c) Uruguay

3. Which country on the graph had the lowest per capita income?

_____ (a) Ecuador

_____ (b) Argentina

_____ (c) Chile

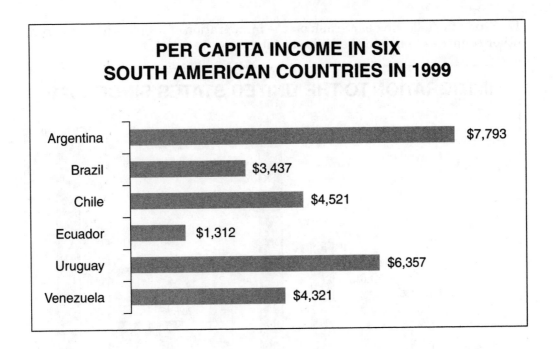

PER CAPITA INCOME IN SIX SOUTH AMERICAN COUNTRIES IN 1999

Argentina — $7,793
Brazil — $3,437
Chile — $4,521
Ecuador — $1,312
Uruguay — $6,357
Venezuela — $4,321

4. Which country on the graph had a per capita income of $3,437?

____ (*a*) Brazil

____ (*b*) Uruguay

____ (*c*) Venezuela

5. Which two of the following countries had the closest per capita incomes?

____ (*a*) Argentina and Uruguay

____ (*b*) Brazil and Chile

____ (*c*) Chile and Venezuela

6. What do you think the following statement means?

"When you know the per capita income of a country, you know a lot more about a country than how much money its people make."

_____

_____

_____

_____

_____

_____

B. Study the following bar graph on the immigration of people who came from other countries to live in the United States.

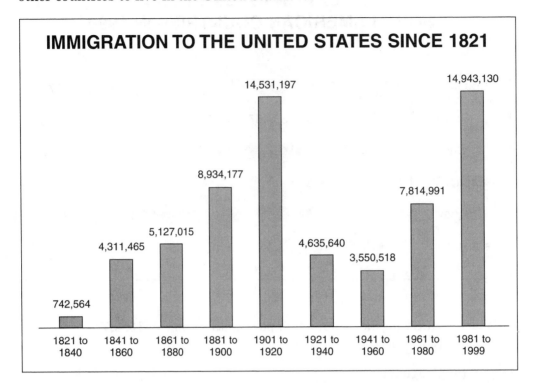

IMMIGRATION TO THE UNITED STATES SINCE 1821

Place a check mark next to the correct answers to questions 1 to 8.

1. The bar graph shows how many people

____ (a) came to the United States between 1821 and 1999.

____ (b) were born in the United States between 1821 and 1999.

____ (c) left the United States between 1821 and 1999.

2. How many bars represent a 20-year period of time?

____ (a) None

____ (b) All except one

____ (c) All

3. The largest immigration to the United States took place between

____ (a) 1881 and 1900.

____ (b) 1901 and 1920.

____ (c) 1981 and 1999.

4. The smallest immigration to the United States took place between

____ (a) 1821 and 1840.

____ (b) 1921 and 1940.

____ (c) 1941 and 1960.

5. How many people immigrated to the United States between 1861 and 1900?

____ (a) 5,127,015

____ (b) 14,061,192

____ (c) 19,188,207

6. How many fewer people immigrated to the United States between 1961 and 1980 than between 1881 and 1900?

_____ (*a*) 1,119,186

_____ (*b*) 1,432,186

_____ (*c*) 1,980,186

7. Immigration to the United States

_____ (*a*) continually increased from 1821 to 1999.

_____ (*b*) was greater between 1961 and 1980 than in any other period in United States history.

_____ (*c*) slowed down between 1921 and 1960.

8. Immigration to the United States

_____ (*a*) has continually decreased since 1921.

_____ (*b*) continually increased between 1821 and 1920.

_____ (*c*) was much greater in the nineteenth century than in the twentieth century.

9. Explain how you know that the choice you picked as the answer to question 8 is true. (Answer in three or four sentences.)

_____

_____

_____

_____

_____

_____

10. Make a chart or pictograph to show the same information that appears on the immigration graph.

C. Study the following double bar graph on life expectancy in five countries.

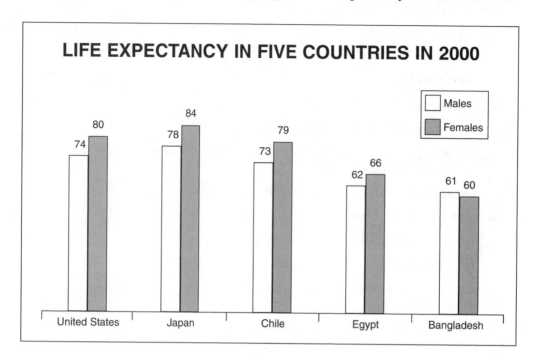

LIFE EXPECTANCY IN FIVE COUNTRIES IN 2000

Place a check mark next to the correct answers to questions 1 to 6.

1. This double bar graph shows the life expectancy of

    ____ (*a*) males only.

    ____ (*b*) females only.

    ____ (*c*) males and females.

2. In which country can females expect to live the longest?

    ____ (*a*) Chile

    ____ (*b*) Egypt

    ____ (*c*) Japan

3. In which *three* countries is the number of years difference between the life expectancy of a man and a woman the same?

    ____ (*a*) United States, Japan, and Chile

    ____ (*b*) Japan, United States, and Egypt

    ____ (*c*) Chile, Egypt, and Bangladesh

4. Which *one* of the following countries has the highest life expectancy for both females and males?

    ____ (*a*) United States

    ____ (*b*) Japan

    ____ (*c*) Egypt

5. Of the countries shown, the life expectancy of a man in Japan is closest to the life expectancy of a woman in

_____ (a) Bangladesh.

_____ (b) Egypt.

_____ (c) Chile.

6. In which *one* of the following countries is the life expectancy of a man the closest to the life expectancy of a woman?

_____ (a) Japan

_____ (b) Chile

_____ (c) Bangladesh

7. In which country can males expect to live the longest? (Answer in one sentence.)

_____

_____

8. In which country is the life expectancy higher for males than it is for females? (Answer in one sentence.)

_____

_____

9. How much longer can males in Japan expect to live than males in Egypt? (Answer in one sentence.)

_____

_____

10. Is the following statement true or false? Explain in one or two sentences.

"The double bar graph shows clearly why people in the United States live longer than people in Chile, Egypt, and Bangladesh."

_____

_____

_____

_____

_____

CHAPTER 15
Line Graphs

Simple Line Graphs

Let us first look at a *line graph*. It is called a line graph because it uses a line to show its information. The following line graph shows increases in world population from the year 1650 to the year 2100.

This graph gives the world population for the years 1650, 1750, 1850, 1950, and 2000. It also shows what the world population is expected to be in the year 2100. All these years are listed along the bottom of the graph. Numbers in billions are listed on both sides of the graph. They stand for the number of people in the world.

Notice that there are six X's on the graph. For each year, an X is drawn across from the population of that year. For example, look at the X above the year 1950. To find the world population in 1950, follow the X across to the population list on the right side of the graph. You can see that the world population in 1950 was just over 2 billion. In the same way, the other X's can help you find the world population of the other years on the graph.

Most line graphs do not use X's. They were put on this graph just to help you with this example. More important than the X's is the line connecting them. Each X shows the world population for only one year. But the line lets you see how fast the world population has increased since 1650 and will continue to increase up to the year 2100.

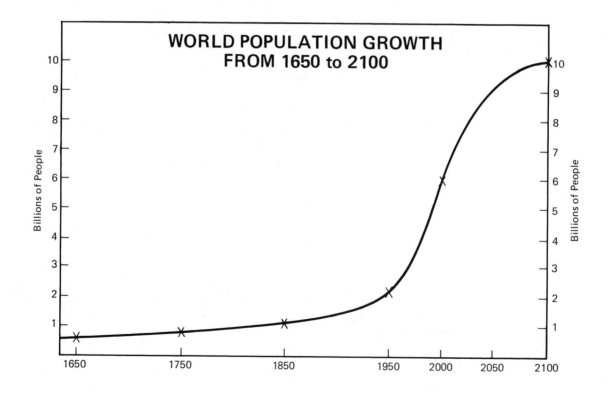

112

Answer the following questions about the line graph.

1. The population figures can be found

_____ (a) along the bottom of the graph.

_____ (b) under each X.

_____ (c) along both sides of the graph.

What was your answer? On this graph the population figures can be found along both sides of the graph. Therefore, the answer to question 1 is (c).

2. What was the world's population in 1850?

_____ (a) About 1 billion

_____ (b) About 2 billion

_____ (c) About 3 billion

What was your answer? Find the year 1850 along the bottom of the graph. Next, find the X above the year 1850. Follow the X across to the numbers on the right or left side of the graph. You can see that the population was about 1 billion. Therefore, the answer to question 2 is (a).

3. In which year is the world population expected to be 10 billion?

_____ (a) 2050

_____ (b) 2100

_____ (c) 2200

Which answer did you choose this time? Find the number 10 billion on the right side of the graph. Now look for the X that is on the same level as the number 10 billion. What year appears under that X? It is the year 2100. So it is in the year 2100 that the world population is expected to be 10 billion. Therefore, the answer to question 3 is (b).

4. The population line graph shows that

_____ (a) the population of the world will stay the same over the next 20 years.

_____ (b) the population of the world has been increasing since 1650.

_____ (c) the population of the world never changes.

Which answer did you choose? If the line on the graph is straight across _____, it means that the population is staying the same. If the line is rising _____, it means that the population is increasing. If the line is falling _____, it means that the population is decreasing (becoming less). What kind of line do you find on this graph? One that is rising. This tells you that the population is increasing. Therefore, the answer to question 4 is (b).

5. How does the population line graph show that there will be a greater need to produce more food in the future? (Answer in one or two sentences.)

_____

_____

_____

_____

_____

_____

_____

What did you write? This graph shows that the population will increase in the future, but it shows nothing about food. When the population grows, however, there is always a need for more food. Sometimes you can use facts on a graph to learn information that is not on the same graph.

Here is an example of a possible answer to question 5.

The line graph shows a great increase in population in the future. When the population increases, there is always a need for more food.

Double Line Graphs

The line of the population graph shows one set of statistics: the changing population between 1650 and 2100. But you may want to put two sets of statistics on a line graph. To do this, you must use a separate line for each.

The graph on the foreign trade of Brazil at the bottom of the page uses two lines: a broken line and a solid line.

The value (cost or worth) of imports is shown by the broken line – – – – . By looking at this line, we can tell how much money Brazil spent in five-year periods between 1980 and 2000 to buy goods from other countries. To find out the value of Brazilian exports, we must look at the solid line ———. It shows how much money Brazil made in five-year periods between 1980 and 2000 by selling goods to other countries. Because this graph uses two lines, it is called a *double line graph*.

1. The double line graph uses two lines to

   _____ (a) show two different years.

   _____ (b) make the graph easier to read.

   _____ (c) show two different sets of statistics.

Which answer did you choose? This foreign trade graph uses two lines to show the imports and exports of Brazil: the broken one for the value of imports and the solid one for the value of exports. Therefore, the answer to question 1 is (c).

2. What was the value of exports in 1985?

   _____ (a) Slightly more than 15 billion U.S. dollars

   _____ (b) Slightly more than 25 billion U.S. dollars

   _____ (c) Slightly more than 35 billion U.S. dollars

Which answer did you choose? Find the year 1985 along the bottom of the graph and the solid line above the year 1985. (The solid line stands for the value of exports.) Place your finger on the solid line over 1985. If you move your finger directly across to the numbers on the left side of the graph, your finger will match up with 25, or more exactly just above 25. This means that the value of exports in 1985 was slightly more than 25 billion U.S. dollars. Therefore, the answer to question 2 is (b).

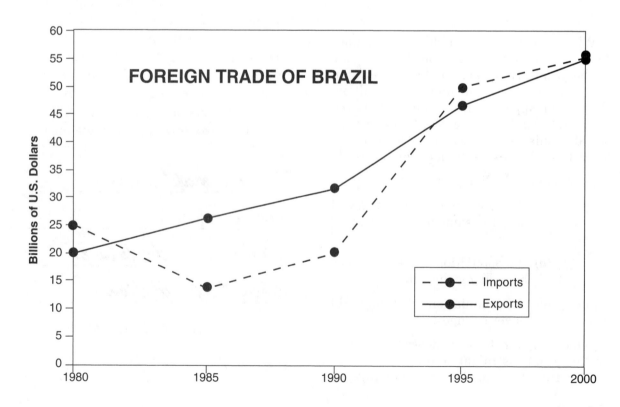

FOREIGN TRADE OF BRAZIL

3. In which year was the value of Brazil's imports 20 billion U.S. dollars?

_____ (a) 1990

_____ (b) 1995

_____ (c) 2000

What was your answer? Find the number 20 on the left side of the graph. The broken line stands for imports, so place your finger on the 20 and move it across the graph until it meets the broken line. Then look at the year below where your finger met the broken line. The year is 1990. This means that in 1990 the value of Brazilian imports was 20 billion U.S. dollars. Therefore, the answer to question 3 is (a).

4. What was the total value of all foreign trade in Brazil in 2000?

_____ (a) 55 billion U.S. dollars

_____ (b) 96 billion U.S. dollars

_____ (c) 111 billion U.S. dollars

What was your answer? To determine the total value of all foreign trade, you add the imports and the exports together. For 2000, the imports are valued at 56 billion U.S. dollars and the exports at 55 billion U.S. dollars. When you add these two numbers together, you get 111 billion U.S. dollars for the total value of all foreign trade in 2000. Therefore, the answer to question 4 is (c).

5. In which two years was the value of imports higher than the value of exports?

_____ (a) 1980 and 1990

_____ (b) 1980 and 1995

_____ (c) 1990 and 1995

What was your answer this time? You know that the broken line stands for imports and the solid line stands for exports. Does the broken line ever appear higher on the graph than the solid line? Yes, over the year 1980 and the year 1995. This means that the value of imports was higher than the value of exports in 1980 and 1995. Therefore, the answer to question 5 is (b).

6. How does the graph show that between 1980 and 2000, exports continually increased, but imports did not **always** increase? (Answer in three or four sentences.)

_____

_____

_____

_____

_____

_____

_____

_____

What did you write? Here is an example of a possible answer to question 6.

The export line went higher for each five-year period between 1980 and 2000. This means that between 1980 and 2000, exports continually increased. On the other hand, the import line dipped between 1980 and 1985. This means that imports did not always increase between 1980 and 2000.

Line graphs are used in many newspapers, books, and magazines. Being able to analyze them is an important Social Studies skill. The following exercises will give you more practice in developing this skill.

USING WHAT YOU HAVE LEARNED

A. Study the following line graph on world production of crude oil.

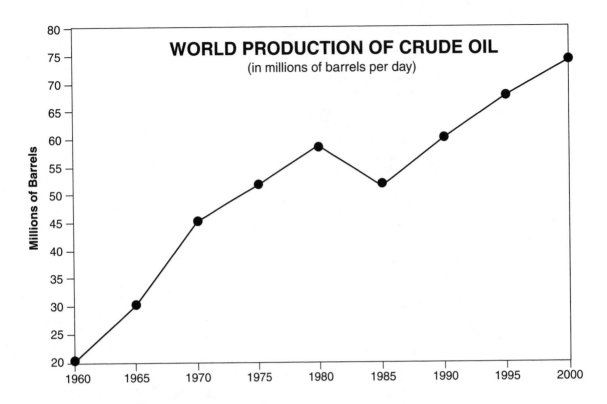

Place a check mark next to the correct answers to questions 1 to 9.

1. The line graph shows how much crude oil

    ____ (a) was used throughout the world between 1960 and 2000.

    ____ (b) the United States exported to other countries between 1960 and 2000.

    ____ (c) was produced throughout the world between 1960 and 2000.

2. Oil production is shown on the graph in

    ____ (a) millions of barrels per day.

    ____ (b) millions of barrels per year.

    ____ (c) billions of barrels per day.

3. The graph is divided into

    ____ (a) one-year time periods.

    ____ (b) five-year time periods.

    ____ (c) ten-year time periods.

4. The line of the graph shows that oil production

    ____ (a) increased for every year given.

    ____ (b) decreased for every year given.

    ____ (c) increased or decreased depending on the year given.

5. How much oil was produced in 1970?

    ____ (a) 21 million barrels per day

    ____ (b) 46 million barrels per day

    ____ (c) 59 million barrels per day

6. In which year were 30 million barrels of oil produced per day?

    ____ (a) 1965

    ____ (b) 1980

    ____ (c) 1995

7. In which one of the following years did oil production decrease from the year (or time period) before?

    ____ (a) 1965

    ____ (b) 1975

    ____ (c) 1985

8. In which two years was the combined oil production almost the same as the total for 1992?

    ____ (a) 1960 and 1970

    ____ (b) 1965 and 1985

    ____ (c) 1980 and 1990

9. How much more oil was produced in 2000 than in 1960?

    ____ (a) 44 million barrels per day

    ____ (b) 54 million barrels per day

    ____ (c) 64 million barrels per day

10. How does the graph show that oil production increased for most of the years between 1960 and 2000? (Answer in two or three sentences.)

_____

_____

_____

_____

_____

B. Study the following double line graph on the foreign trade of Japan.

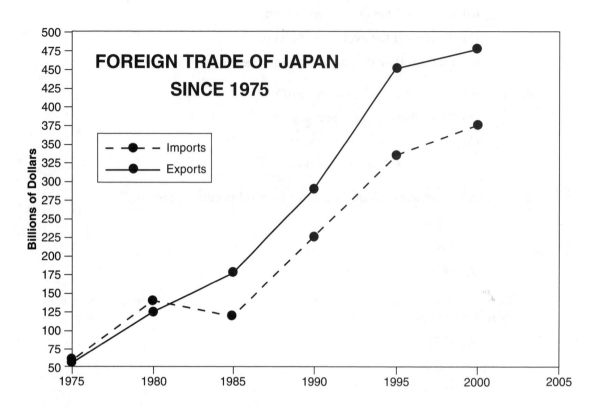

Place a check mark next to the correct answers to questions 1 to 9.

1. The graph shows Japan's imports and exports for

    ____ (*a*) 5 years.

    ____ (*b*) 15 years.

    ____ (*c*) 25 years.

2. The solid line shows the value of Japan's

    ____ (*a*) imports.

    ____ (*b*) exports.

    ____ (*c*) total foreign trade.

3. In which year were Japan's imports greater than its exports?

    ____ (*a*) 1980

    ____ (*b*) 1990

    ____ (*c*) 2000

4. What was the value of Japan's exports in 1985?

    ____ (*a*) Slightly more than 50 billion dollars

    ____ (*b*) Slightly more than 175 billion dollars

    ____ (*c*) Slightly more than 285 billion dollars

5. In which year was the value of Japan's imports about 375 million dollars?

_____ (a) 1990

_____ (b) 1995

_____ (c) 2000

6. What was the total of all foreign trade in Japan in 1995?

_____ (a) Nearly 800 billion dollars

_____ (b) Nearly 444 billion dollars

_____ (c) Nearly 107 billion dollars

7. Japan's exports increased the most between

_____ (a) 1975 and 1980.

_____ (b) 1985 and 1990.

_____ (c) 1990 and 1995.

8. In which year was the difference between the value of Japan's imports and exports about 53 million dollars?

_____ (a) 1980

_____ (b) 1990

_____ (c) 1995

9. Between which two years did Japan's imports decrease in value while its exports continued to increase in value?

_____ (a) 1980 and 1985

_____ (b) 1985 and 1990

_____ (c) 1995 and 2000

10. A *trend* is the general direction in which something moves. On occasion, the direction may change, but for the most part it remains the same. When the direction changes permanently, we say that a new trend has begun. Describe one trend that the time line shows involving Japanese imports and/or exports. (Answer in one or two sentences.)

_____

_____

_____

_____

_____

C. Study the following triple line graph. Use the same rules in studying this graph as you did in studying a double line graph.

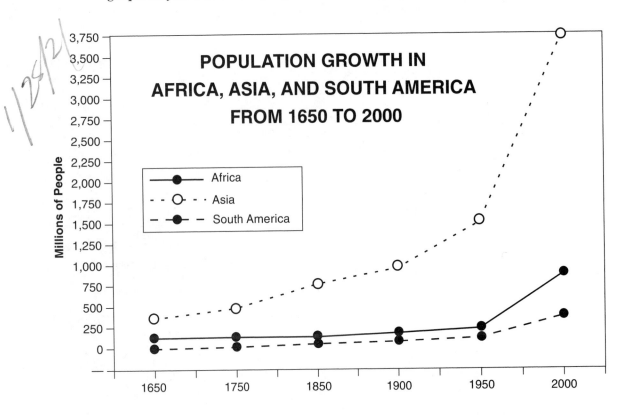

Place a check mark next to the correct answers to questions 1 to 10.

1. South America is shown by the line

____ (*a*) - - - -

____ (*b*) ———

____ (*c*) – – –

2. The population of Asia in 1850 was about

____ (*a*) 550 million.

____ (*b*) 750 million.

____ (*c*) 950 million.

3. The population of Africa in 2000 was slightly higher than

____ (*a*) 400 million.

____ (*b*) 800 million.

____ (*c*) 1.8 billion.

4. Which continent was the least populated in 1950?

____ (*a*) Africa

____ (*b*) Asia

____ (*c*) South America

5. The biggest increase in the population of Asia took place between

____ (a) 1650 and 1850.

____ (b) 1850 and 1950.

____ (c) 1950 and 2000.

6. South America had a population of 347 million in 2000. But Asia had a population of 335 million in

____ (a) 1650.

____ (b) 1750.

____ (c) 1850.

7. In 1650, the population of Africa was about

____ (a) 200 million less than the population of Asia.

____ (b) 450 million less than the population of Asia.

____ (c) 650 million less than the population of Asia.

8. The population of Asia in 1900 was nearly

____ (a) 1 million.

____ (b) 100 million.

____ (c) 1 billion.

9. Which statement is supported by the graph?

____ (a) The population of Africa, Asia, and South America grew more between 1950 and 2000 than between 1650 and 1950.

____ (b) In 1750, the total population of Africa and South America was almost the same as the population of Asia.

____ (c) Since 1900, the population of South America has been greater than the population of Africa.

10. In 2000, the world population reached nearly 6 billion. From the graph, you can see that the majority of the world's population lives in

____ (a) Africa.

____ (b) Asia.

____ (c) Africa and South America.

CHAPTER 16
Photographs and Drawings

Pictures can tell a story or give information quickly and clearly. Many paragraphs may be needed to explain in writing what one picture shows. This is why pictures such as photographs and drawings are often used to teach Social Studies skills.

Photographs

Photographs show scenes and events as they look to the "eye" of the camera and to the person taking the picture. Look at the photograph at the right.

What does it show? At first the answer seems easy. An Arab man in the desert is using a telephone. But does the photograph have any deeper meaning? Perhaps one or two sentences (called a caption) next to or below the photograph would help you find the deeper meaning. Here is a possible caption: "Desert life finally benefits from the sun. New solar-powered radiophones (phones powered by energy from the sun) make life less difficult for those who live and travel in the Arabian Desert."

This caption makes you think a little more about what is shown in the photograph. Throughout history, the sun has been a source of trouble for people in the desert. Finding ways to protect plants, animals, and humans from the heat of the sun is an important part of desert life. Note that the clothing of the man in the photograph is designed to protect him from the sun.

The photograph also shows that with the arrival of solar-powered phones, people in the Arabian Desert have finally begun to benefit from the sun. Can you think of how solar-powered phones help improve the

© Robert Azzi 1980 Woodfin Camp & Associates

quality of life in the desert? Surely the man in the photograph knows that as long as he can use the phone, he is not far from any help he may need.

By just looking at the photograph, you might have understood its meaning, but the caption probably made you think more deeply about what you saw.

Sometimes it is difficult to understand what a photograph is about unless it has a caption. Look at the photograph on page 123.

Although you can see that the subject of this photograph is a parade, you may still wonder what the picture is all about. Where

Tass from Sovfoto

did this parade take place? What was the reason for having it? A caption can give you the answers to these questions.

Here is the caption that goes with this photograph: "A parade in the Soviet Union in the 1960's. The Soviet government used parades to show its great military power to the rest of the world."

Answer the following questions about this photograph.

1. The parade is made up of

_____ (a) bands playing music.

_____ (b) people marching.

_____ (c) missiles being pulled by trucks.

Which answer did you choose? You can find the answer by looking at the photograph, which shows you that the parade is made up of missiles being pulled by trucks. Therefore, the answer to question 1 is (c).

2. The Soviet government probably used this parade

_____ (a) to give the people a day off from work.

_____ (b) to show that the Soviet Union was a great military power.

_____ (c) to show its support of military education.

What was your answer? This time the answer is contained in the caption, which states that the Soviet Union used parades to show its great military power. Because the

photograph shows giant missiles, you might have been able to answer this question without the help of the caption. Many people believe that the Soviet Union paraded its giant missiles to let the whole world see its military power. Therefore, the answer to question 2 is (b).

3. Describe in your own words what you see in the photograph.

_____

_____

_____

_____

_____

_____

_____

_____

_____

What did you write? You should study a photograph very carefully. If you look at a photograph too quickly, you may miss important information. Here is a possible answer to question 3.

The photograph shows a great parade. Giant missiles are being pulled by trucks. Large crowds of people are gathered in a large open area in front of buildings to watch the parade.

Drawings

You know that photographs are pictures taken with a camera. But the camera was invented only about 160 years ago, so it is impossible to have photographs of events that happened hundreds or thousands of years ago. Even since the invention of the camera, it has not always been possible to photograph every important event, person, or place.

Pictures made by an artist, or *drawings,* can take the place of photographs. Artists may be present at an event while it is happening. But if not, the artist has to read and study about the event before making a drawing of it. Remember that drawings, even though they may look like photographs, show only what the artist decided to put into the picture.

Look at the following drawing and its caption.

EBONY Magazine

Timbuktu in the sixteenth century. This great African city was destroyed by wars in the 1500's and was since rebuilt.

1. The drawing shows

_____ (*a*) a city, but it is impossible to know the name of the city.

_____ (*b*) the city of Timbuktu as it looked in the sixteenth century.

_____ (*c*) the city of Timbuktu as it looks today.

Which answer did you choose? The drawing shows a city. But you need a caption to find out the name of the city and to give you information about the city. Captions are just as important to drawings as they are to photographs. The caption of this drawing tells you that the city is Timbuktu as it looked in the sixteenth century. Therefore, the answer to question 1 is (*b*).

2. When you look at this drawing of Timbuktu,

_____ (a) you can be sure that this is how Timbuktu really looked.

_____ (b) you can compare this drawing with a photograph of Timbuktu.

_____ (c) you are seeing only what the artist wanted people to see.

Which answer did you choose this time? No one alive today has seen the city of Timbuktu as it was in the 1500's. No photographs exist of the city as it looked then because the camera had not yet been invented. Only through drawings do we know what the city may have been like. Some of these drawings were done centuries ago by people who saw Timbuktu with their own eyes. But proving that their drawings show Timbuktu as it really was would be difficult. You can be sure, however, that the artists drew Timbuktu as they wanted others to see it. Therefore, the best answer to question 2 is (c).

To get more information from pictures, ask yourself questions such as these when you look at a drawing or photograph:

Does the picture show a present-day scene or something that happened in the past?
Is it a country scene or a city scene?
What kinds of buildings are shown? What are they probably used for?
What kinds of people are shown? What are they doing? How are they dressed?
What time of year is shown?

USING WHAT YOU HAVE LEARNED

A. Look at the following photograph and read the caption under it.

United Nations

A marketplace in Abidjan, capital of Côte d'Ivoire.

Place a check mark next to the correct answers to questions 1 to 3.

1. The photograph shows a marketplace in

   ____ (a) Nairobi, Kenya.

   ____ (b) Cairo, Egypt.

   ____ (c) Abidjan, Côte d'Ivoire.

2. What is being sold in the marketplace?

   ____ (a) Fruits and vegetables

   ____ (b) Pots and pans

   ____ (c) Clothes

3. The photograph shows women

   ____ (a) in traditional African dress only.

   ____ (b) in modern American dress only.

   ____ (c) in traditional African and modern American dress.

4. Why could you use this photograph to show that cities in Africa are becoming modern? (Answer in two or three sentences.)

   _____

   _____

   _____

   _____

   _____

   _____

   _____

5. How does this photograph show that many Africans hold on to their traditions? (Answer in two or three sentences.)

   _____

   _____

   _____

   _____

   _____

   _____

Wide World Photos

The first atomic bomb was dropped on Hiroshima, Japan, on August 6, 1945. The United States dropped the bomb, hoping to bring an end to World War II. A week later, the Japanese surrendered and World War II was over.

B. Look at the photograph above and read the caption under it.

Place a check mark next to the correct answers to questions 1 to 3.

1. The destruction (damage, ruin) in the photograph was caused by

    ____ (*a*) an earthquake.   (*c*) an atomic bomb.

    ____ (*b*) a hurricane.

2. The photograph shows part of the city of

    ____ (*a*) Beijing.   ____ (*b*) Hiroshima.   ____ (*c*) Saigon.

3. The atomic bomb was dropped because

    ____ (*a*) the United States wanted to start a war with Japan.

    ____ (*b*) Japan had dropped an atomic bomb on the United States.

    ____ (*c*) the United States thought it would end World War II more quickly.

4. What details in the photograph indicate that the area shown was part of a city? (Answer in two or three sentences.)

_____

_____

_____

_____

_____

5. How does this photograph show that war is terrible? (Answer in two or three sentences.)

_____

_____

_____

_____

_____

_____

C. Study the following drawing and read the caption under it.

Culver Pictures, Inc.

Napoleon's army retreating from Russia in 1812. Nearly one-half million French soldiers died trying to conquer Russia.

Place a check mark next to the correct answers to questions 1 to 5.

1. This drawing shows

_____ (*a*) Napoleon's army on its way to Moscow.

_____ (*b*) Napoleon's army retreating from Russia.

_____ (*c*) the Russian army invading France.

2. The scene in the drawing took place in the

____ (*a*) winter.

____ (*b*) spring.

____ (*c*) summer.

3. You know that nearly one-half million French soldiers died in Russia because

____ (*a*) all the dead soldiers are shown in the drawing.

____ (*b*) the caption tells you.

____ (*c*) Napoleon is telling his generals the sad news.

4. There is no photograph of the event shown in the drawing because

____ (*a*) no one remembered to bring a camera.

____ (*b*) drawings are more interesting than photographs.

____ (*c*) the camera had not yet been invented.

5. Which one of the following statements is true?

____ (*a*) We know for sure that the artist was with Napoleon in Russia.

____ (*b*) The drawing shows only what the artist wanted us to see.

____ (*c*) Drawings never show events as they really happened.

6. History books tell us that Napoleon and his army suffered greatly during their invasion of Russia. How does this drawing show some of the suffering experienced by Napoleon and his army? (Answer in two or three sentences.)

_____

_____

_____

_____

_____

D. Look at the pictures on page 130 and read the captions under them.

Place a check mark next to the correct answers to questions 1 to 5.

1. Which statement is true?

____ (*a*) Pictures A and B are both photographs.

____ (*b*) Picture A is a photograph, and Picture B is a drawing.

____ (*c*) Picture A is a drawing, and Picture B is a photograph.

2. Picture A shows

____ (*a*) the arrival of Commodore Matthew Perry in Japan in 1853.

____ (*b*) the end of World War II in Japan.

____ (*c*) a scene in Japan today.

Corbis/Bettmann

Picture A
Commodore Matthew C. Perry of the United States sailed to Japan in 1853.
This visit marked the first time an American was allowed to enter Japan.

Japan National Tourist Organization

Picture B
Japan has become one of the most modern nations in the world.
Today Japanese cities look like many American cities.

3. The caption to Picture A states that

  ____ (*a*) Japan has borrowed many things from the United States.

  ____ (*b*) the United States has become interested in Japan only in the last 25 years.

  ____ (*c*) the visit of Perry was the first time an American was allowed to visit Japan.

4. Picture B shows

  ____ (*a*) a scene in the United States today.

  ____ (*b*) a scene in Japan at the time of Perry's arrival.

  ____ (*c*) a scene in Japan today.

5. What is the weather like in Picture B?

  ____ (*a*) Cool

  ____ (*b*) Hot

  ____ (*c*) Very cold

6. Describe in your own words what you see in Picture A.

  _____

  _____

  _____

  _____

  _____

  _____

7. How does Picture B show that Japan has been influenced by U.S. customs? (Answer in one or two sentences.)

  _____

  _____

  _____

  _____

  _____

  _____

8. How do the two pictures show that life in Japan has changed over the last 150 years? (Answer in two or three sentences.)

_____

_____

_____

_____

_____

_____

_____

CHAPTER 17
Social Studies Cartoons

Sometimes artists express their feelings or opinions about current events in drawings. These drawings, called *cartoons,* exaggerate (overstate) ideas and present them in a simplified form. Cartoons are usually funny, but they can also be serious. Often they can be used to teach important Social Studies ideas.

To understand the meaning of the ideas in cartoons, you have to think about the pictures in a special way. For example, look at the following cartoon.

What is this cartoon saying? It seems to be just a drawing of a man pulling a ball and chain, but the artist who drew the cartoon is trying to show more. The man and the ball and chain are symbols, pictures that stand for, or represent, other things. The man represents the poor countries of the world. The ball and chain represent the problems facing these countries. According to the cartoon symbols, the artist's opinion is that certain problems are holding back many poor countries of the world and keeping them from becoming modern nations.

Answer the following questions about this cartoon.

1. The problems of the poor countries of the world are represented in the cartoon by a

   _____ (*a*) man.

   _____ (*b*) wall.

   _____ (*c*) ball and chain.

Which answer did you choose? If the cartoon had nothing written on it, it would be impossible to know its real meaning. But the words "illiteracy," "disease," and "hunger" are written on the ball. (Illiteracy means not being able to read and write.) Because illiteracy, disease, and hunger are all problems of poor countries, the ball and chain represent the problems of the poor countries of the world. Therefore, the answer to question 1 is (*c*).

2. Which one of the following statements is true?

   _____ (*a*) A cartoon is always based on fact.

   _____ (*b*) A cartoon is an artist's opinion and is not fact.

   _____ (*c*) A cartoon is an artist's opinion, but it can still be based on fact.

Which answer did you choose? A cartoon shows an artist's opinion, which may or may not be based on fact. In this cartoon, the opinion of the artist can easily be proved to be true by records and statistics. Therefore, the answer to question 2 is (c).

3. How can the chain in the cartoon be broken? That is, how can the problem be solved? (Answer in one or two sentences.)

_____

_____

_____

_____

_____

_____

_____

_____

What did you write? Your answer should not have described the details of the cartoon, such as the man, the ball and chain, or the buildings. Instead your answer should have dealt with the ideas or events that these details stand for. Here is a possible answer to question 3.

The chain could be broken by building schools and hospitals. Also, rich countries could be asked to help build factories and increase food production so more people could have jobs and enough to eat.

Sometimes it is necessary to use more than one drawing in a cartoon to present an idea. Study the following cartoon, which is made up of four drawings. It shows Mao Zedong, the dictator (all-powerful ruler) of China for many years.

Courtesy of Jim Ivey, reprinted by permission

1. This cartoon shows that

_____ (a) a dictator is happy to hear criticism (disapproving or unfavorable comments).

_____ (b) a dictator may invite criticism but really does not want it.

_____ (c) people never try to criticize a dictator.

Which answer did you choose? If you saw only Drawings A and B, you would think that a dictator is happy to hear criticism.

But Drawing C shows a person who has a criticism being punished. Drawing D shows that there are no more criticisms because everyone is afraid of being punished. Taken together, the four drawings show that the answer to question 1 is (b).

Sometimes you may see two or more cartoons with opposite opinions on the same subject. Cartoonists, just like people who write essays, may use the same facts to form different opinions. Study the following cartoons to see two views of the same idea.

CARTOON A

"I am only interested in the United States. The rest of the world can take care of itself."

CARTOON B

"I am glad to meet all of you. I am always interested in helping other countries."

1. In Cartoons A and B, Uncle Sam represents

   _____ (a) the American people and/or their government.

   _____ (b) people all over the world.

   _____ (c) the United Nations.

Which answer did you choose? Uncle Sam appears in many cartoons. He is usually shown as an old man with a white beard who is dressed in a suit and tall hat that look like the U.S. flag. Uncle Sam is the symbol used to represent the American people and the U.S. government. Therefore, the answer to question 1 is (a).

2. In Cartoon A, Uncle Sam

   _____ (a) wants to help other countries.

   _____ (b) wants to help only some other countries.

   _____ (c) does not want to be involved with other countries.

Which answer did you choose? Cartoon A shows Uncle Sam building a wall around the United States. A wall is often used as a symbol for keeping out someone or something. In the caption, Uncle Sam says that he is interested only in the United States. He is building the wall to keep out the problems of other countries. Therefore, the answer to question 2 is (c).

3. In Cartoon B, Uncle Sam

   _____ (a) does not want to help other countries.

   _____ (b) wants to help other countries.

   _____ (c) wants to go to war against weak countries.

Which answer did you choose this time? Cartoon B shows Uncle Sam greeting people from other countries. In the caption, Uncle Sam says that he is glad to meet them and is interested in helping them. Therefore, the answer to question 3 is (b).

4. Which cartoon do you agree with the most? Why? (Answer in two or three sentences.)

   _____

   _____

   _____

   _____

   _____

   _____

   _____

   _____

What did you write? Because you were asked for your opinion, you could have agreed with either Cartoon A or Cartoon B. What matters is that your opinion is reasonable and carefully thought out.

The exercises that follow will give you more practice in studying and interpreting Social Studies cartoons.

USING WHAT YOU HAVE LEARNED

A. Look at the following cartoon.

Burck in the *Chicago Sun-Times*

Place a check mark next to the correct answers to questions 1 and 2.

1. The woman with wings represents

_____ (*a*) war.

_____ (*b*) hatred.

_____ (*c*) world peace.

2. The woman cannot fly because

_____ (*a*) her feet are chained to the problems on the ground.

_____ (*b*) she does not know how to fly.

_____ (*c*) her wings are too small.

3. What four problems stop the woman from flying?

_____

_____

_____

_____

4. How can the chains be broken, the problems solved? (Answer in two or three sentences.)

_____

_____

_____

_____

_____

5. What would be a good title for this cartoon?

_____

_____

B. Look at the cartoon on page 138.

Place a check mark next to the correct answers to questions 1 to 4.

1. This cartoon contains
   _____ (*a*) two drawings.
   _____ (*b*) four drawings.
   _____ (*c*) six drawings.

2. The first drawing tells you that
   _____ (*a*) people talk a lot about pollution but do not do much to stop it.
   _____ (*b*) people are working hard to stop pollution.
   _____ (*c*) people do not like to talk about pollution.

3. The cartoon tells you that the source of pollution is
   _____ (*a*) cars.
   _____ (*b*) factories.
   _____ (*c*) people.

Pogo

Reprinted by permission of Selby Kelly, Executrix © 1970 by Walt Kelly

4. The cartoon suggests that we solve the problem of pollution by

____ (*a*) picking up litter.

____ (*b*) doing away with the source—people.

____ (*c*) passing laws.

5. Do you agree or disagree that we cannot really do much about pollution? Why? (Answer in two or three sentences.)

_____

_____

_____

_____

_____

_____

C. Look at the following cartoon dealing with Latin America.

Place a check next to the correct answer to questions 1 to 4.

1. The people atop the left side of the platform represent the

   ____ (*a*) governments of many Latin American countries.

   ____ (*b*) wealthy classes in Latin America.

   ____ (*c*) poor classes in Latin America.

2. The people atop the right side of the platform represent

   ____ (*a*) newly arrived immigrants in Latin America.

   ____ (*b*) the educated classes in Latin America.

   ____ (*c*) the poor classes in Latin America.

3. Political stability usually means

   ____ (*a*) keeping the government and society just as they are.

   ____ (*b*) replacing one government with another.

   ____ (*c*) having more than one person run for a political office.

4. More than likely, in drawing the person balancing the platform in the same kind of clothes as the people atop the right side of the platform, the artist is saying that

   ____ (*a*) the power to improve the lives of the people atop the right side of the platform is in their own hands.

   ____ (*b*) there is no middle class in Latin America.

   ____ (*c*) the wealthy play no role in keeping a country politically stable.

5. The couple atop the left side of the platform are fearful that if the people atop the right side make a move, political stability will be lost. In your opinion, is that the only thing the couple are fearful of losing? (Answer in one or two sentences.)

_____

_____

_____

6. In your opinion, what is the meaning of this cartoon? (Answer in two or three sentences.)

_____

_____

_____

_____

D. In recent years, the U.S. government has spent 18% of its revenue (money) on defense and 2% on education. The following cartoons deal with this issue.

CARTOON A

CARTOON B

"Uncle Sam, don't you think that you should take a little of that defense money and put it into education?"

"Uncle Sam, we know that your most important job is to keep our country free and strong."

Place a check mark next to the correct answers to questions 1 to 5.

1. In Cartoons A and B, Uncle Sam represents

_____ (*a*) the United Nations.

_____ (*b*) the U.S. government.

_____ (*c*) state governments.

2. In Cartoon A, the girl and boy are asking Uncle Sam to

____ (a) protect the independence of the United States.

____ (b) give equal consideration to defending the United States and improving education.

____ (c) consider spending more money on education.

3. In Cartoon A, the artist probably thinks that

____ (a) too much money is spent on defense in the United States.

____ (b) the U.S. government spends too much money on education.

____ (c) more money should be spent on defense and education.

4. In Cartoon B, the girl and boy believe that

____ (a) Uncle Sam's first responsibility is to protect the independence of the United States.

____ (b) their school needs many improvements.

____ (c) educational reform is the responsibility of state governments.

5. In Cartoon B, the artist probably thinks that

____ (a) too much money is spent on the defense in the United States.

____ (b) the U.S. government spends too much money on defense and education.

____ (c) the U.S. government should spend whatever money is needed to provide a strong defense.

6. How do these two cartoons show that a caption is important in understanding the meaning of a cartoon? (Answer in two or three sentences.)

_____

_____

_____

_____

_____

7. Which cartoon comes closer to expressing your feeling on how much money the U.S. government should spend on defense and education? (Explain your answer in two or three sentences.)

_____

_____

_____

_____

_____

CHAPTER 18
Introducing Globes and Maps

Our planet Earth is one of a group of planets that travel around the sun. For hundreds of years, people have been studying our planet. Some of their findings have been put on drawings of the earth called *maps*. Maps come in all shapes, sizes, and colors and show many useful and interesting things about the earth.

Globes

The best representation of the earth is a *globe*, which is a small model of the earth. A globe is shaped like a ball because the earth looks almost like a ball, or a sphere. (See Picture A.) As you turn a globe, you can see what the entire earth looks like. A globe is the *only* type of map that shows the correct size, shape, and location of land and water areas on the earth.

Although it is the best representation of the earth, a globe is not always the easiest to use. First, a globe is difficult to carry about. Second, unless a globe is very big, it cannot show close-up views of different areas of the earth. To overcome these problems, people have created other types of maps.

Flat Maps

One other type of map is called a *flat map* because it is printed on flat sheets of paper or cloth. Flat maps can be folded or carried

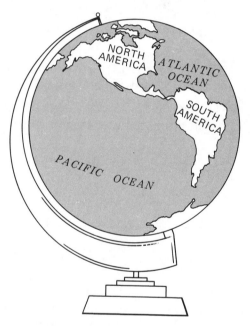

PICTURE A GLOBE

along wherever you go or printed in books. They can show close-up views of places and many other kinds of information. But there is one serious problem to keep in mind when using flat maps. On them, the shape, size, and location of the earth's land and water areas may be distorted (twisted out of shape) and inaccurate (not correct, wrong). Let us look at some of these flat maps so you can learn some of their good and bad points.

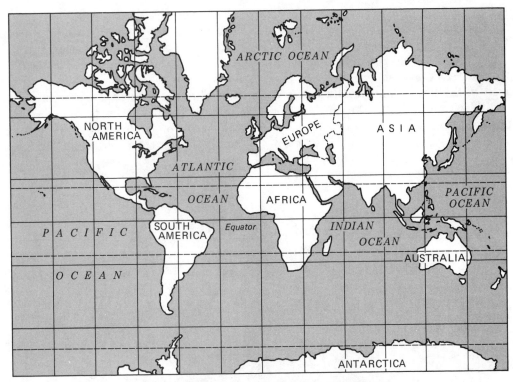

PICTURE B MERCATOR MAP

One of the oldest flat maps is the *Mercator map,* shown in Picture B. It was first used more than 400 years ago to help sailors find their way across oceans. The grid of straight lines going north to south (top to bottom) and east to west (across) made it easier to chart a course and, therefore, sail in the right direction.

The major problem with the Mercator map is the distortion of the size and shape of land and water areas. Though the size and shape of the land and water areas across the center of the map are correct, the land and water areas at the top and bottom of the map appear much larger than they actually are.

Compare the distorted land and water areas on a Mercator map with the same areas on a globe. For example, on a Mercator map, North America looks larger than Africa. A globe, which shows the true size and shape of land areas, lets us see that North America is really smaller than Africa.

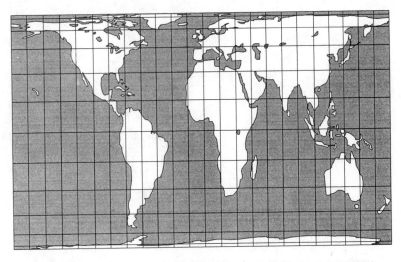

PICTURE C PETERS PROJECTION MAP

The *Peters Projection map,* shown in Picture C, corrects some of the distortions of the Mercator map. It gives the correct size of land and ocean areas. North America, Europe, and Asia are shown in true size compared with South America and Africa. The grid of straight lines, like the grid on the Mercator map, is used to provide accurate directions. The problem with the Peters Projection map is that the land areas across the center of the map are stretched longer than they really are. Also the land areas at the top and bottom of the map are pressed flatter than on the Mercator map.

A third flat map, called a *Mollweide,* or *equal area, map,* has an oval shape, that is, the shape of an egg. This map, shown in Picture D, gives the true size of land and water areas. It also shows the lines running north to south as curved. This is a more accurate view of the earth because the earth is curved.

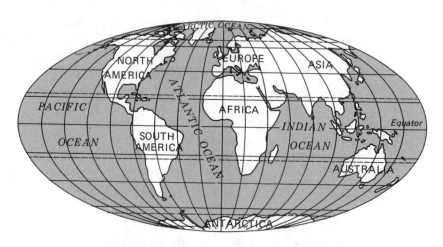

PICTURE D MOLLWEIDE MAP

The problem with the Mollweide map is that land shapes are slightly distorted and untrue. This distortion can be corrected by using a *broken projection,* or *interrupted projection, map.* Such a map shows most land shapes correctly by breaking the oval into several parts. But as you can see in Picture E, the water areas then are cut up and not accurately shown.

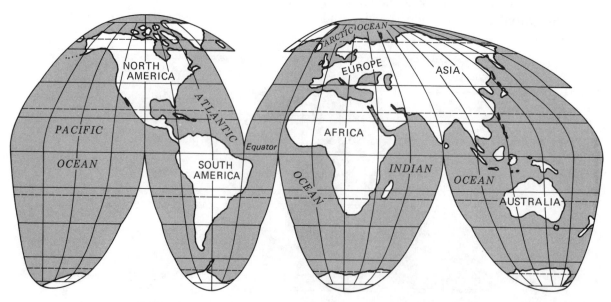

PICTURE E BROKEN PROJECTION MAP

Another important flat map is the *polar map,* shown in Picture F. The North Pole or the South Pole is the center of a polar map.

Go back to the Mercator map and notice how far North America and Asia appear to be from each other. The Mercator map makes you think that an airplane trip between the two continents would take a long time. Now look at the polar map, which shows how close North America and Asia really are to each other. It is easy to see why pilots use a polar map when flying between North America and Asia. A polar map helps them find the shortest and most direct routes.

A polar map also has distortions. The land and water areas at the outer sections of the map are too large and have inaccurate shapes.

Despite their distortions and problems, maps give us the most useful drawings of the earth. They can be very helpful in your Social Studies classes as you learn about places on the earth.

Checking on Globes and Maps

Answer the following questions to see how much you have learned about globes and maps.

1. A globe is the best representation of the earth because

   _____ (*a*) it is the easiest map to use.

   _____ (*b*) it gives more information than any other type of map.

   _____ (*c*) it looks most like the earth.

Which answer did you choose? A globe can be very inconvenient as well as difficult to carry about. So choice (*a*) cannot be the answer. As for choice (*b*), the fact is that flat maps can be drawn to show many things that globes never show. For example, flat maps can show local streets, whereas globes are too small to do that. So the correct answer cannot be choice (*b*). Earlier in this chapter, you read that a globe is shaped like the earth. Because a globe looks most like the earth and shows the land and water areas in their true size, shape, and location, it is the best representation. Therefore, the answer to question 1 is (*c*).

2. A major problem with a Mercator map is

   _____ (*a*) the lines running across the map.

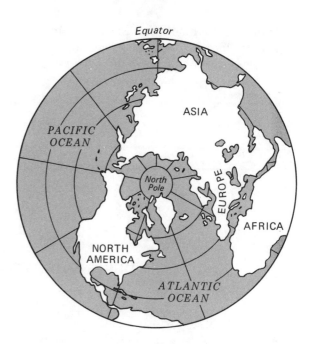

PICTURE F   POLAR MAP

   _____ (*b*) the distortion of land and water areas at the top and bottom.

   _____ (*c*) the distortion of land and water areas across the center.

Which answer did you choose? Look at the examples of a globe and a Mercator map in the chapter. The land and water areas on the globe and across the center of the Mercator map are shown in their correct size and shape. But see how the land and water areas at the top and bottom of the Mercator map are distorted. This means that the answer to question 2 must be (*b*).

3. Which flat map shows how close North America, Europe, and Asia actually are to one another?

   _____ (*a*) Mollweide

   _____ (*b*) Polar

   _____ (*c*) Peters

Which answer did you choose this time? The best way to answer this question is to look at all three maps and compare them. You will see that a polar map shows how close North America, Europe, and Asia are to one another. Therefore, the answer to question 3 is (*b*).

4. What problem on the Mercator map is solved by the Peters Projection map? (Answer in one or two sentences.)

_____

_____

_____

What did you write? A good answer might state that the Mercator map shows North America as larger than Africa. On a Peters Projection map, North America is shown in its true size as compared with Africa.

Reading maps correctly is an important Social Studies skill. The following exercises will give you practice in improving this skill.

USING WHAT YOU HAVE LEARNED

A. Place a check mark next to the correct answers to questions 1 to 10.

1. A globe is

____ (a) a flat map of the earth.

____ (b) a small model of the earth.

____ (c) the same size as the earth.

2. A globe is the only type of map that shows

____ (a) the correct size and shape of land and water areas on the earth.

____ (b) cities and countries on the earth.

____ (c) continents and oceans.

3. Flat maps are used in place of globes because

____ (a) they always show the correct size and shape of land areas.

____ (b) they rarely need to be updated.

____ (c) they can show more information than a globe.

4. In a Peters Projection map, North America is

____ (a) shown as being larger than Africa.

____ (b) shown at its true size compared with Africa.

____ (c) shown at its true size and shape.

5. The polar map gets its name from the fact that

____ (a) North America and Asia are near the North Pole.

____ (b) the South Pole is near the center of Antarctica.

____ (c) the North Pole or the South Pole is in the center of it.

6. The flat map that is in the shape of an oval is

____ (a) the Mercator map.

____ (b) the Mollweide map.

____ (c) the polar map.

7. Mollweide maps show

    ____ (*a*) the correct size and shape of land areas on the earth.

    ____ (*b*) the correct size of land and water areas on the earth.

    ____ (*c*) the correct shape of land and water areas on the earth.

8. You might find a Mercator or Peters Projection map useful if you were

    ____ (*a*) an astronaut.

    ____ (*b*) the captain of a ship.

    ____ (*c*) a racing car driver.

9. Which flat map shows the correct shape of almost all land areas on the earth?

    ____ (*a*) Mercator map

    ____ (*b*) Mollweide map

    ____ (*c*) broken projection map

10. A disadvantage of the interrupted projection map is the distortion of

    ____ (*a*) water area shapes.

    ____ (*b*) land area shapes.

    ____ (*c*) water and land area shapes.

B. The following are the six kinds of maps you learned about in this chapter. In the spaces provided, write the name of each map and list its good and bad points.

MAP A_____

Good Point (s) _____

_____

_____

Bad Point (s) _____

_____

_____

MAP A

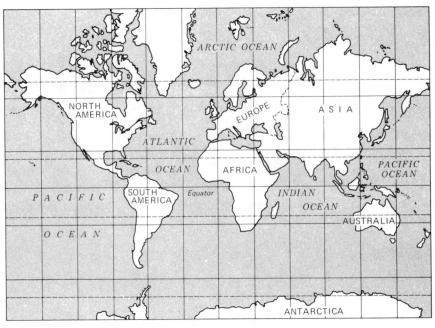

MAP B

MAP B _____

Good Point (s) _____

_____

_____

Bad Point (s) _____

_____

MAP C _____

Good Point (s) _____

_____

_____

_____

Bad Point (s) _____

_____

_____

MAP C

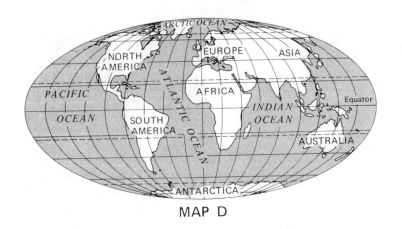

MAP D

MAP D _____

Good Point (s) _____

_____

Bad Point (s) _____

_____

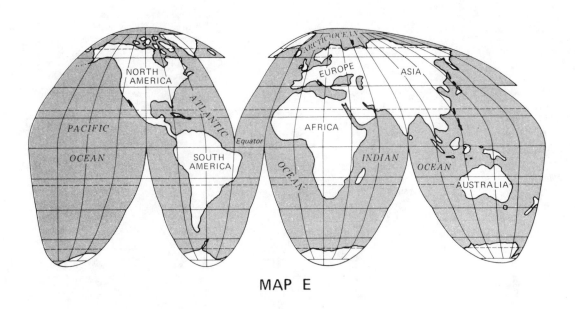

MAP E

MAP E _____

Good Point (s) _____

_____

Bad Point (s) _____

_____

MAP F_____

Good Point (s)_____

_____

_____

Bad Point (s)_____

_____

_____

MAP F

CHAPTER 19
Landforms

The planet Earth is made up of land and water. *Landforms* are important to the human beings, animals, and plants of the earth. On the landforms we grow food, build cities, and manufacture products.

Continents

The largest landforms on the earth are called *continents,* or mainlands. There are seven continents: Asia, Africa, North America, South America, Antarctica, Europe, and Australia. Asia is the largest continent, and Australia is the smallest. Picture A shows the shape and land area of each continent.

Inside the continents are *countries.* The countries are separated on a map by *boundary lines,* which are decided by governments.

On the map of the world on page 152, you can see that there are many countries contained inside most continents. The boundary lines on this map are shown by broken lines.

CONTINENT	AREA	CONTINENT	AREA
Asia	16,988,000 Square Miles	South America	6,795,000 Square Miles
Africa	11,506,000 Square Miles	Antarctica	5,500,000 Square Miles
North America	9,390,000 Square Miles	Europe	3,745,000 Square Miles
		Australia	2,968,000 Square Miles

PICTURE A

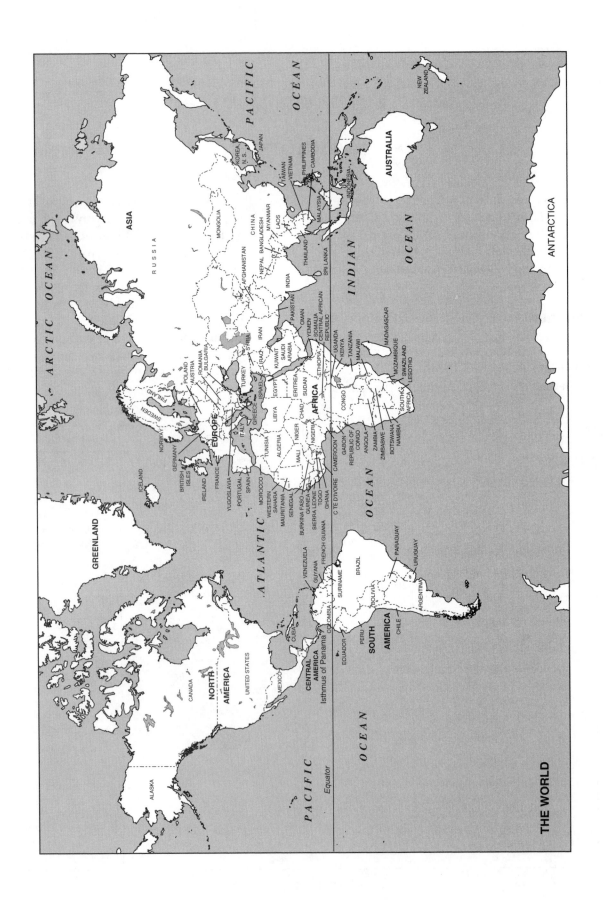

THE WORLD

Notice on the map the countries inside the continent of North America. The three largest countries in North America are Canada, the United States, and Mexico. In the lower part of North America are the countries that make up Central America. These are Panama, Costa Rica, Honduras, Guatemala, Nicaragua, Belize, and El Salvador. The continent of South America contains 13 countries. The continent of Africa is made up of about 50 countries. Over 40 countries are in Asia, and more than 30 are in Europe.

The boundary lines of many countries have changed over the years because of wars, invasions, or agreements among more powerful countries. Remember that continents are large landforms made by nature, but countries are parts of continents and are created by governments.

The continents of Europe and Asia share some countries. Both Turkey and Russia are countries partly in Europe and partly in Asia. Because Europe and Asia look as if they are part of one large continent, they are sometimes called Eurasia.

Notice on the map on page 152 that the continent of Australia contains only one country, with the same name—Australia. The continent of Antarctica is not always shown on maps. Because the climate is very cold in Antarctica, almost no one lives there. Also, the location of Antarctica makes it difficult to include on a map of other continents.

Let us see how much you have learned about continents. Answer the following questions with the help of the map on page 152.

_____ 1. True or False: A continent is the same thing as a country.

What was your answer? It is true that the continent of Australia is the same as the country of Australia. But this is not true of any other continent. Antarctica has no countries at all, and all five other continents are made up of many countries. A continent is a large landform made by nature. A country is created by governments and is only part of a continent. Therefore, the answer to question 1 is False.

2. Which one of the following statements is true?

_____ (a) Russia is a continent.

_____ (b) Africa is a country.

_____ (c) South America is a continent.

Which answer did you choose? Two choices are false and only one choice is true. It is difficult to remember all the countries in the world. But it should not be difficult to remember the names of the seven continents: Asia, Africa, North America, South America, Antarctica, Europe, and Australia. These seven—and only these seven—are the names of the continents. Any other name cannot be the name of a continent. Choice (a) is "Russia is a continent." Is Russia named as one of the seven continents? No, it is not. Russia is a country. So choice (a) is not true. Choice (b) is "Africa is a country." Is Africa listed above as one of the continents? Yes, it is. Africa is a continent and *not* a country. So choice (b) is not true. Choice (c) is "South America is a continent." Is South America listed as a continent? Yes, it is. Therefore, choice (c) is true and the answer to question 2.

Answer again these two important questions. What is the difference between a continent and a country? What are the names of the seven continents?

Other Landforms

You now know that the earth contains seven very large landforms called continents. It also contains other important landforms called *islands*. An island is a body of land completely surrounded by water. Most islands belong to a particular continent. For example, the island of Greenland is part of

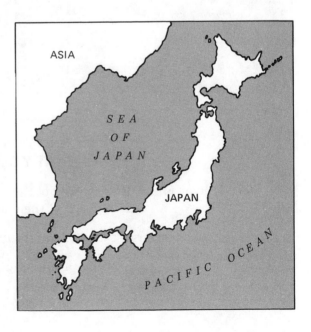

North America, and the islands of Japan are part of Asia.

Locate the following islands on the map on page 152. Then, in the space provided, write the continent to which each island belongs.

Island

1. Sri Lanka

2. Madagascar

3. Sumatra (Indonesia)

Continent

1. _____

2. _____

3. _____

The map on page 152 shows that Sri Lanka and Sumatra are part of Asia and that Madagascar is part of Africa.

Some islands are not part of a continent. For example, the islands of New Zealand are located near Australia. But they are not part of Australia.

Two other important land shapes are drawn and explained below.

1. A *peninsula* is a body of land sticking out into the sea. It is almost completely surrounded by water. For example, Florida is a peninsula. Locate Florida on the map on page 152. Then try to locate three more peninsulas on the same map.

2. An *isthmus* is a narrow strip of land connecting two large landforms. For example, the Isthmus of Panama connects North America and South America. Find the Isthmus of Panama on the map on page 152. Another important isthmus connects Africa and Asia. It is called the Isthmus of Suez. Find the Isthmus of Suez on the map on page 175.

The following exercises will help you learn more about landforms and land shapes.

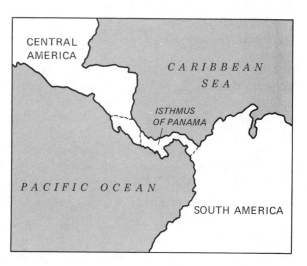

USING WHAT YOU HAVE LEARNED

A. True or False: If every part of the statement is true, write **T.**
If any part of the statement is false, write **F.**

_____ 1. The largest landforms on the earth are called countries.

_____ 2. Another word for a continent is mainland.

_____ 3. The largest continent is Africa.

_____ 4. The smallest continent is South America.

_____ 5. Most continents contain many countries.

_____ 6. Two countries that are in both Europe and Asia are Turkey and China.

_____ 7. Few people live in Antarctica because of the great heat.

_____ 8. A body of land completely surrounded by water is an island.

_____ 9. A body of land almost completely surrounded by water is a peninsula.

_____ 10. A narrow strip of land connecting two large landforms is called an isthmus.

B. Place a check mark next to the correct answers to questions 1 to 5.

1. Europe and Asia together are sometimes called

____ (a) Russia.

____ (b) Eurasia.

____ (c) Greater Asia.

2. Which one of the following statements is true?

____ (a) Continents and countries are made by governments.

____ (b) Continents and countries are made by nature.

____ (c) Continents are made by nature, but countries are made by governments.

3. The three largest countries in North America are

____ (a) Canada, the United States, and Mexico.

____ (b) Canada, the United States, and Nicaragua.

____ (c) the United States, Mexico, and Panama.

4. Which one of the following statements is true?

____ (a) The islands of Japan are part of the continent of Asia.

____ (b) The islands of New Zealand are part of the continent of Australia.

____ (c) The island of Greenland is part of the continent of Europe.

5. Which one of the following statements is false?

____ (a) Florida is a peninsula.

____ (b) The Isthmus of Panama connects North America and South America.

____ (c) The Isthmus of Suez connects Europe and Asia.

C. Match the names of the continents in the list with their shapes below.

a. North America

b. Africa

c. South America

d. Asia

e. Australia

f. Europe

g. Antarctica

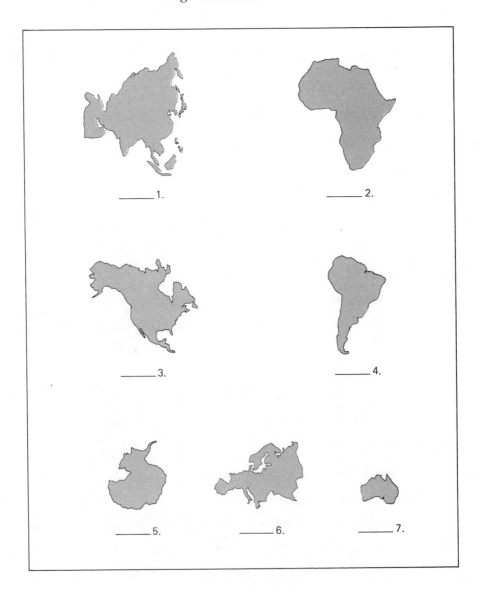

_____ 1.

_____ 2.

_____ 3.

_____ 4.

_____ 5.

_____ 6.

_____ 7.

D. Next to the name of each country in South America, write the number that matches its location on the map. If you need help, look at South America on the map on page 152.

Countries of South America

_____ Argentina

_____ Bolivia

_____ Brazil

_____ Chile

_____ Colombia

_____ Ecuador

_____ French Guiana

_____ Guyana

_____ Paraguay

_____ Peru

_____ Surinam

_____ Uruguay

_____ Venezuela

E. Essay. "Why is it unfair to compare the United States and the continent of Africa?" (Answer in two or three sentences.)

_____

_____

_____

_____

_____

_____

CHAPTER 20
Water Forms

Although the main landforms on the earth, the continents, are huge, they do not cover even half of the earth's surface. Only 30% of the earth is covered with land. The remaining 70% is water.

The largest and most important bodies of water, or *water forms,* on the earth are called *oceans.* There are four: the Pacific (the largest), the Atlantic, the Indian, and the Arctic.

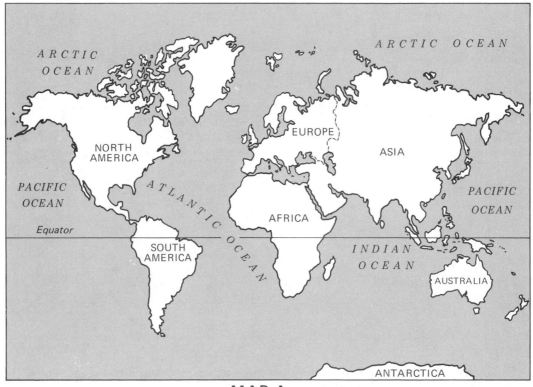

MAP A

The location of the oceans on the earth is shown on Map A.

Three other types of large bodies of water are *seas, gulfs,* and *bays.* Gulfs and bays are parts of larger bodies of water that extend into land. Some seas, such as the Caspian Sea, are completely surrounded by landforms. Most seas, like all gulfs and bays, are only partly surrounded by landforms or extend deep into landforms. On Map B, you can see the Bering Sea, the Gulf of Alaska, and Bristol Bay. They are all parts of the Pacific Ocean.

Another type of body of water is a *strait.* Made by nature, it is a narrow stretch of water connecting two larger bodies of water. The Bering Strait, on Map B, connects the

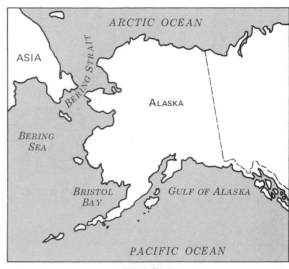

MAP B

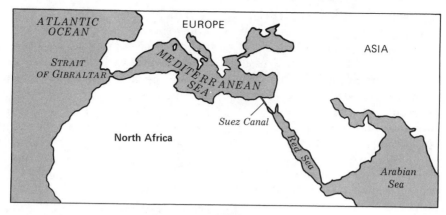

MAP C

Arctic Ocean and the Bering Sea. The Strait of Gibraltar, shown on Map C, connects the Atlantic Ocean and the Mediterranean Sea.

A second type of narrow body of water connecting two larger bodies of water is a *canal*. It is different from a strait because it is made by humans. You can see on Map C that the Suez Canal allows ships to sail from the Mediterranean Sea to the Red Sea. Can you think of any other famous canals or straits?

Many bodies of water lie within landforms. A body of water completely surrounded by land is called a *lake*. Map D shows Lake Nyanza in East Africa. Map D also shows another important body of water inside land: the Nile River. On a map, a *river* is usually shown by a blue or black line. The place where a river begins is called the *source* of the river. This might be water running down from the mountains or a lake. The main source of the Nile River is Lake Nyanza.

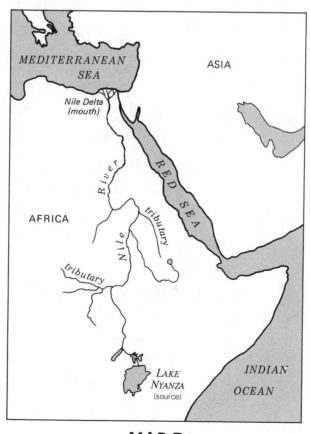

MAP D

The Nile River flows into the Mediterranean Sea. The place where a river ends, or flows into a larger body of water, is called the *mouth* of the river. At the mouth of a river may be a large area of fertile soil that is good for growing plants. This area of fertile soil at the mouth of a river is called a *delta*. Find the Nile Delta on Map D.

Along the Nile River you can see other smaller rivers flowing into it. These smaller rivers that flow into a larger river are called *tributaries*. Some tributaries of the Nile are shown on Map D.

Answer the following questions to find out how much you have learned about water forms on the earth.

1. The largest water forms on the earth are

_____ (a) lakes.

_____ (b) oceans.

_____ (c) seas.

Which answer did you choose? On most maps, water is shown by the color blue or by a light shade of gray. Look at the large gray areas on Map A at the beginning of this chapter. These large gray areas have the following words written on them: *PACIFIC OCEAN, ATLANTIC OCEAN, INDIAN OCEAN, ARCTIC OCEAN*. These oceans are the largest water forms on the earth. Therefore, the answer to question 1 is (b).

2. Part of a large body of water that extends into the land is called

_____ (a) a strait or a canal.

_____ (b) a lake or a river.

_____ (c) a bay or a gulf.

Which answer did you choose? Do you know the meaning of each water form listed in the choices? You can find the meanings in this chapter. Choice (a) is "a strait or a canal." Because straits and canals are narrow bodies of water connecting two larger bodies of water, choice (a) cannot be the answer. Choice (b) is "a lake or a river." Lakes and rivers start inside land, and a river flows out to the sea. So choice (b) cannot be the answer. Choice (c) is "a bay or a gulf." Both bays and gulfs are bodies of water that extend into the land. Therefore, the answer to question 2 is (c).

3. Match the terms related to rivers in Column B with their meanings in Column A.

Column A

_____ 1. a fertile area of land at the mouth of a river

_____ 2. a place where a river begins

_____ 3. a smaller river flowing into a larger river

_____ 4. a place where a river ends

Column B

a. mouth

b. source

c. delta

d. tributary

An explanation of each of these terms is given in this chapter. Read over the chapter if you have forgotten their meanings. The correct answers are 1. *c*, 2. *b*, 3. *d*, 4. *a*.

The following exercises will help you learn more about the important water forms on the earth.

USING WHAT YOU HAVE LEARNED

A. Place a check mark next to the correct answers to questions 1 to 5.

1. The largest bodies of water on the earth are

____ (a) bays.

____ (b) lakes.

____ (c) oceans.

2. The largest ocean is the

_____ (*a*) Atlantic Ocean.

_____ (*b*) Pacific Ocean.

_____ (*c*) Indian Ocean.

3. The percentage of the earth covered by water is about

_____ (*a*) 20%.

_____ (*b*) 50%.

_____ (*c*) 70%.

4. Which one of the following is NOT a water form?

_____ (*a*) A strait

_____ (*b*) A bay

_____ (*c*) An isthmus

5. Which one of the following is made by humans?

_____ (*a*) A gulf

_____ (*b*) A strait

_____ (*c*) A canal

B. Terms Related to Rivers.

Write the following terms in the correct place on this map of a river. Then tell what each word means on the lines to the right of the terms.

Source _____

_____

Mouth_____

_____

Delta _____

_____

Tributary _____

_____

C. Types of Water Forms.

Find an example of each of the following water forms on the map. Write the name of each example you find on the line to the left of the water form. Then write the definition of each water form on the line to the right of it. The first one is done for you.

Name	Water Form	Definition
Bengal	Bay	*A large body of water extending into the land*
	Strait	
	River	
	Ocean	
	Gulf	
	Sea	

CHAPTER 21
Using Directions

Directions

Being able to use *directions* correctly will help you locate places more easily. This is true whether you are trying to find your way around a city or looking for a city on a map. But how do you know what directions to use?

Look at Picture A, which shows a line, called an *axis,* running through the center of the earth. This is an imaginary line because it does not really exist in the earth. At the top end of the axis is the North Pole, and at the bottom is the South Pole.

All directions heading toward the North Pole are north (N). All directions heading toward the South Pole are south (S). If you face the North Pole, the direction on your left is west (W), and the one on your right is east (E). The directions north, south, west, and east are called *cardinal,* or the most important, *directions.* They can be seen in Picture B. If you are facing south, which direction is on your right? If you are facing west, which direction is on your left?

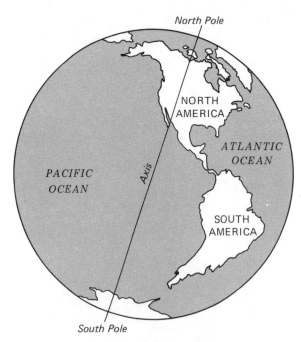

PICTURE A

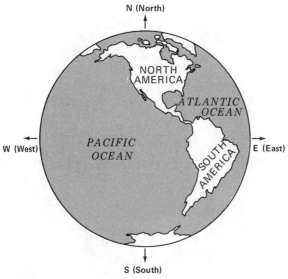

PICTURE B

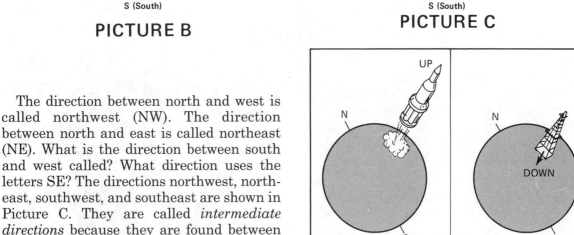

PICTURE C

The direction between north and west is called northwest (NW). The direction between north and east is called northeast (NE). What is the direction between south and west called? What direction uses the letters SE? The directions northwest, northeast, southwest, and southeast are shown in Picture C. They are called *intermediate directions* because they are found between the cardinal directions.

Most maps have a directional compass or arrow on them to let you know where north is. On the maps you generally use, north is at the top. As you have learned, if you know where north is, you can easily determine where the other directions are.

Two other important directions are up and down. They are not the same as north and south. If you leave or go away from the earth, the direction is up. If you then go toward the earth, the direction is down. Picture D can help you understand what the directions up and down mean.

Hemispheres

Halfway between the North Pole and the South Pole is an imaginary line called the *equator*. In Picture E, you can see that the equator goes around the center of the earth. It divides the earth into two equal parts, called *hemispheres*. Hemisphere means half of a sphere or half of the earth.

PICTURE D

PICTURE E

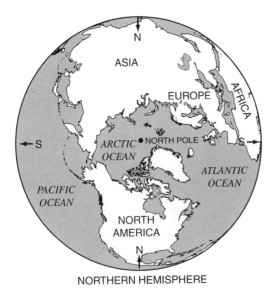

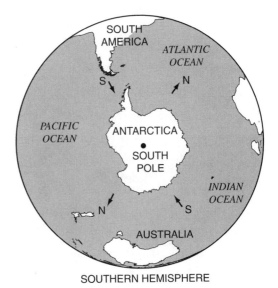

NORTHERN HEMISPHERE

SOUTHERN HEMISPHERE

PICTURE F

The Northern Hemisphere and the Southern Hemisphere can each be shown in another way. Picture F shows the Northern Hemisphere with the North Pole in the center and the Southern Hemisphere with the South Pole in the middle.

Picture G shows that the earth can also be divided into the Western Hemisphere and the Eastern Hemisphere.

Picture H turns the Western Hemisphere and the Eastern Hemisphere around to show all of each hemisphere.

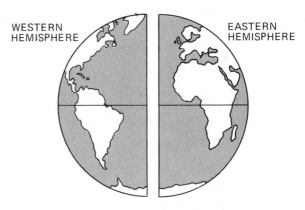

PICTURE G

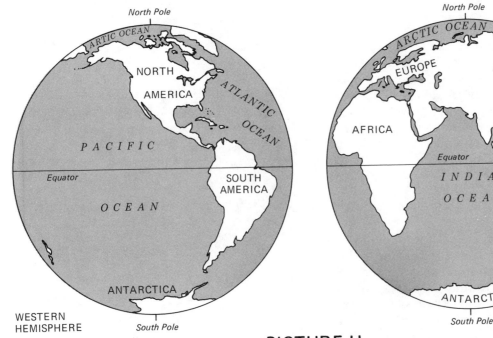

PICTURE H

Answer the following questions to see how much you have learned about directions.

1. When you are facing north, the direction to your right is

    _____ (a) north.

    _____ (b) west.

    _____ (c) east.

Which answer did you choose? Look at Picture B in this chapter. It shows the direction north at the top of the earth. The direction on the right side of the earth is east. Therefore, the answer to question 1 is (c).

2. If a country is located below, or south of, the equator, it is in

    _____ (a) the Northern Hemisphere.

    _____ (b) the Southern Hemisphere.

    _____ (c) both the Northern Hemisphere and the Southern Hemisphere.

Which answer did you choose? Picture E shows how the equator divides the earth into the Northern Hemisphere and the Southern Hemisphere. Any part of the earth above, or north of, the equator is in the Northern Hemisphere. Any part of the earth below, or south of, the equator is in the Southern Hemisphere. Therefore, the answer to question 2 is (b).

Answer questions 3 and 4 by using the following map.

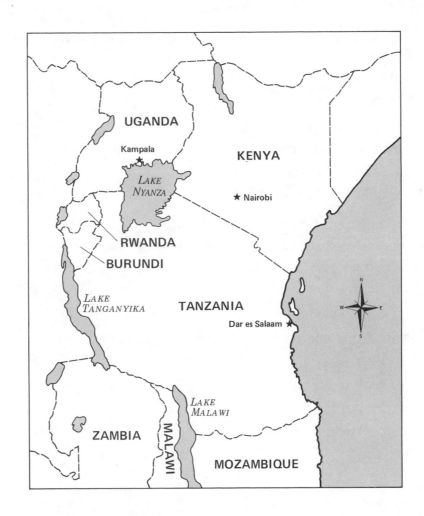

3. Fill in the blank with the correct cardinal direction: north, south, west, east.

    Kenya is _____ of Tanzania.

    Which direction did you choose? Is Kenya above (north of) Tanzania? Or is it below (south of) Tanzania? Or is Kenya left (west) or right (east) of Tanzania? You can see on the map that Kenya is above Tanzania. Therefore, Kenya is north of Tanzania.

4. Fill in the blank with the correct intermediate direction: northwest, northeast, southwest, southeast.

Dar es Salaam is _____ of Nairobi.

Which direction did you choose? Remember that intermediate directions are found between the cardinal directions. You can see on the map that Dar es Salaam is below Nairobi. Therefore, Dar es Salaam is south of Nairobi. But this is only part of the answer. Now you must find out if Dar es Salaam is southwest or southeast of Nairobi. The direction west is to the left on the above map. The direction east is to the right. The map shows that Dar es Salaam is to the south and to the right of Nairobi. Therefore, the correct answer is that Dar es Salaam is southeast of Nairobi.

Using directions correctly is an important Social Studies skill because directions help you locate places on the earth. The following exercises will give you more practice in learning this important skill.

USING WHAT YOU HAVE LEARNED

A. Place a check mark next to the correct answers to questions 1 to 10.

1. The imaginary line running through the earth from the North Pole to the South Pole is

_____ (a) an axis.

_____ (b) the equator.

_____ (c) a hemisphere.

2. The directions north, south, west, and east are called

_____ (a) cardinal directions.

_____ (b) intermediate directions.

_____ (c) subordinate directions.

3. When you travel north, you are heading toward the

_____ (a) moon.

_____ (b) North Pole.

_____ (c) South Pole.

4. If you are facing south, which direction is to your right?

_____ (a) West

_____ (b) East

_____ (c) North

5. If you are traveling to the moon, you are going

_____ (a) east.

_____ (b) up.

_____ (c) north.

6. The directions northwest, northeast, southwest, and southeast are called intermediate directions because they are

_____ (a) located at the North Pole and the South Pole.

_____ (b) found in the middle of the earth.

_____ (c) found between the cardinal directions.

7. The letters that stand for the direction northeast are

_____ (a) NW.

_____ (b) EN.

_____ (c) NE.

8. The imaginary line called the equator divides the earth into the

_____ (a) Northern Hemisphere and the Southern Hemisphere.

_____ (b) Eastern Hemisphere and the Western Hemisphere.

_____ (c) Northern Hemisphere and the Eastern Hemisphere.

9. The center of the Southern Hemisphere is the

_____ (a) equator.

_____ (b) North Pole.

_____ (c) South Pole.

10. If a country is located above, or north of, the equator, it is in

_____ (a) the Northern Hemisphere.

_____ (b) the Southern Hemisphere.

_____ (c) both the Northern Hemisphere and the Southern Hemisphere.

B. Cardinal and Intermediate Directions.

B-1. Using the map of Asia on page 170, fill in the correct cardinal direction. The first one is done for you.

North   South   West   East

1. Russia is _____*North*_____ of China.

2. India is _____ of Russia.

3. Saudi Arabia is _____ of China.

4. Afghanistan is _____ of Iran.

5. Mongolia is _____ of Russia and _____ _____ of China.

6. The Philippines are _____ of Indonesia and _____ _____ of Japan.

B-2. Using the map of Asia on page 170, fill in the correct intermediate direction. The first one is done for you.

Northwest   Northeast   Southwest   Southeast

1. India is _____*Southwest*_____ of China.

2. Pakistan is _____ of Sri Lanka.

ASIA

3. Saudi Arabia is _____ of Russia.

4. North Korea is _____ of Pakistan.

5. Iran is _____ of Japan and _____ of Turkey.

6. Malaysia is _____ of India and _____ of the Philippines.

C. Cardinal and Intermediate Directions.

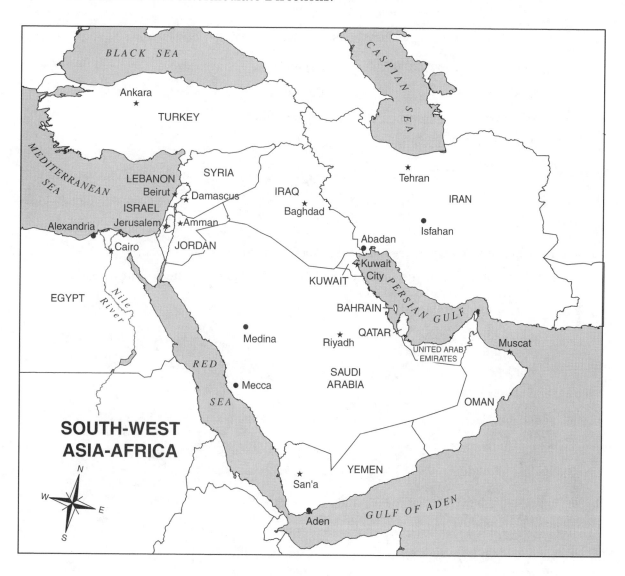

C-1. Using this map of South-West Asia/Africa, fill in the correct cardinal direction. The first one is done for you. (Two directions may seem to fit each answer. Pick the one that is more correct than the other.) North South West East

1. Cairo is _____*South*_____ of Ankara.

2. Damascus is _____ of Baghdad.

3. Tehran is _____ of Abadan.

4. San'a is _____ of Mecca.

5. Jerusalem is _____ of Baghdad.

6. Muscat is _____ of Mecca.

C-2. Using the map of South-West Asia/Africa, fill in the correct intermediate directions. The first one is done for you.

Northwest   Northeast   Southwest   Southeast

1. Cairo is _____*Southwest*_____ of Damascus.

2. San'a is _____ of Muscat.

3. Ankara is _____ of Baghdad.

4. Abadan is _____ of Baghdad.

5. Jerusalem is _____ of Cairo.

6. Mecca is _____ of Cairo.

D. Using the Hemispheres to Learn About Continents.

Study these maps of the four hemispheres. Then place a check mark next to the correct answers to questions 1 to 10.

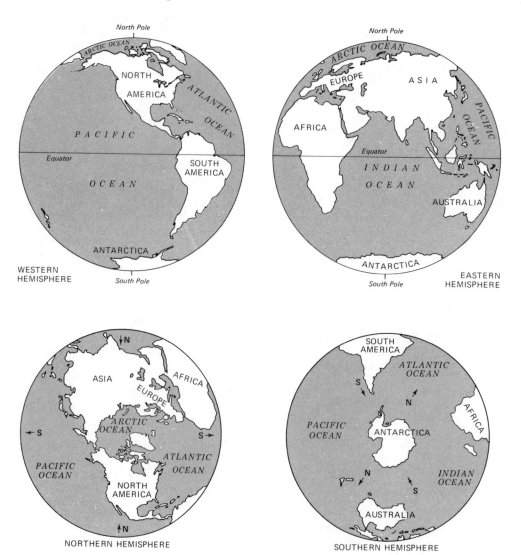

1. North America is in the
   _____ (a) Western Hemisphere.
   _____ (b) Southern Hemisphere.
   _____ (c) Eastern Hemisphere.

2. Asia is mostly in the
   _____ (a) Western Hemisphere.
   _____ (b) Southern Hemisphere.
   _____ (c) Eastern Hemisphere.

3. Australia is in the
   _____ (a) Northern Hemisphere.
   _____ (b) Western Hemisphere.
   _____ (c) Southern Hemisphere.

4. Most of South America is in the
   _____ (a) Northern Hemisphere.
   _____ (b) Southern Hemisphere.
   _____ (c) Eastern Hemisphere.

5. Europe is in both the
   _____ (a) Northern Hemisphere and the Southern Hemisphere.
   _____ (b) Eastern Hemisphere and the Western Hemisphere.
   _____ (c) Northern Hemisphere and the Eastern Hemisphere.

6. Which continent is found in the Northern Hemisphere, the Southern Hemisphere, and the Eastern Hemisphere?
   _____ (a) Africa
   _____ (b) North America
   _____ (c) Australia

7. The equator does NOT pass through
   _____ (a) South America.
   _____ (b) Africa.
   _____ (c) Australia.

8. Traveling east from Asia, you would first come to
   _____ (a) North America.
   _____ (b) Africa.
   _____ (c) Europe.

9. Africa is located
   _____ (a) northeast of Asia.
   _____ (b) southeast of Asia.
   _____ (c) southwest of Asia.

10. The hemisphere with the most landforms is the
   _____ (a) Western Hemisphere.
   _____ (b) Northern Hemisphere.
   _____ (c) Southern Hemisphere.

CHAPTER 22
Map Keys and Scales

As you know, a map is a drawing that shows part or all of the surface of the earth. It can be very simple and show only a small part of a country, city, or town, or it can give a lot of details about all the countries of the world.

Map Keys

Let us first look at a simple map of a part of Egypt. (See page 175.)

What does this map of northern Egypt show? On it are many symbols. Some of them are:

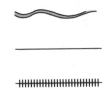

Without knowing the meaning of the symbols, it is impossible to understand what the map is supposed to show.

A very important part of the map is missing: the *key,* or legend, to explain the meaning of each symbol on the map. By looking at the key, you would know what the map shows.

Here is the key that belongs to the map of northern Egypt.

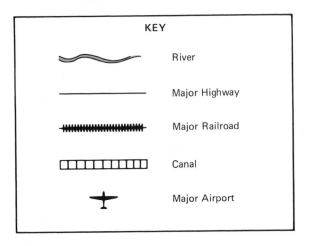

Use this key to help you answer the following questions about the map of Egypt.

1. The symbols used on the map of Egypt show

   _____ (a) how many people live in Egypt.

   _____ (b) how much food is grown in Egypt.

   _____ (c) many of the ways people travel in Egypt.

   Which answer did you choose? The key shows different symbols that clearly stand for ways of traveling. These symbols represent rivers, highways, railroads, canals, and airports. Therefore, the answer to question 1 is (c).

2. The symbol for a canal on the map is

   _____ (a) ───────────

   _____ (b) ▰▰▰▰▰▰▰▰▰▰

   _____ (c) ▭▭▭▭▭▭▭▭

   Which answer did you choose? To find the meaning of a symbol on the map, you have to look at the key. The key shows that the symbol for a canal is ▭▭▭▭▭▭▭▭. Therefore, the answer to question 2 is (c).

3. Which one of the following cities on the map has a major airport?

   _____ (a) Cairo

   _____ (b) Tanta

   _____ (c) El Mansura

   What was your answer? The key tells you that ✈ is the symbol for an airport. Now check to see if any of the cities in question 3 has this symbol next to it on the map. You can see that, of the cities named, only Cairo has the airport symbol next to it. Therefore, the answer to question 3 is (a).

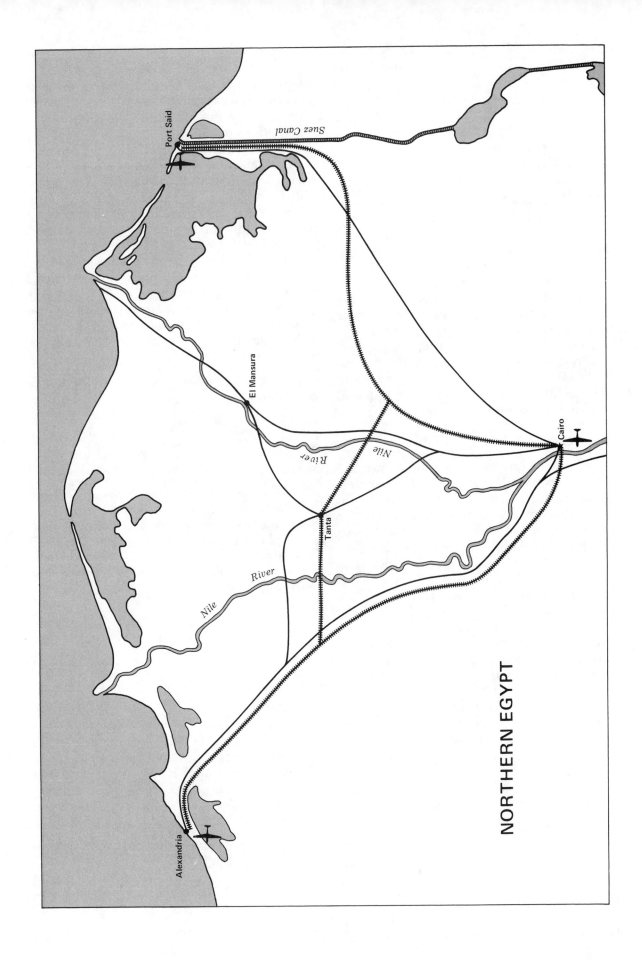

NORTHERN EGYPT

4. According to the map, which city does NOT seem to be as important as the other three?

____ (a) Alexandria

____ (b) Tanta

____ (c) Cairo

____ (d) Port Said

Which answer did you choose this time? Important cities tend to have many means of traveling. According to the map, Alexandria, Cairo, and Port Said have more means of traveling than Tanta. All four cities have major highways and railroads, but only Alexandria, Cairo, and Port Said have major airports. Therefore, the answer to question 4 is (b).

These four questions have shown you how important keys are in understanding maps. Fortunately for us, most maps have keys to help us interpret the symbols and special markings on them.

Map Scales

Let us imagine that you want to use the map on page 175 to plan a trip around northern Egypt. Before you visit all the cities, you might want to know how far apart they are. How can you use this map to answer your question? The key for it on page 174 does not help because it does not show the distances between the cities on the map. Something else is needed to find this information.

Before we find out what this item is, we need to know how distance is measured. In the United States, long distances are usually measured in miles. But in almost every other country in the world, long distances are measured in kilometers. (This is a unit of measurement in the metric system.) One mile is equal to 1.6 kilometers.

To measure distance on a map, you need a *scale* of miles and kilometers. A scale tells you how many miles or kilometers on the earth a certain area on a map represents. The scale for the map of Egypt on page 175 looks like this:

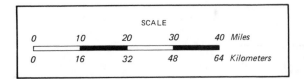

Each black or white section on the scale stands for 10 miles, or 16 kilometers, on the earth. By finding out how many sections there are between cities on the map, you can find out how many miles or kilometers apart the cities are.

On the scale for the map of northern Egypt, each black or white section is a half inch long. So you can also say that each half inch on the map stands for 10 miles, or 16 kilometers, on the earth. An inch (one black section and one white section together) stands for 20 miles, or 32 kilometers.

The map on page 177 shows the five important cities that appear on the map of northern Egypt on page 175. A scale is shown below the cities, and sections of the scale are drawn between some of the cities. See if you can answer the questions that follow by using the scale.

1. How many miles apart are Tanta and El Mansura?

_____ (a) 10 miles

_____ (b) 30 miles

_____ (c) 50 miles

Which answer did you choose? The scale shows that each black and each white section stands for 10 miles on the earth. There are three sections between Tanta and El Mansura on the map. Three sections times 10 miles equals 30 miles. Therefore, the answer to question 1 is (b).

2. How many kilometers apart are Tanta and Cairo?

_____ (a) 88 kilometers

_____ (b) 108 kilometers

_____ (c) 168 kilometers

Which answer did you choose? You can count five and one-half black and white sections between Tanta and Cairo on the map. Each section stands for 16 kilometers. Five and one-half sections times 16 kilometers equals 88 kilometers. Therefore, the answer to question 2 is (a).

3. How many miles apart are El Mansura and Port Said?

_____ (a) 35 miles

_____ (b) 55 miles

_____ (c) 110 miles

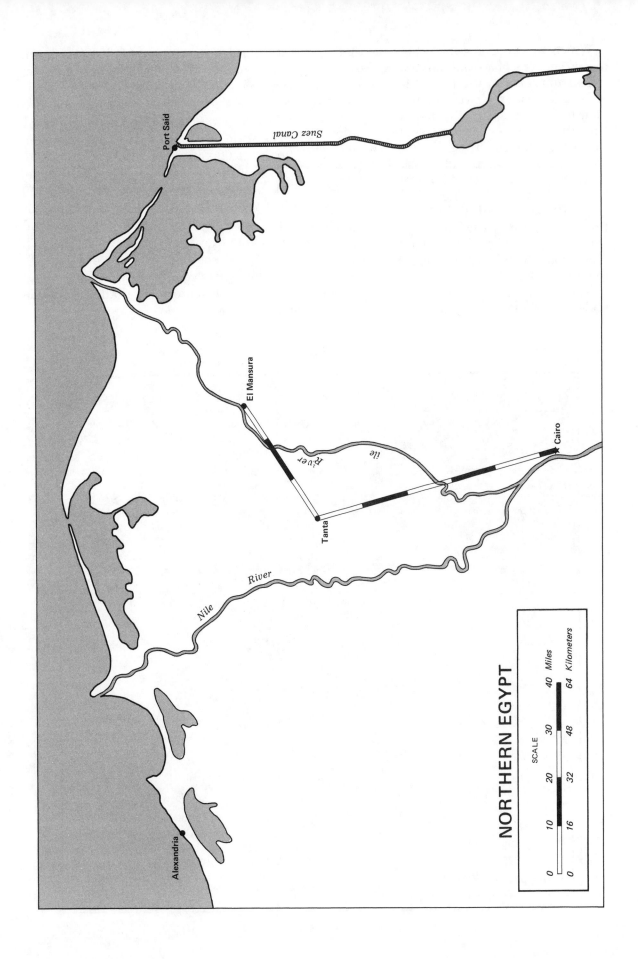

NORTHERN EGYPT

SCALE

| 0 | 10 | 20 | 30 | 40 | Miles |
| 0 | 16 | 32 | 48 | 64 | Kilometers |

Port Said

Suez Canal

El Mansura

River

ile

Cairo

Tanta

River

Nile

Alexandria

Which was your answer? This time there are no sections of a scale connecting the two cities. You have to use the scale below the cities and a ruler, a piece of paper, or maybe your finger to measure the distance between the cities. (Remember to measure from dot to dot.) If you measure carefully, you will see that it will take five and one-half sections (2¾ inches) to connect El Mansura and Port Said on the map. Five and one-half sections times 10 miles equals 55 miles. You can also find the answer by using inches. Two and three-fourths inches times 20 miles for each inch equals 55 miles. Therefore, the answer to question 3 is (b).

Not all maps have the same scale. The scales on two maps may stand for different distances depending on what is to be shown on the maps. The following two maps of Egypt have different scales.

The scale on Map A shows that each inch stands for 300 miles, or 480 kilometers.

The scale on Map B shows that each inch stands for 600 miles, or 960 kilometers.

Look at the map on page 177. On its scale, each black or white section stands for 10 miles, or 16 kilometers. How is it different from the maps of Egypt on pages 178 and 179? While they show all of Egypt, the map on page 177 shows only a part of Egypt. To show the whole country at this scale would take up much more room than is available on these pages.

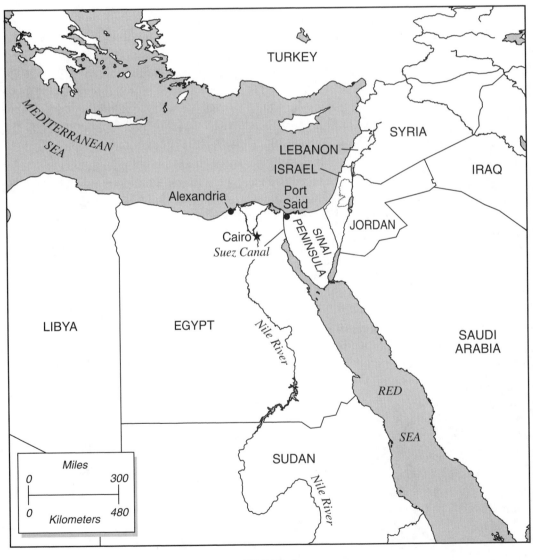

MAP A

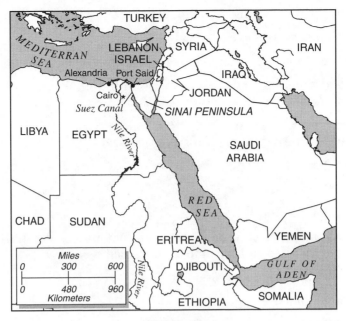

MAP B

How is Map A on page 178 different from Map B on page 179? More countries can be seen on Map B than on Map A. Each inch on the scale for Map B stands for 600 miles, or 960 kilometers. This is a longer distance than an inch on the scale for Map A stands for. Fewer details can be shown on a map picturing a large area than on a map the same size that pictures a smaller area. For example, Ethiopia does not even appear on Map A. But the countries that do appear, such as Egypt and Jordan, are larger on Map A than on Map B.

Map keys help you to understand the symbols used on maps. Scales help you find the distances between places on the maps. Before you answer the following questions, study the keys and scales on the maps.

USING WHAT YOU HAVE LEARNED

A. Place a check mark next to the correct answers to questions 1 to 5.

1. Symbols used on a map are

   ____ (a) explained in the dictionary.

   ____ (b) explained in the key.

   ____ (c) not explained at all.

2. A scale on a map is used to

   ____ (a) explain symbols on the map.

   ____ (b) tell how many miles or kilometers on earth a certain space on the map represents.

   ____ (c) tell what kind of map it is.

3. Which one of the following statements is true?

_____ (*a*) All maps use the same scale.

_____ (*b*) Two maps of different countries can never use the same scale.

_____ (*c*) The scales on maps may stand for different distances depending on what is to be shown on the maps.

4. On a certain map, 1 inch is equal to 150 miles on earth. If there are 2 inches between cities on that map, then the cities are

_____ (*a*) 150 miles apart.

_____ (*b*) 300 miles apart.

_____ (*c*) 450 miles apart.

5. On a certain map, 1 inch is equal to 250 kilometers on earth. If there are 3 inches between cities on that map, then the cities are

_____ (*a*) 250 kilometers apart.

_____ (*b*) 500 kilometers apart.

_____ (*c*) 750 kilometers apart.

B. Study the following map of Russia, Ukraine, and Belarus.

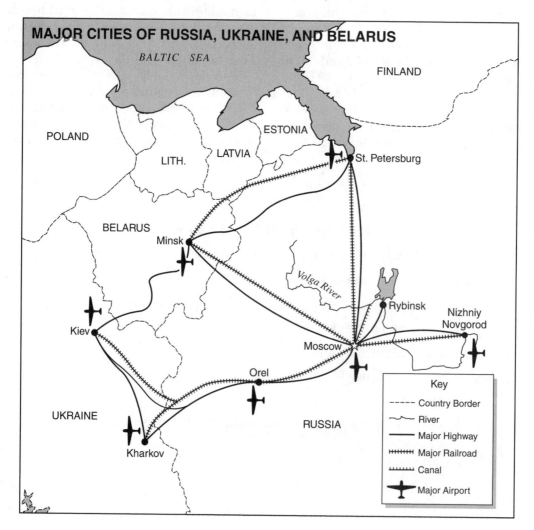

Place a check mark next to the correct answers to questions 1 to 8.

1. The map of parts of Russia, Ukraine, and Belarus shows

    ____ (a) ways of traveling between major cities.

    ____ (b) how many railroads link the major cities.

    ____ (c) how many highways link the major cities.

2. All the symbols on the map are

    ____ (a) explained in a dictionary.

    ____ (b) explained in the key.

    ____ (c) not explained at all.

3. The symbol for a major airport is

    ____ (a) ┼┼┼┼┼┼┼┼┼┼┼┼┼┼

    ____ (b) ~~~~

    ____ (c) ✈

4. The symbol for a major highway is

    ____ (a) ———

    ____ (b) ▪▪▪▪▪▪▪▪

    ____ (c) ▴▴▴▴▴

5. Which city on the map does NOT have a major airport?

    ____ (a) Moscow   ____ (b) Kiev   ____ (c) Rybinsk

6. Which one of the following is the name of a river found on the map?

    ____ (a) Nizhniy Novgorod   ____ (b) Minsk   ____ (c) Volga

7. The canal on the map is located near the city of

    ____ (a) Moscow.   ____ (b) Minsk.   ____ (c) Kiev.

8. According to the map, you cannot travel directly between Minsk and Kiev by

    ____ (a) airplane.

    ____ (b) a major highway.

    ____ (c) a major railroad.

9. List three ways you can travel between Moscow and St. Petersburg.

    _____

    _____

    _____

10. How does the map show that Moscow must be the most important city in the area shown?

_____

_____

_____

_____

C. Look at the following cities as they would be shown on a map of Russia, Ukraine, and Belarus. Study the scale under the cities.

Place a check mark next to the correct answers to questions 1 to 10.

1. The scale under the cities shows how

____ (*a*) big each country is.

____ (*b*) many miles or kilometers each inch on the map represents.

____ (*c*) people travel from Moscow to Minsk.

2. Each inch on the scale stands for

____ (a) 100 miles, or 160 kilometers.

____ (b) 200 miles, or 320 kilometers.

____ (c) 300 miles, or 480 kilometers.

3. On the map, how many inches are there between Moscow and Minsk?

____ (a) 1 inch

____ (b) 2 inches

____ (c) 3 inches

4. About how many miles apart are Moscow and Minsk?

____ (a) 100 miles

____ (b) 200 miles

____ (c) 400 miles

5. About how many kilometers apart are Minsk and Orel?

____ (a) 160 kilometers

____ (b) 560 kilometers

____ (c) 800 kilometers

6. How many miles apart are Moscow and Nizhniy Novgorod?

____ (a) About 250 miles

____ (b) About 350 miles

____ (c) About 400 miles

7. How many kilometers apart are St. Petersburg and Nizhniy Novgorod?

____ (a) 160 kilometers

____ (b) 480 kilometers

____ (c) 880 kilometers

8. How many miles apart are Kiev and St. Petersburg?

____ (a) About 250 miles

____ (b) About 450 miles

____ (c) About 650 miles

9. If you could travel only to cities within 300 miles of Moscow, which cities could you visit?

____ (a) Orel, Nizhniy Novgorod, Rybinsk

____ (b) Kiev, Minsk, Rybinsk

____ (c) St. Petersburg, Orel, Kiev

10. If you traveled from Kiev to Minsk to St. Petersburg, how many miles would you travel?

____ (a) 300 miles

____ (b) 700 miles

____ (c) 960 miles

D. Study the following map of Africa.

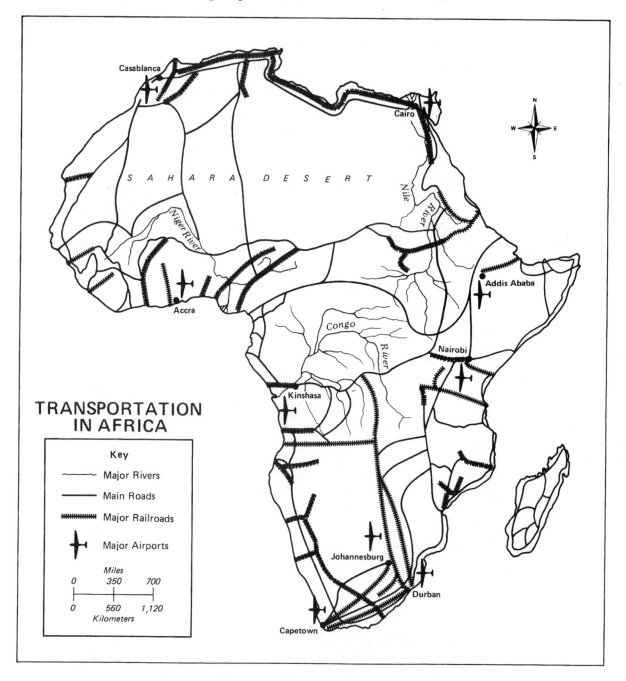

TRANSPORTATION
IN AFRICA

Key

~~~~ Major Rivers

——— Main Roads

+++++++ Major Railroads

✈ Major Airports

Miles
0   350   700

0   560   1,120
Kilometers

Place a check mark next to the correct answers to questions 1 to 6.

1. The map shows

____ (a) how many railroads there are in Africa.

____ (b) how many people live in Africa.

____ (c) the major ways of traveling in Africa.

2. The symbols on the map are

____ (a) explained in the text.

____ (b) explained in the key.

____ (c) not explained at all.

3. The symbol ——————— on the map stands for

____ (a) main roads.

____ (b) major railroads.

____ (c) major rivers.

4. The symbol ✛ stands for

____ (a) major cities.

____ (b) major airports.

____ (c) major canals.

5. The scale tells you

____ (a) distance in miles or kilometers.

____ (b) the weight of an area of a country.

____ (c) the population of a country.

6. Which two cities are on major rivers?

____ (a) Addis Ababa and Accra

____ (b) Durban and Capetown

____ (c) Kinshasa and Cairo

7. List the three major rivers shown on the map.

_____

_____

_____

8. List three different ways you could travel between Cairo and Casablanca.

_____

_____

_____

9. Why do you think there are few symbols on the area of the map marked Sahara? (Answer in one or two sentences.)

_____

_____

_____

_____

10. Why is having an airport important to many cities in Africa? (Answer in two or three sentences.)

_____

_____

_____

_____

_____

_____

Answer questions 11 to 15 with the help of the scale in the key on page 184. (Clue: See how many times the scale will fit between each of the cities named in the questions.) Place a check mark next to the correct answers.

11. About how many miles apart are Addis Ababa and Nairobi?

____ (a) 100 miles

____ (b) 300 miles

____ (c) 500 miles

____ (d) 700 miles

12. About how many kilometers apart are Durban and Capetown?

____ (a) 560 kilometers

____ (b) 1,260 kilometers

____ (c) 1,600 kilometers

____ (d) 2,200 kilometers

13. How many miles apart are Cairo and Casablanca?

____ (a) About 350

____ (b) About 700

____ (c) About 2,300

____ (d) About 3,360

14. About how many kilometers apart are Kinshasa and Nairobi?

____ (a) 1,120 kilometers

____ (b) 2,520 kilometers

____ (c) 3,360 kilometers

____ (d) 4,000 kilometers

15. The distance between Accra and Johannesburg can be expressed as

____ (a) 2,975 miles or 4,760 kilometers.

____ (b) 3,500 miles or 5,600 kilometers.

____ (c) 4,000 miles or 6,400 kilometers.

____ (d) 7,000 miles or 11,200 kilometers.

CHAPTER 23
Political Maps

Most people use maps to find cities and countries. A map that shows mainly cities and countries is a *political map*. (The word "political" means having to do with government.) A political map uses symbols to show where cities are located and lines to show the size and shape of each country. These symbols and lines are explained in a key on the map.

On most political maps, the key looks like the one on the map below.

The symbol used in the key to show a city is a dot ● . A star ★ indicates the capital city of a country. This is where the national government is located. Lines are used to show the boundaries of countries, that is, where a country begins and ends. These dividing lines may look like any one of the following: ——— ——— ——–·—

The names of countries are usually written in capital letters, such as VIETNAM. Sometimes colors are used on a map to help you see the size and shape of countries. (Of course, these lines and colors do not really exist on the earth.)

The following political map shows mainland Southeast Asia as it is today. ("Mainland" means the part connected to the continent. It does not include any of the

island nations of Southeast Asia.) In the bottom right corner of the map is a key that explains the symbols and lines used on the map. Study the map and its key.

1. The political map on page 187 shows

    _____ (a) how many people live in mainland Southeast Asia.

    _____ (b) the important rivers of mainland Southeast Asia.

    _____ (c) the countries and major cities of mainland Southeast Asia.

Which answer did you choose? Look at the key on the map. It shows the symbols for boundary lines and cities in mainland Southeast Asia. Therefore, the answer to question 1 is (c).

2. Which two countries share the same boundary line?

    _____ (a) Myanmar and Vietnam

    _____ (b) Laos and Cambodia

    _____ (c) Thailand and Vietnam

What was your answer? First, you have to locate the countries listed in choices (a), (b),

and (c). They are written on the map in capital letters. Then, you have to study the boundary lines of each country. The boundary line on the map looks like this ‒‒‒ . You should be able to see that only Laos and Cambodia share the same boundary. The southern part of Laos borders on the northern part of Cambodia. Therefore, the answer to question 2 is (b).

    _____ 3. True or False: Ho Chi Minh City is the capital of Vietnam.

What was your answer this time? The key uses a dot to show a city and a star to show the capital city of a country. Ho Chi Minh City has a dot, and Hanoi has a star. Therefore, Hanoi is the capital of Vietnam, and the answer to question 3 is False.

The political map on page 187 shows the countries of mainland Southeast Asia as they are today. A political map showing Southeast Asia in the 1920's would look very different. Because boundaries of many countries have changed over the years, it is always important to know what time period a map is dealing with.

Look at the map of mainland Southeast Asia as it was in 1925. (See below.) Notice

how it is different from the map of Southeast Asia today. The key is also different. It shows which areas of mainland Southeast Asia were controlled by European countries in 1925.

1. The map shows mainland Southeast Asia

   _____ (a) today.

   _____ (b) in 1925.

   _____ (c) in 1700.

What was your answer? Perhaps the most important fact on a political map is the date. The date tells you what year or century the information on the map reflects. If a political map has no date, it usually means that the map is showing cities and countries as they appear today. In the map title, the year 1925 appears. This tells you that the map shows the countries of Southeast Asia as they were in 1925. Therefore, the answer to question 1 is (b).

2. The key on this map shows

   _____ (a) the boundary lines of the countries.

   _____ (b) the capital cities of the countries.

   _____ (c) which European countries controlled parts of Southeast Asia in 1925.

What was your answer? The key shows that parts of Southeast Asia were controlled by European countries in 1925. Therefore, the answer to question 2 is (c).

3. Which one of the following areas on the map was *not* controlled by a European country in 1925?

   _____ (a) Burma

   _____ (b) Indochina

   _____ (c) Siam

Which answer did you choose? Here again the key helps you to answer the question. The key shows that the area colored dark gray on the map was independent, or free from European control, in 1925. Only Siam is colored dark gray on the map. Therefore, the answer to question 3 is (c).

It is important to point out that the country named Siam on the 1925 map is named Thailand on today's map. Over the years, some countries have changed their names.

4. The area named Indochina on the 1925 map is now the three countries of

   _____ (a) Vietnam, Thailand, and Myanmar.

   _____ (b) Vietnam, Laos, and Cambodia.

   _____ (c) Myanmar, Thailand, and Cambodia.

What was your answer? You have to look at both maps of mainland Southeast Asia to answer this question. First, look at the area named Indochina on the 1925 map. Notice the size and shape of Indochina. Now look at the same area on the map of Southeast Asia as it looks today. You can see that the same area has been divided into three countries: Vietnam, Laos, and Cambodia. Therefore, the answer to question 4 is (b).

When you study a political map, be sure to look closely at the key. Also, be sure that you know the year or the time period the map is showing.

You will study political maps more than any other kind of map in your Social Studies classes. The following exercises will give you practice in using political maps.

USING WHAT YOU HAVE LEARNED

A. True or False: If every part of the statement is true, write **T**.
If any part of the statement is false, write **F**.

_____ 1. A political map only shows how many people live in a city or country.

_____ 2. Boundary lines between countries never change.

_____ 3. On the map of mainland Southeast Asia at the beginning of this chapter, you know that Myanmar is a country because its name is written in capital letters across its land area.

_____ 4. On the map of mainland Southeast Asia at the beginning of this chapter, the symbol used to show a capital city is a dot.

_____ 5. A political map can be drawn to show cities and boundaries at different times in history.

B. Study the following political map of South-West Asia/Africa.

Place a check mark next to the correct answers to questions 1 to 9.

1. The map shows

____ (*a*) all the cities of South-West Asia/Africa.

____ (*b*) the countries and important cities of South-West Asia/Africa.

____ (*c*) oil production in South-West Asia/Africa.

2. The symbol on the map used to show a capital city is a

____ (a) •

____ (b) ⋆

____ (c) ----

3. The boundary line between countries on this map looks most like

____ (a) ———

____ (b) ----------

____ (c) ——··——

4. Which one of the following cities is the capital of Iraq?

____ (a) Cairo

____ (b) Riyadh

____ (c) Baghdad

5. Which one of the following cities is the capital of Saudi Arabia?

____ (a) San'a

____ (b) Riyadh

____ (c) Damascus

6. Which one of the following cities is NOT a capital city?

____ (a) Ankara

____ (b) Tehran

____ (c) Mecca

7. How many countries are shown and labeled on this map?

____ (a) 10

____ (b) 15

____ (c) 20

8. Which two of these countries on the map share the same boundary line?

____ (a) Egypt and Iran

____ (b) Turkey and Saudi Arabia

____ (c) Saudi Arabia and Jordan

9. Which country is north of Syria?

____ (a) Turkey

____ (b) Oman

____ (c) Iran

10. List the six countries on the map that share a boundary line with Iraq.

_____

_____

_____

C. Study the political maps of Africa on pages 192 and 193.

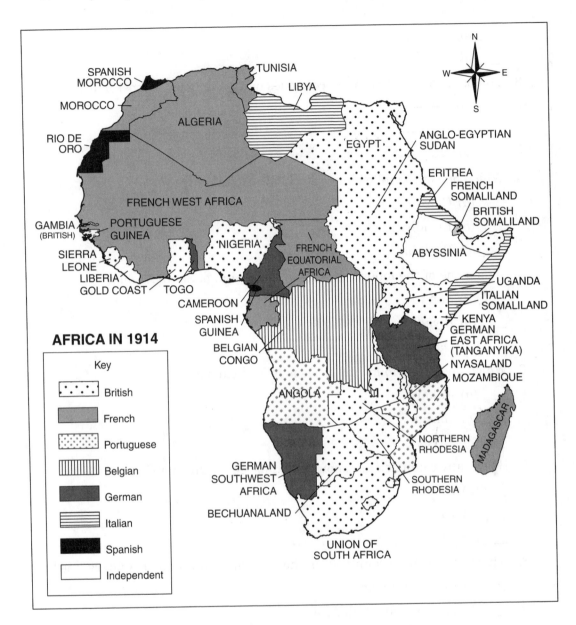

MAP A

Place a check mark next to the correct answers to questions 1 to 8.

1. The two maps of Africa show that

_____ (a) the boundaries of countries in Africa have not changed at all between 1914 and today.

_____ (b) most of Africa is still controlled by Europeans today.

_____ (c) there have been many political changes in Africa between 1914 and today.

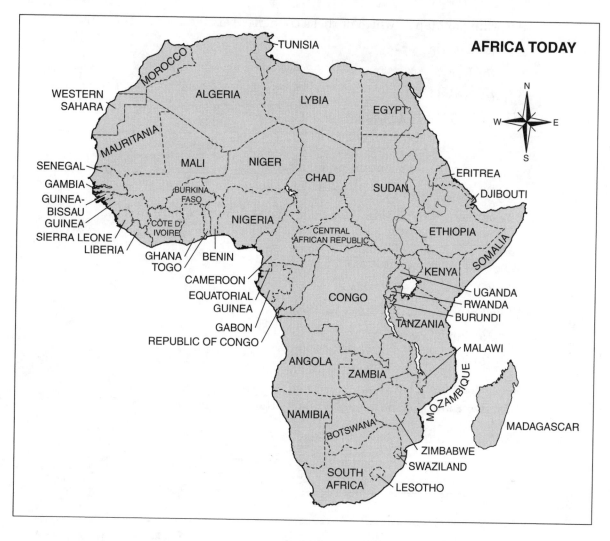

MAP B

2. Map A shows Africa in 1914, and Map B shows Africa

   ____ (*a*) in 1924.

   ____ (*b*) in 1950.

   ____ (*c*) today.

3. Map A shows that Africa

   ____ (*a*) was once controlled by European countries.

   ____ (*b*) was always independent.

   ____ (*c*) is independent today.

4. According to Map A, which European country controlled the areas of Africa with the pattern [   ] ?

   ____ (*a*) Britain

   ____ (*b*) France

   ____ (*c*) Italy

5. According to Map A, which of these countries was independent in 1914?

_____ (*a*) Liberia

_____ (*b*) Kenya

_____ (*c*) Angola

6. Map B shows that Africa is

_____ (*a*) one large country.

_____ (*b*) a continent containing many countries.

_____ (*c*) a continent containing few countries.

7. The country Mali in Map B was once part of the area in Map A named

_____ (*a*) German East Africa.

_____ (*b*) French Equatorial Africa.

_____ (*c*) French West Africa.

8. Which country did Northern Rhodesia become?

_____ (*a*) Zimbabwe

_____ (*b*) Zambia

_____ (*c*) Tanzania

9. List five countries, now independent, that were controlled by Britain in 1914.

_____

_____

_____

10. Why are there more boundary lines on today's map of Africa than there are on the 1914 map? (Answer in one or two sentences.)

_____

_____

_____

_____

D. Study the political maps of South America on pages 195 and 197.

D-1. Study Map A and its key. Then place a check mark next to the correct answers to questions 1 to 5.

1. Map A shows the political boundaries of South America

_____ (*a*) in 1800.

_____ (*b*) in 1900.

_____ (*c*) today.

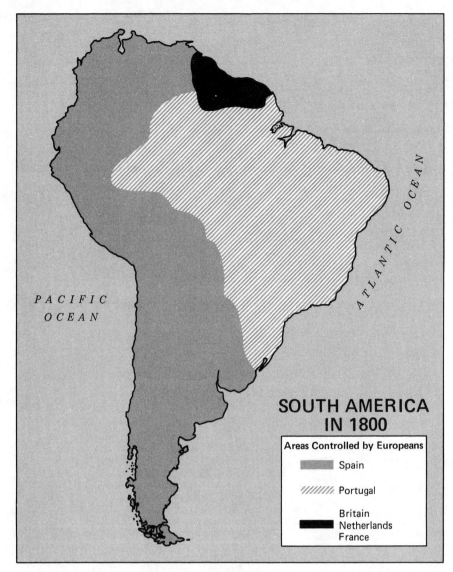

MAP A

2. The patterns in the key show

____ (a) the crops produced in South America in 1800.

____ (b) the size of countries in South America today.

____ (c) the areas in South America controlled by European countries in 1800.

3. The area colored gray on Map A was under the control of

____ (a) Spain.

____ (b) Portugal.

____ (c) Britain.

4. Britain, the Netherlands, and France controlled the area on the map that looks like this:

____ (a) ▰▰▰

____ (b) ▨▨▨

____ (c) ▰▰

5. Which country controlled the smallest area of land in South America in 1800?

____ (a) France

____ (b) Portugal

____ (c) Spain

D-2. Study Map B and its key on page 197.

Place a check mark next to the correct answers to questions 1 to 5.

1. The broken lines on the map show the

____ (a) important rivers of South America.

____ (b) main railroads of South America.

____ (c) main highways of South America.

____ (d) boundaries between countries of South America.

2. The capital of Brazil is

____ (a) Rio de Janeiro.

____ (b) São Paulo.

____ (c) Brasília.

____ (d) Montevideo.

3. The country in South America with two capital cities is

____ (a) Brazil.

____ (b) Ecuador.

____ (c) Argentina.

____ (d) Bolivia.

4. Ecuador shares a boundary line with

____ (a) Peru.

____ (b) Argentina.

____ (c) Paraguay.

____ (d) Venezuela.

5. Bogotá is the capital city of

____ (a) Venezuela.

____ (b) Colombia.

____ (c) Chile.

____ (d) Peru.

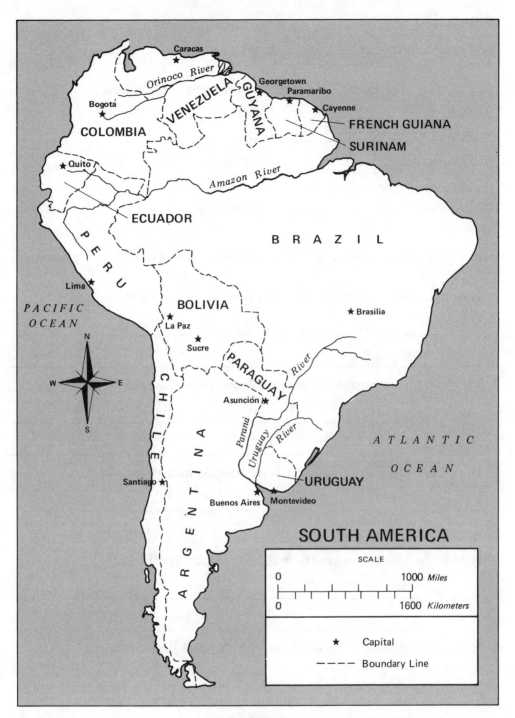

MAP B

D-3. Use the directional compass on Map B to help you answer questions 1 to 10. Write the correct cardinal and intermediate directions in the blanks.

North   South   West   East

1. Brazil is _____ of Paraguay.

2. Guyana is _____ of Venezuela.

3. Peru is _____ of Colombia.

4. Chile is _____ of Argentina.

5. Surinam is _____ of Uruguay.

Northwest   Northeast   Southwest   Southeast

6. Sucre is _____ of Asunción.

7. Bogotá is _____ of Quito.

8. Bogotá is _____ of Caracas.

9. Buenos Aires is _____ of Lima.

10. Brasília is _____ of Santiago.

D-4. Study the scale on Map B. Then answer each of the following questions in a sentence.

1. How many miles are there between Buenos Aires and Montevideo?

_____

_____

2. How many miles are there between Bogotá and Cayenne?

_____

_____

3. How many miles are there between Asunción and Montevideo?

_____

_____

4. How many kilometers are there between Quito and Lima?

_____

_____

5. How many miles are there between La Paz and Brasília?

_____

_____

CHAPTER 24
Latitude on Globes and Maps

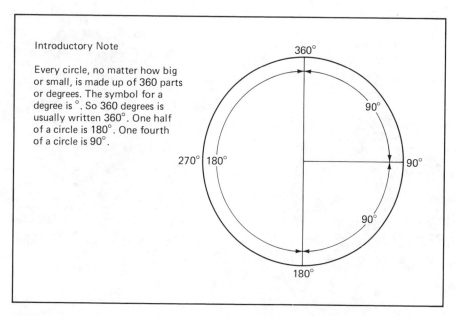

Introductory Note

Every circle, no matter how big or small, is made up of 360 parts or degrees. The symbol for a degree is °. So 360 degrees is usually written 360°. One half of a circle is 180°. One fourth of a circle is 90°.

The earth is such a large place that directions alone will not help you find exact locations of places. Other guides are also needed. They are supplied by a system of imaginary lines that are drawn on many maps and globes.

You already know of one imaginary line called the equator, which divides the earth into the Northern Hemisphere and the Southern Hemisphere. Picture A shows the location of the equator on the earth. All other imaginary lines in Picture A are used to show distances north or south of the equator. The distance north or south of the equator is called *latitude*. That is why these imaginary lines are called *lines of latitude*. They are also called *parallels*

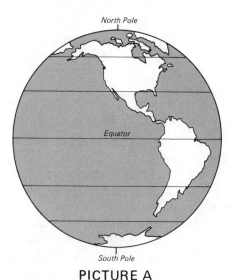

PICTURE A

of latitude because they never meet. They remain the same distance from each other all the way around the earth.

Latitude, or distance from the equator, is measured in degrees. Each parallel of latitude is one degree from the parallel above or below it. One degree of latitude equals about 69 miles on the earth's surface. Since latitude measurement starts at the equator, the equator is marked 0°. Every other line of latitude is numbered from 1° to 90°. 90° represents one-fourth of a circle, or one-fourth of 360°. (See the Introductory Note.)

There are 90° between the equator and the North Pole and 90° between the equator and the South Pole. As a result, 90 lines of latitude could be drawn north of the equator or south of the equator on a map of the earth. But this could make the map too crowded. So maps and globes generally show only some of the lines of latitude. Picture B, of the Western Hemisphere, shows lines of latitude for every 20° north of the equator. Other maps may show different degrees of latitude.

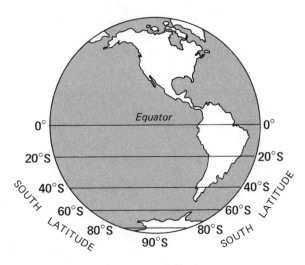

PICTURE C

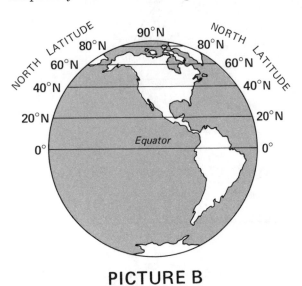

PICTURE B

A degree of latitude north of the equator may have an N after it. For example, 60°N would mean 60° north of the equator.

Picture C shows that there are also 90° from the equator to the South Pole. A degree of latitude south of the equator may have an S after it. For example, 60°S would mean 60° south of the equator.

Picture D shows why it is important to look for the letter N or S after a degree of latitude. Both the Northern Hemisphere and the Southern Hemisphere contain 0° to

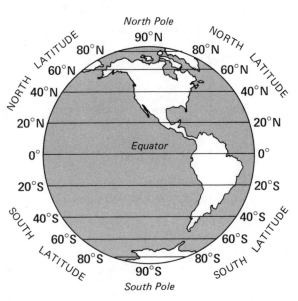

PICTURE D

90°. The N or S tells you in which hemisphere a degree of latitude is located.

Use the information you have learned in this chapter to answer the following questions.

1. Lines of latitude are used on a map

_____ (a) to show that maps are better than globes.

_____ (b) to find distances north or south of the equator.

_____ (c) to find distances west or east of the equator.

Which answer did you choose? A line of latitude alone means nothing. It has meaning only when it is used along with the equator. This is because a line of latitude tells you only one thing—how far some place is north or south of the equator. Therefore, the answer to question 1 is (b).

2. Lines of latitude are also called parallel lines because

_____ (a) they cross one another halfway around the earth.

_____ (b) they meet at the North Pole.

_____ (c) they remain the same distance from each other all the way around the earth.

Which answer did you choose? Lines of latitude never meet. They remain the same distance from each other all around the earth, which is why they are called parallel lines. Therefore, the best answer to question 2 is (c).

3. Look at the diagram. Then decide which ship is in trouble at 45°N.

_____ (a) Ship A

_____ (b) Ship B

_____ (c) Ship C

Which answer did you choose this time?

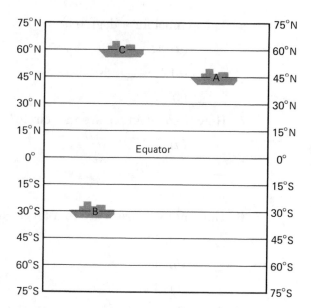

You are looking for the ship that is in trouble at 45°N. The N after 45°N tells you that you must look north of the equator. Starting at the equator, move your finger north. Stop when you come to the line marked 45°N. You will see that it is Ship A that is on the 45°N line of latitude. Therefore, the answer to question 3 is (a).

The following exercises will give you practice in finding distances and locations with the help of latitude.

USING WHAT YOU HAVE LEARNED

A. Place a check mark next to the correct answers to questions 1 to 10.

1. The imaginary line that goes around the center of the earth is

_____ (a) an axis.

_____ (b) a pole.

_____ (c) the equator.

2. The imaginary lines used on a map to show distance north or south of the equator are called

_____ (a) lines, or parallels, of latitude.

_____ (b) degrees.

_____ (c) circles.

3. Latitude is measured in

_____ (a) miles.

_____ (b) inches.

_____ (c) degrees.

4. The symbol for a degree is

_____ (a) +.

_____ (b) °.

_____ (c) '.

5. How many degrees are in a circle?

_____ (a) 90°

_____ (b) 180°

_____ (c) 360°

6. How many degrees are in a large circle?

_____ (a) 360°

_____ (b) 400°

_____ (c) 460°

7. From the equator to the North Pole, there are

_____ (a) 90°.

_____ (b) 180°.

_____ (c) 360°.

8. From the equator to the South Pole, there are

_____ (a) 90°.

_____ (b) 180°.

_____ (c) 360°.

9. From the North Pole to the South Pole, there are

_____ (a) 90°.

_____ (b) 180°.

_____ (c) 360°.

10. A degree of latitude north or south of the equator

_____ (a) touches the North Pole or the South Pole.

_____ (b) runs from the North Pole to the South Pole.

_____ (c) is often followed by an N or an S.

B. Latitude and Location.

In the spaces provided, write the degrees of latitude at which ships 1 to 10 are located. (See top of page 203.) The first one is done for you.

Ship 1 _____15°N_____   Ship 6 _____

Ship 2 _____   Ship 7 _____

Ship 3 _____   Ship 8 _____

Ship 4 _____   Ship 9 _____

Ship 5 _____   Ship 10 _____

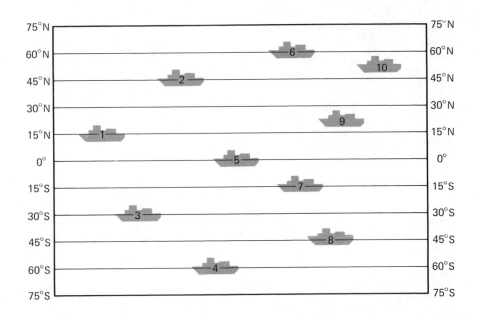

C. Latitude and Location.

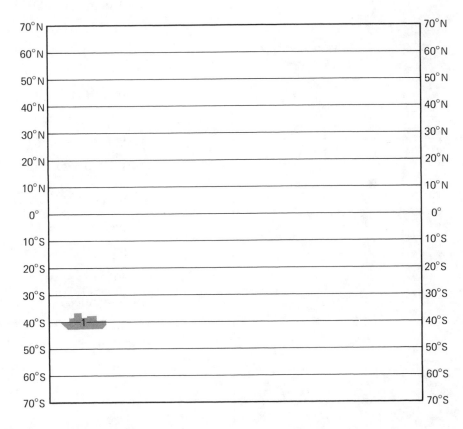

Locate the following degrees of latitude on the chart above by placing the number before each degree on the correct line of latitude. The first one is done for you.

1. 40°S   6. 0°   11. 30°S
2. 60°N   7. 25°S   12. 55°S
3. 30°N   8. 48°N   13. 18°N
4. 20°N   9. 5°N   14. 62°S
5. 70°N   10. 60°S   15. 27°N

D. In this chapter, you learned that every degree of latitude on a map equals 69 miles on the earth. If two cities are one degree apart on a map, then they are 69 miles apart on the earth. If two cities are two degrees apart on a map, then they are 138 miles apart on the earth. Here is how it is done: 69 miles × 2 = 138 miles. Look at the map of Chile, in South America. Use this map to answer the following questions on finding distances.

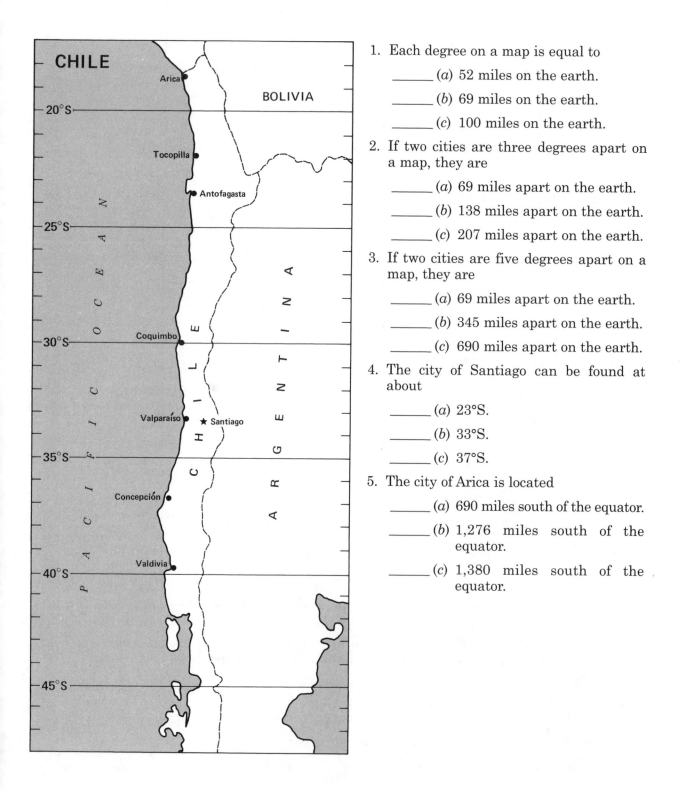

1. Each degree on a map is equal to

   _____ (*a*) 52 miles on the earth.

   _____ (*b*) 69 miles on the earth.

   _____ (*c*) 100 miles on the earth.

2. If two cities are three degrees apart on a map, they are

   _____ (*a*) 69 miles apart on the earth.

   _____ (*b*) 138 miles apart on the earth.

   _____ (*c*) 207 miles apart on the earth.

3. If two cities are five degrees apart on a map, they are

   _____ (*a*) 69 miles apart on the earth.

   _____ (*b*) 345 miles apart on the earth.

   _____ (*c*) 690 miles apart on the earth.

4. The city of Santiago can be found at about

   _____ (*a*) 23°S.

   _____ (*b*) 33°S.

   _____ (*c*) 37°S.

5. The city of Arica is located

   _____ (*a*) 690 miles south of the equator.

   _____ (*b*) 1,276 miles south of the equator.

   _____ (*c*) 1,380 miles south of the equator.

For questions 6-8, you should mark two answers. One is to show how many degrees apart the cities are. The second is to show how many miles apart the cities are.

6. The city of Tocopilla and the city of Antofagasta are about

___ (a) one degree apart.   ___ (d) 138 miles apart.

___ (b) two degrees apart.   ___ (e) 69 miles apart.

___ (c) three degrees apart.   ___ (f) 207 miles apart.

7. The city of Coquimbo and the city of Valparaíso are about

___ (a) one degree apart.   ___ (d) 207 miles apart.

___ (b) two degrees apart.   ___ (e) 69 miles apart.

___ (c) three degrees apart.   ___ (f) 138 miles apart.

8. The city of Valdivia and the city of Concepción are about

___ (a) three degrees apart.   ___ (d) 207 miles apart.

___ (b) four degrees apart.   ___ (e) 345 miles apart.

___ (c) five degrees apart.   ___ (f) 276 miles apart.

9. What do we mean when we say that Concepción is located at 37°S? (Answer in one or two sentences.)

_____

_____

_____

_____

10. Imagine that the degrees on the map had been written without the letter S. For example, the map showed 30° instead of 30°S. How would you still be able to tell by the degrees that Chile is in the Southern Hemisphere? (Answer in two or three sentences.)

_____

_____

_____

_____

_____

_____

CHAPTER 25
Latitude and Climate

Is there one line of latitude that is more important than any other line of latitude? By now you should be able to answer that the equator is the most important line of latitude. All other lines of latitude are drawn parallel to the equator.

In addition to the equator, there are several other important parallels of latitude. (See Picture A.) They are: the *Tropic of Cancer*, the *Tropic of Capricorn*, the *Arctic Circle*, and the *Antarctic Circle*. These imaginary lines are used to show different climate areas on the earth. (*Climate* is the weather in an area over a long period of time.)

Let us look first at the Tropic of Cancer and the Tropic of Capricorn. The Tropic of Cancer is a line of latitude 23½°N of the equator. The Tropic of Capricorn is a line of latitude 23½°S of the equator. As shown in

Picture B, the area of the earth between these two parallel lines is called the *low latitudes*. The climate in this area is almost always warm or hot.

Two other important parallels are the Arctic Circle and the Antarctic Circle. The Arctic Circle is a line of latitude 66½°N of the equator. Between 66½°N and the North Pole is the area called the Arctic. The North Pole is the center of the Arctic, as shown in Picture C.

The Antarctic Circle is a line of latitude 66½°S of the equator. The area between 66½°S and the South Pole is called the Antarctic. At the center of the Antarctic is the South Pole, as shown in Picture C.

The areas of the Arctic and the Antarctic are called the *high latitudes,* or the *polar zones.* Few people live in the high latitudes because of the extremely cold climate that exists for most of the year. Picture C shows where the high latitudes are located on the earth.

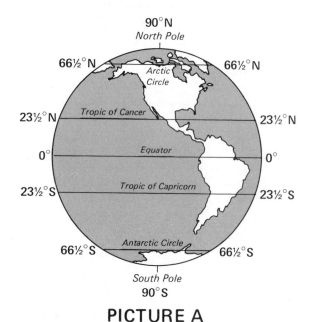

PICTURE A

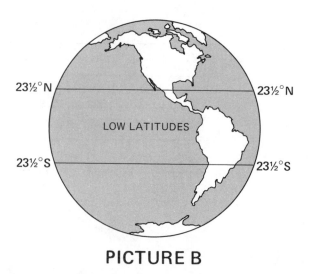

PICTURE B

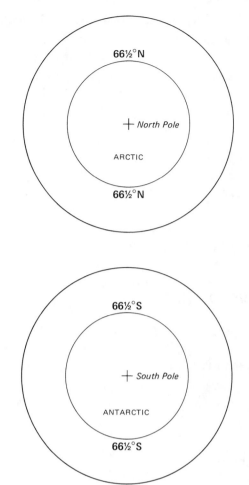

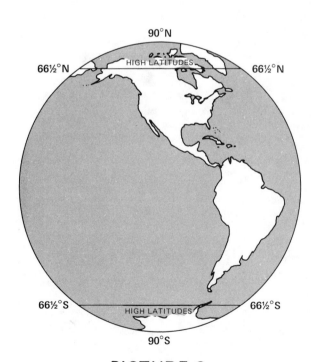

PICTURE C

The areas between 23½° and 66½° in both the Northern Hemisphere and the Southern Hemisphere are called the *middle latitudes.* (See Picture D.) They have this name because they are between the high latitudes and the low latitudes. The middle latitudes have four seasons—spring, summer, fall, and winter. Most of the people in the world live in the middle latitudes because of the favorable (good, pleasing) climate.

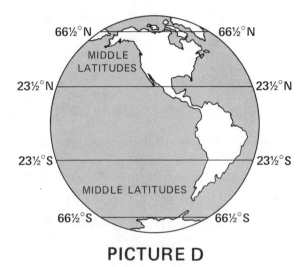

PICTURE D

Using the information you learned in this chapter, answer the following questions.

1. In this chapter, you have seen that certain lines of latitude are used

   _____ (*a*) to show the time.

   _____ (*b*) to locate sinking ships.

   _____ (*c*) to show different climate areas on the earth.

Which answer did you choose? Different areas of the earth have different climates. You have read in this chapter that lines of latitude are used to show where these climate areas are located on the earth. Therefore, the answer to question 1 is (*c*).

_____ 2. True or False: Few people live in the high latitudes because the climate is extremely cold most of the year.

What was your answer? The high latitudes are found between the Arctic Circle and the North Pole and between the Antarctic Circle and the South Pole. The areas of the earth around the North Pole and the South Pole are extremely cold most of the year. This is why few people live in the high latitudes. Therefore, the answer to question 2 is True.

3. A city located on the earth between the Tropic of Cancer and the Arctic Circle is likely to have

_____ (a) only a hot climate.

_____ (b) only a cold climate.

_____ (c) a climate with four seasons.

Which answer did you choose this time? The area on the earth between the Tropic of Cancer and the Arctic Circle is called the middle latitudes. The middle latitudes do not have the extreme heat of the low latitudes or the extreme cold of the high latitudes. Instead, the middle latitudes have four seasons with changing temperatures. Therefore, the answer to question 3 is (c).

You have seen in this chapter how certain lines of latitude are used to show climate areas on the earth. The following exercises will give you more practice in learning about latitude and climate.

USING WHAT YOU HAVE LEARNED

A. Place a check mark next to the correct answers to questions 1 to 5.

1. The name given to the line of latitude at 23½°N is the

____ (a) Arctic Circle.

____ (b) Tropic of Cancer.

____ (c) equator.

2. The name given to the line of latitude at 66½°S is the

____ (a) Tropic of Capricorn.

____ (b) Antarctic Circle.

____ (c) Arctic Circle.

3. The Tropic of Capricorn is located at

____ (a) 23½°.

____ (b) 23½°N.

____ (c) 23½°S.

4. The Arctic Circle is located at

____ (a) 66½°.

____ (b) 66½°N.

____ (c) 66½°S.

5. The term "middle latitudes" refers to the area of the earth between

____ (a) 23½°N to 66½° N and 23½°S to 66½°S.

____ (b) 23½°N to 66½°N only.

____ (c) 23½°S to 66½°S only.

B. True or False: If every part of the statement is true, write **T**.
If any part of the statement is false, write **F**.

_____ 1. The area of the earth between 23½°N and 23½°S is called the middle latitudes.

_____ 2. The climate of the low latitudes is generally extremely cold.

_____ 3. The area of the earth north of 66½°N is called both the Arctic and the high latitudes.

_____ 4. The area of the earth between 66½°S and the South Pole is likely to have only a hot season.

_____ 5. There are four seasons in the middle latitudes.

C. Important Lines of Latitude and Climate Areas.

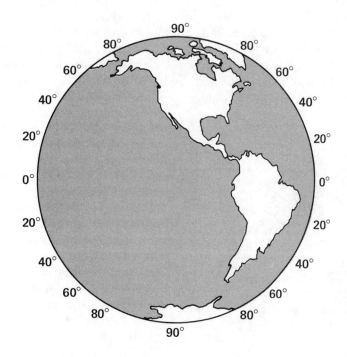

C-1. On the map, draw and label the following important lines of latitude:

Equator	Arctic Circle
Tropic of Cancer	Antarctic Circle
Tropic of Capricorn	

C-2. Then label on the map the following climate areas:

low latitudes   middle latitudes   high latitudes

CHAPTER 26
Longitude on Globes and Maps

Lines of latitude show only distances north and south of the equator. To measure east and west distances, it is necessary to have another system of imaginary lines on the earth. Distance east or west is called *longitude,* and the lines to measure this distance are called *meridians of longitude.* In Picture A, you see that lines of longitude run north and south between the North Pole and the South Pole.

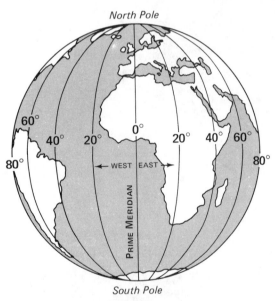

North Pole

South Pole

PICTURE A

To measure longitude, you need a starting line. You learned that parallels of latitude are measured north or south from the equator. The equator is the starting line for measuring latitude. For measuring longitude, the starting line is the *Prime Meridian,* a line of longitude that runs through Greenwich, England. Picture A shows where the Prime Meridian is located on the earth.

All lines of longitude are measured in degrees east or west of the Prime Meridian. Each meridian is one degree from the meridian next to it. Starting from the Prime Meridian, which is marked 0°, meridians are marked going east from 1° to 180°E. Going west, the meridians are marked from 1° to 180°W.

It is important to use W (west) or E (east) after a degree of longitude. For example, if you were told to find 120° on the map, you would have trouble because 120° appears twice on the map. The W or E tells you if you are looking for 120° west or 120° east of the Prime Meridian.

Meridians are not parallel lines; that is, they are not always the same distance from one another. Look again at Picture A, and you will see that the meridians are farthest apart at the equator and closest together at the poles. At the equator, one degree of longitude equals about 69 miles on the earth. Near the poles, one degree of longitude equals only a few miles.

In Picture A you see nearly one half of the earth and less than one half of 360°. You see 80° west of the Prime Meridian and 80° east of the Prime Meridian. Both parts add up to 160°. On a different kind of map of the earth, a Mollweide map, for example, all 360° can be shown. In Picture B you can see 180° west of the Prime Meridian and 180° east of the Prime Meridian.

Understanding how to use lines of longitude is an important Social Studies skill. But it would be impossible to find the exact location of a place on the earth with only a line of longitude. To find the exact location of a place, it is necessary to use both a line of latitude and a line of longitude. Here is an example to show why you need the two lines.

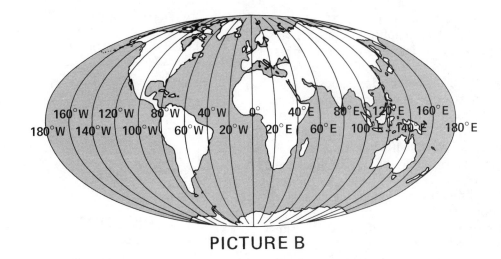

PICTURE B

Suppose you live in a town that has the streets mapped in Picture C. You asked your friend to meet you on 10th Avenue. Would it be easy for your friend to find you? Probably not. Since 10th Avenue runs for at least five blocks, your friend would have to walk blocks to find you. But what if you told your friend to meet you where 10th Avenue meets Jay Street, or at the intersection of 10th and Jay? Your friend would walk along 10th Avenue until he got to Jay Street. Then he would stop and wait for you. By using the intersection of two streets or two lines in giving your location, your friend would be able to find you easily.

Picture D shows how latitude and longitude lines look when they are put together on the same map. They meet and cross like street intersections. Let us use the lines of latitude and longitude in Picture D to locate something on the earth. Imagine that a ship is sinking. It sends out a radio message that it is at 20°N 40°W. This means that the ship is 20' north of the equator and 40° west of the Prime Meridian. It is located where the 20°N latitude line meets and crosses the 40°W longitude line. Latitude is always given first and longitude second.

The captain of the rescue ship finds the 20°N line on a map. (Remember that latitude

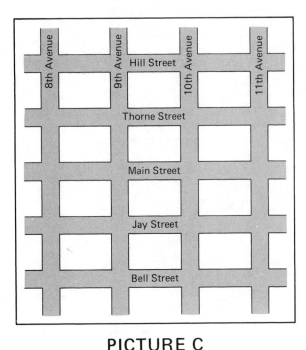

PICTURE C

PICTURE D

lines run east and west across a map, or from left to right.) The captain knows to look north of the equator because of the N after 20°. After the captain finds 20°N, he looks for the 40°W line of longitude. (Lines of longitude run north and south, or from the top to the bottom of the map.) The captain knows that there are two 40° lines on the map, but he wants the 40° line that is west of the Prime Meridian, or 40°W. He puts one finger on the 40°W line and another finger on the 20°N line and moves his fingers along the two lines until they meet. At the place where the two lines meet (20°N 40°W), the captain will find the sinking ship.

Let us see if you can use lines of latitude and longitude to locate a ship. A ship is in trouble at 40°S 60°E. Mark an X on the map in Picture D where you think this ship can be found.

Where did you place the X? The first degree (40°S) is a line of latitude. The S tells you that it is a line of latitude south of the equator. The second degree (60°E) is a line of longitude. The E tells you that it is a line of longitude east of the Prime Meridian.

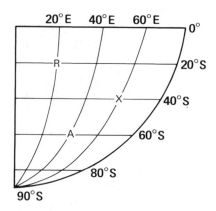

PICTURE E

You will find the ship where these two lines meet. If you put an X on the map in Picture D in the same place as the letter X in Picture E, then you found the ship.

You have seen in this chapter that it is necessary to use two lines on a map to find the exact location of a thing or a place. These two lines are a parallel of latitude and a meridian of longitude. The following exercises will give you more practice in finding the exact location of places on the earth.

USING WHAT YOU HAVE LEARNED

A. Place a check mark next to the correct answers to questions 1 to 8.

1. Lines of longitude are used to find distance

   ____ (*a*) east or west of the Prime Meridian.

   ____ (*b*) north or south of the equator.

   ____ (*c*) north or south of the Prime Meridian.

2. The most important line of longitude is the

   ____ (*a*) equator.

   ____ (*b*) axis.

   ____ (*c*) Prime Meridian.

3. Lines of longitude are also called

   ____ (*a*) parallels.

   ____ (*b*) meridians.

   ____ (*c*) latitudes.

4. Lines of longitude run

_____ (a) north to south.

_____ (b) east to west around the earth.

_____ (c) west to east around the earth.

5. Lines of longitude are NOT parallel lines because they

_____ (a) run in the same direction.

_____ (b) get closer to one another as they near the poles.

_____ (c) never meet.

6. On a map, the Prime Meridian is at

_____ (a) 0°.

_____ (b) 15°W.

_____ (c) 30°E.

7. The Prime Meridian runs through

_____ (a) Bombay, India.

_____ (b) Chicago, Illinois.

_____ (c) Greenwich, England.

8. If an oil spill is located at 60°W, this means that the spill is

_____ (a) 60° west of the equator.

_____ (b) 60 miles west of the Prime Meridian.

_____ (c) 60° west of the Prime Meridian.

9. Is the following statement true or false? "It is not necessary to write W (west) or E (east) after a degree showing longitude." (Explain in one or two sentences.)

_____

_____

_____

_____

10. Is the following statement true or false? Explain your answer in one or two sentences. "You need to know only the degree of longitude of a place to know its exact location."

_____

_____

_____

_____

B. Longitude and Location.

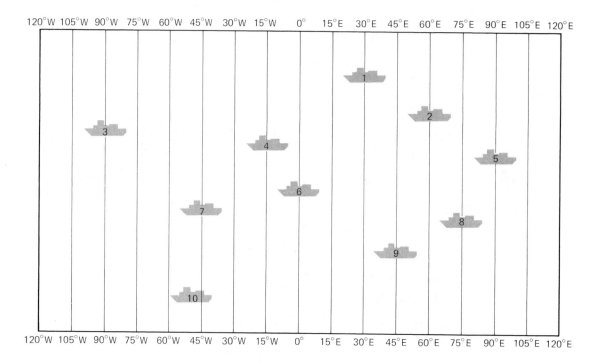

In the spaces provided, write the degrees of longitude where ships 1 to 10 are located. The first one is done for you.

Ship 1 _____30°E_____ Ship 5 _____ Ship 8 _____

Ship 2 _____ Ship 6 _____ Ship 9 _____

Ship 3 _____ Ship 7 _____ Ship 10 _____

Ship 4 _____

C. Latitude, Longitude, and Location.

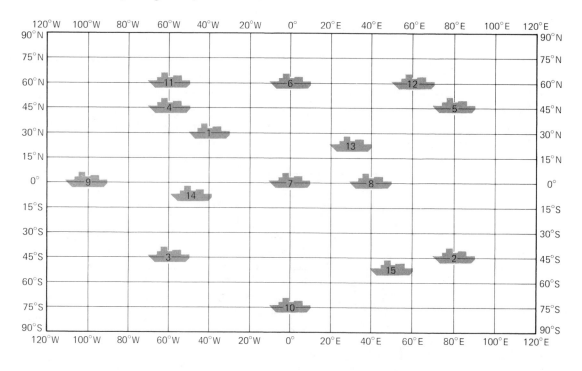

In the spaces provided, write the latitude and longitude of ships 1 to 15 shown on the graph at the bottom of page 214. The first two are done for you.

	Latitude	Longitude
Ship 1	30°N	40°W
Ship 2	45°S	80°E
Ship 3	_____	_____
Ship 4	_____	_____
Ship 5	_____	_____
Ship 6	_____	_____
Ship 7	_____	_____
Ship 8	_____	_____
Ship 9	_____	_____
Ship 10	_____	_____
Ship 11	_____	_____
Ship 12	_____	_____
Ship 13	_____	_____
Ship 14	_____	_____
Ship 15	_____	_____

D. Degrees of Latitude and Longitude.

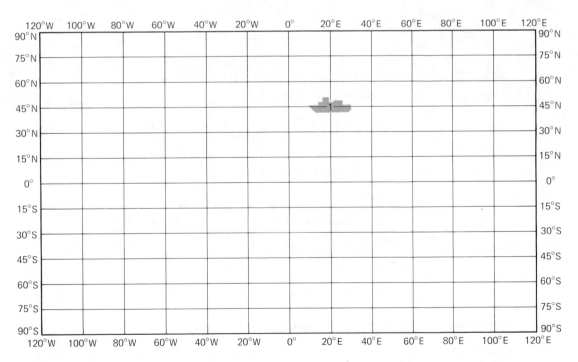

Locate the following degrees of latitude and longitude on the above graph. Write the number before each degree of latitude and longitude in the correct place on the graph. The first one is done for you.

1. 45°N 20°E   6. 30°N 80°E   11. 50°N 40°E
2. 60°N 60°E   7. 60°S 100°E   12. 50°S 50°E
3. 45°S 40°E   8. 75°N 0°   13. 70°N 110°W
4. 75°S 75°W   9. 0° 0°   14. 80°S 0°
5. 0° 20°W   10. 15°N 80°W   15. 25°N 75°E

E. Study the following map of Mexico and the Caribbean World.

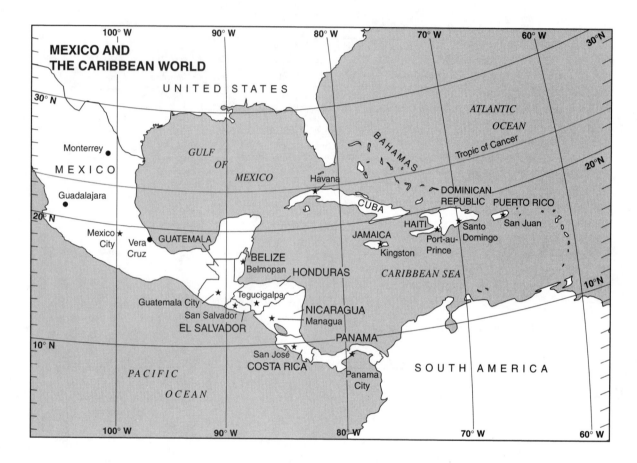

Place a check mark next to the correct answers to questions 1 to 10.

1. The equator (0°) divides the earth into the Northern Hemisphere and the Southern Hemisphere. Therefore, the area on the map is in the

    ____ (*a*) Northern Hemisphere.

    ____ (*b*) Southern Hemisphere.

    ____ (*c*) Northern Hemisphere and the Southern Hemisphere.

2. The Tropic of Cancer runs through

    ____ (*a*) Cuba.

    ____ (*b*) Jamaica.

    ____ (*c*) Mexico.

3. Monterrey, Mexico, is located in

_____ (a) the low latitudes.

_____ (b) the middle latitudes.

_____ (c) the high latitudes.

4. San Juan, Puerto Rico, is located in

_____ (a) the low latitudes.

_____ (b) the middle latitudes.

_____ (c) the high latitudes.

5. Mexico City is located at

_____ (a) 19°N 99°W.

_____ (b) 99°N 19°W.

_____ (c) 19°N 19°W.

6. Havana, Cuba, is located at

_____ (a) 83°N 22°W.

_____ (b) 23°N 83°W.

_____ (c) 22°N 22°W.

7. Which city on the map is located at 10°N 84°W?

_____ (a) Panama City, Panama

_____ (b) San José, Costa Rica

_____ (c) Belmopan, Belize

8. Which city on the map is located at 18°N 70°W?

_____ (a) Kingston, Jamaica

_____ (b) San Salvador, El Salvador

_____ (c) Santo Domingo, Dominican Republic

9. Each degree of latitude on a map stands for 69 miles on the earth. Therefore, the distance between Monterrey, Mexico, and Mexico City is about

_____ (a) 210 miles.

_____ (b) 414 miles.

_____ (c) 690 miles.

10. Each degree of latitude stands for 69 miles on the earth. The distance between Havana, Cuba, and San José, Costa Rica, is about

_____ (a) 300 miles.

_____ (b) 600 miles.

_____ (c) 900 miles.

CHAPTER 27
Longitude and Time

If you were to visit a television news station, you might see clocks on the wall like the ones in the drawing. They show different times in different cities in the world. The clocks show that when it is 4 A.M. in San Francisco, it is 7 A.M. in New York, 1 P.M. in Rome, 2 P.M. in Cairo, and 8 P.M. in Beijing. These time differences can be shown on a map with the help of lines of longitude.

In the last chapter, you learned that lines of longitude are used to measure distance east or west of the Prime Meridian. Besides measuring distance, lines of longitude are used to help you find what time it is in different parts of the world. Map A shows how lines of longitude are used to show time.

The lines of longitude on Map A are 15° apart. They run 15°, 30°, 45°, and so on. Each of these lines of longitude has a differ-

ent time. For example, the line of longitude marked 0° is 12 noon. The line marked 30°W is 10 A.M. The line 45°E is 3 P.M.

You may wonder why there is a line every 15° on a map showing time. The earth turns, or rotates, on its axis from west to east. Every 24 hours the earth makes a complete 360° turn. By dividing 24 into 360, you get 15. This means that for every 15° of longitude, there is a difference in time of one hour.

Each 15° line of longitude is at the center of a *time zone,* which spreads 7½° west and 7½° east of the center line. For example: the center line of longitude, or standard meridian, for the Mountain Time Zone in the United States is 105°W. The area covered by the Mountain Time Zone is between 97½°W and 112½°W. All of the places in the Mountain Time Zone have the same time.

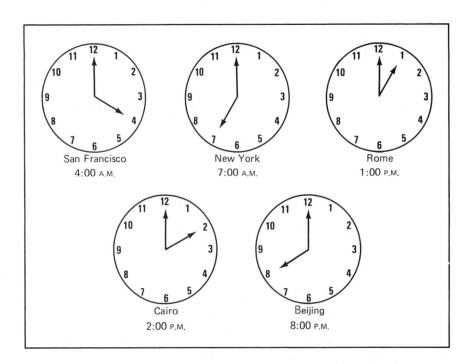

San Francisco
4:00 A.M.

New York
7:00 A.M.

Rome
1:00 P.M.

Cairo
2:00 P.M.

Beijing
8:00 P.M.

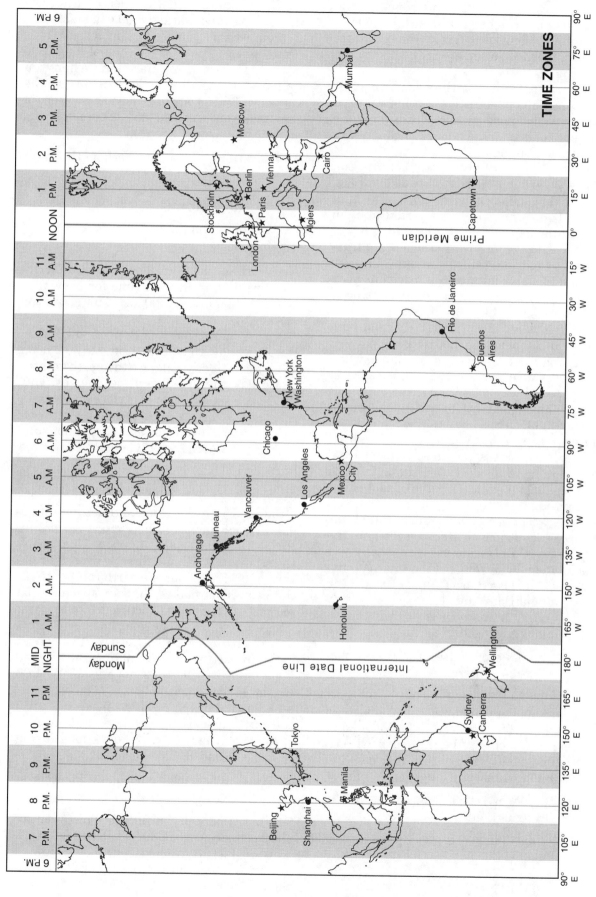

TIME ZONES

MAP A

Actually, none of the 24 time zones on the earth has a straight north-south boundary. Zone lines zig-zag to meet the needs of the people living in the areas affected by the time changes.

When it is noon in a time zone, the 11½ time zones to the left (the west) of it are in *ante meridiem* time, or A.M. This is any time between midnight and noon. Times that are A.M. are said to be in the morning. The 11½ time zones to the right (the east) of the noon time zone are in *post meridiem* time, or P.M. This is any time between noon and midnight. Times that are P.M. are said to be in the afternoon, evening, or night.

You can see on Map A that when you travel east, or to the right, the time continues to become one hour later as you move into each time zone. For example, when it is 12 noon in London, it is 1:00 P.M. in Vienna. When you travel west, or to the left, the time continues to become one hour earlier as you move from zone to zone. For example, when it is 9:00 A.M. in Rio de Janeiro, it is 8:00 A.M. in Buenos Aires.

On Map A, look at the line of longitude marked 180°. This line is called the *International Date Line*. When you travel from east to west across the International Date Line, you jump ahead to the same time the next day. If it is 2 P.M. on Sunday east of the International Date Line, it is 2 P.M. on Monday west of the International Date Line. Likewise, if you travel west to east across the International Date Line, you go back a day. If it is 9 A.M. on Friday west of the International Date Line, it is 9 A.M. on Thursday east of the International Date Line.

Use Map A to answer the following questions on longitude and time.

_____ 1. True or False: There is a one-hour difference in time for every 30° of longitude.

What was your answer? If you divide 24 hours into 360°, you get 15° for each hour. You can also see on Map A that each one-hour time zone covers 15° and not 30°. Therefore, the answer to question 1 is False.

2. On Map A, it is 3:00 P.M. on the line of longitude marked

_____ (a) 15°.

_____ (b) 45°.

_____ (c) 135°.

Which answer did you choose? Find the line of longitude marked 3:00 P.M. on Map A. Remember that you are looking for 3:00 P.M., not 3:00 A.M. The 3:00 P.M. line of longitude is east of the Prime Meridian. When you find the 3:00 P.M. line, follow the line all the way down with your finger. At the bottom of the line, you will see 45°. Therefore, the answer to question 2 is (b).

3. What time is it in New York on the map?

_____ (a) 2:00 A.M.

_____ (b) 7:00 A.M.

_____ (c) 1:00 P.M.

Which answer did you choose? First find New York on the map. The standard meridian that determines the time for New York is 75°. It is marked 7:00 A.M. Therefore, the answer to question 3 is (b).

Map A shows that it is 12 noon in London. But you know that it does not stay 12 noon in London all day long. As the earth rotates on its axis, the time in a place changes. This is because the position of a place on earth in relation to the sun changes. The rotation turns a place toward or away from the sun.

Study Pictures A and B on page 221 to see how time changes.

You see that Pictures A and B show the same degrees of longitude. Each line of longitude is 15° apart. But the times are different in each picture. On Picture A, 0° (the Prime Meridian) shows 12 noon. This means that the sun is shining directly over the time zone of 0°. Each hour the earth rotates 15° to the east. This makes the sun appear to be moving to the west. Picture B shows you where it is 12 noon one hour later. The direct sun is now over 15°W. So it is 12 noon at 15°W in Picture B and 1:00 P.M. at 0°. One hour later, it will be 12 noon at 30°W, 1:00 P.M. at 15°W, and 2:00 P.M. at 0°. This hour-by-hour change happens 24 times a day until the earth makes one complete rotation.

Answer the following questions using Pictures A and B.

1. When it is 10:00 A.M. at 30°W, it is at _____ 30°E.

What time did you fill in? Which picture shows 10:00 A.M. at 30°W? It is Picture A. Now on Picture A look for the 30°E line of longitude. Since 30°E has a time of 2:00 P.M., the answer to question 1 is 2:00 P.M.

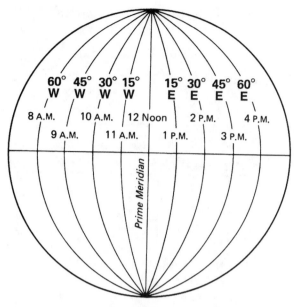

PICTURE A

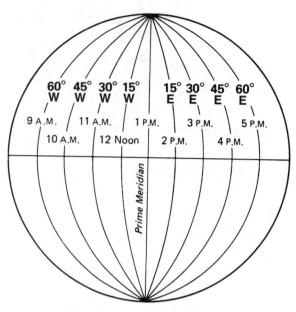

PICTURE B ONE HOUR LATER

You could also find the answer to question 1 in another way. When you travel from 30°W to 30°E, you pass through four lines of longitude. These four lines are 15°W, 0°, 15°E, and 30°E. Each of these lines represents one hour. By adding these four hours to the 10:00 A.M. at 30°W, you come to 2:00 P.M. at 30°E.

Suppose it is 2:00 P.M. at 30°E, and you are asked what time it is at 30°W. To find out, you subtract four hours from 2:00 P.M. You would then know it is 10:00 A.M. at 30°W.

2. When it is 2:00 P.M. at 45°W, it is _____ _____ at 45°E.

What time did you fill in? Neither Picture A nor Picture B shows 2:00 P.M. at 45°W. Picture B shows that it is 10:00 A.M. at

45°W and 4:00 P.M. at 45°E. How many hours difference is there between 10:00 A.M. and 2:00 P.M.? There is a difference of four hours. So the time you want to find out is four hours after the time shown in Picture B. You must add four hours to the 4:00 P.M. found at 45°E. This gives you 8:00 P.M. Therefore, when it is 2:00 P.M. at 45°W, it is 8:00 P.M. at 45°E.

You could also have found the answer to question 2 in another way. You could have counted the time zones between 45°W and 45°E. There are six of them. Then you could have added that number to 2:00 P.M.

The following exercises will give you more practice in understanding longitude and time zones.

USING WHAT YOU HAVE LEARNED

A. True or False: If every part of the statement is true, write **T.**
If any part of the statement is false, write **F.**

_____ 1. The earth makes one complete rotation every 24 hours.

_____ 2. For every 15° of longitude, there is a difference of one hour in time.

_____ 3. Time zones always have straight boundaries.

_____ 4. It is 12 noon everywhere on the earth at the same time.

_____ 5. The letters A.M. stand for the 12 hours before 12 noon.

_____ 6. Post meridiem means the 12 hours after 12 noon.

_____ 7. The line of longitude at 180° is called the Prime Meridian.

_____ 8. When you travel across the International Date Line, you stay in the same day.

_____ 9. When you cross the Prime Meridian, you stay in the same day.

_____ 10. It takes one hour for the earth to rotate 15°.

B. Longitude and Time Change.

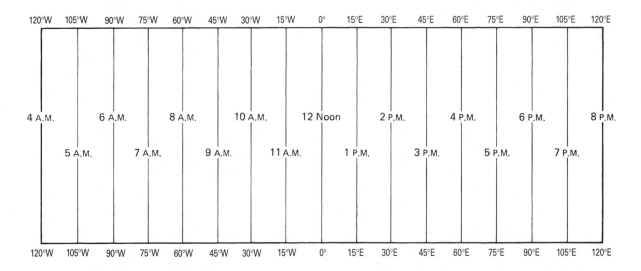

Use the graph to help you answer the following questions. Write the correct answer in the space provided.

1. On the graph, it is 12 noon at _____ degrees.

2. The sun is directly overhead at _____ degrees.

3. When it is 9 A.M. at 45°W, it is _____ at 45°E.

4. When it is 10 A.M. at 30°W, it is _____ at 60°E.

5. When it is 5 P.M at 75°E, it is _____ at 75°W.

6. When it is 10 A.M. at 45°W, it is _____ at 45°E.

7. When it is 10 A.M. at 60°W, it is _____ at 75°E.

8. When it is 7 P.M at 45°E, it is _____ at 0°.

9. When it is 4 P.M. at 15°W, it is _____ at 15°E.

10. When it is 7 P.M at 60°W, it is _____ at 60°E.

C. Time Zones in the United States.

C-1. Place a check mark next to the correct answers to questions 1 to 10. Use the map on page 223 to help you answer the questions.

1. From the map, you can see that the 48 states of the United States that border each other have

____ (*a*) one time zone.

____ (*b*) four time zones.

____ (*c*) ten time zones.

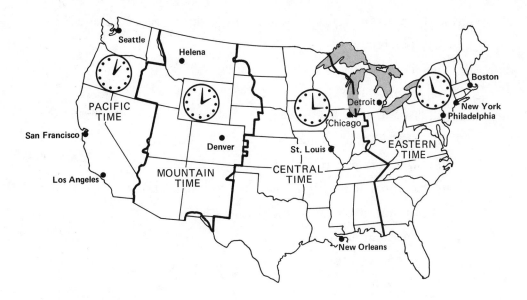

2. New York is in the

    ____ (a) Eastern Time Zone.

    ____ (b) Central Time Zone.

    ____ (c) Pacific Time Zone.

3. Chicago is in the

    ____ (a) Eastern Time Zone.

    ____ (b) Central Time Zone.

    ____ (c) Mountain Time Zone.

4. Denver is in the

    ____ (a) Eastern Time Zone.

    ____ (b) Mountain Time Zone.

    ____ (c) Pacific Time Zone.

5. San Francisco is in the

    ____ (a) Central Time Zone.

    ____ (b) Mountain Time Zone.

    ____ (c) Pacific Time Zone.

6. Which one of the following statements is true?

    ____ (a) It is the same time everywhere in the United States.

    ____ (b) Chicago and Denver always have the same time.

    ____ (c) There is a time difference of one hour between neighboring time zones on the map.

7. The map shows that it is

    ____ (a) 2 o'clock in Boston.

    ____ (b) 3 o'clock in Boston.

    ____ (c) 4 o'clock in Boston.

8. What is the time difference between New York and San Francisco?

_____ (a) Two hours

_____ (b) Three hours

_____ (c) Four hours

9. Mountain Time means the time it is

_____ (a) at the top of a mountain.

_____ (b) where there are mountains.

_____ (c) in a particular time zone in the United States.

10. If it is 11 A.M. in Detroit, in New Orleans it is

_____ (a) one hour earlier.

_____ (b) one hour later.

_____ (c) the same time.

C-2. Fill in the correct times based on the Time Zone map.

1. When it is 1 o'clock in Los Angeles, it is _____ o'clock in Chicago.

2. When it is 5 o'clock in Philadelphia, it is _____ o'clock in New Orleans.

3. When it is 2 o'clock in San Francisco, it is _____ o'clock in Denver.

4. When it is 5 o'clock in Denver, it is _____ o'clock in New York.

5. When it is 4 o'clock in St. Louis, it is _____ o'clock in Seattle.

D. In your own words, explain why different places in the United States show different hours on the clock at the same time. In other words, why is it 9 A.M. in Seattle and 11 A.M. in St. Louis when it is noon in Philadelphia? (Answer in three or four sentences.)

_____

_____

_____

_____

_____

_____

_____

_____

_____

CHAPTER 28
Population Maps

So far you have seen maps that were drawn to show the shapes of landforms and water forms, the boundaries of countries, and the location of cities. Another important type of information that can be shown on a map is population, or the total number of people living in a place. A map that shows the population of cities and countries is called a *population map*.

Symbols

The key on the following population map of China includes symbols commonly used to show population figures for cities. Note that each symbol stands for a different number of people.

Study the map and then answer the following questions about it.

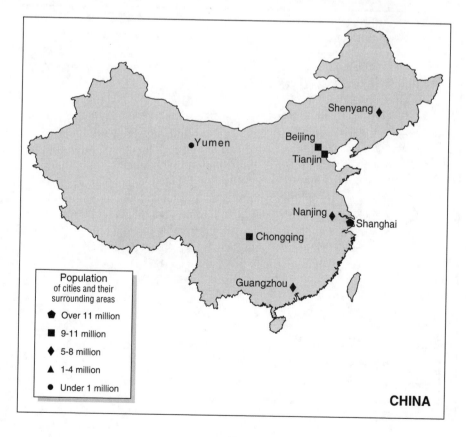

Population
of cities and their
surrounding areas

⬟ Over 11 million

■ 9-11 million

◆ 5-8 million

▲ 1-4 million

● Under 1 million

CHINA

1. The map shows

_____ (a) the entire population of China.

_____ (b) how many people live in eastern China.

_____ (c) the population of eight cities in China.

Which answer did you choose? The map shows only eight cities in China. Each one has a symbol next to it. These symbols and the population that each represents are explained in the key. Since the map shows only the population of these eight cities, the answer to question one is (c).

2. The city of Beijing has a population

_____ (a) between 5 million and 8 million.

_____ (b) between 9 million and 11 million.

_____ (c) over 11 million.

Which answer did you choose? Look on the map for the city of Beijing and the symbol next to it. The key shows that this symbol ■ stands for a population between 9 million and 11 million. Therefore, the answer to question 2 is (b).

_____ 3. True or False: Three cities on the map have a population between 1 million and 4 million.

What was your answer? A population between 1 million and 4 million would have the symbol ▲, but no city on the map has that symbol. Therefore, the answer to question 3 is False. However, name the three cities with a population between 5 million and 8 million.

Dots

The map you just studied shows the population of eight important cities in China. But people live not only in cities but throughout a country. Population maps can be drawn to show the average population of a small area or of an entire country. This kind of map is called a *population density map*. (Population density means the average number of people living in a certain area of land.) The following is a population density map of China.

This map uses dots to show how many people live in certain areas of China. Each dot stands for a particular number of people. Areas on the map with few dots have few people living in them. Areas with many dots have many people living in them.

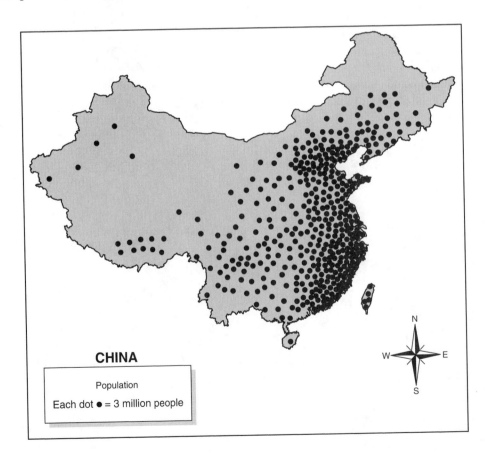

CHINA

Population

Each dot ● = 3 million people

Use the dot population density map of China to help you answer the following questions.

1. Each dot on the map stands for

_____ (a) 1 million people.

_____ (b) 2 million people.

_____ (c) 3 million people.

What was your answer? The key on the map shows that each dot stands for 3 million people. Therefore, the answer to question 1 is (c).

2. Most people in China live in

_____ (a) northern China.

_____ (b) western China.

_____ (c) eastern China.

Which answer did you choose? Remember that the area of the country with the most dots has the most people. Because the map shows that eastern China has the most dots, the answer to question 2 is (c).

Patterns

Sometimes a population density map uses patterns (designs) or colors instead of dots. The patterns or colors on the map show how many people live in a certain area of land. On this kind of population density map, the key may look something like the following:

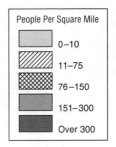

The patterns and population statistics may be different on different maps. But the key will always explain what population statistics the patterns represent.

Let us look at an example to see how this key works. In the key, the pattern stands for 11 to 75 people per square mile. This means that wherever this pattern appears on the map between 11 and 75 people live on every square mile of land.

Study the following population density map of China. The key on it is the same as the one above.

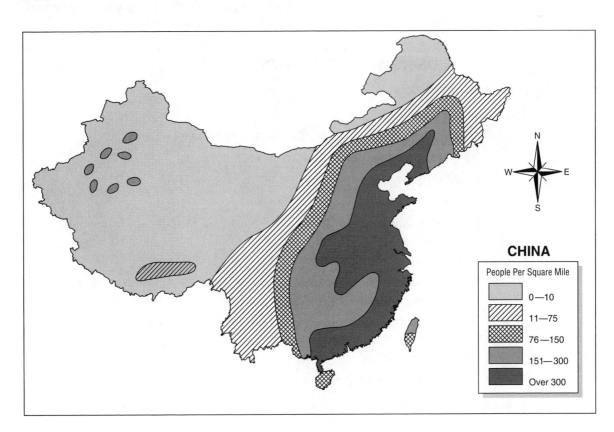

1. This population density map of China shows how many people live

_____ (*a*) in cities.

_____ (*b*) on farms.

_____ (*c*) in certain areas of the country.

Which answer did you choose? The key shows that patterns on the map stand for different populations in different areas of China. By using the key, you can see how many people live in a certain area of China. Therefore, the answer to question 1 is (*c*).

2. The pattern  stands for

_____ (*a*) 11 to 75 people per square mile.

_____ (*b*) 76 to 150 people per square mile.

_____ (*c*) 151 to 300 people per square mile.

Which answer did you choose? The key shows that the pattern  stands for 76 to 150 people per square mile. This means that wherever this pattern appears on the map there are between 76 and 150 people per square mile of land. Therefore, the answer to question 2 is (*b*).

3. Which area of China has the fewest people?

_____ (*a*) eastern China

_____ (*b*) western China

_____ (*c*) southern China

Which answer did you choose? According to the key, the area of China with the fewest people (0 to 10) is shown on the map by the pattern  . This pattern is found mainly in western China. It can be assumed then that the section of China with the fewest people is in the west. So the answer to question 3 is (*b*).

In question 3, you learned that the lowest population density in China is generally in the western part of the country. But you did not learn why western China has the fewest people. A population map shows where people live in a country, but it does not show why people live in certain areas. Before you can know why people live in an area, you need to know more about what the area is like. In general, people live where they can grow food or earn a living in some other way.

In this chapter, you have studied three different kinds of population maps. These maps use symbols, dots, or patterns to show population and population density. The following exercises will give you practice in using these three important kinds of population maps.

USING WHAT YOU HAVE LEARNED

A. Place a check mark next to the correct answers to questions 1 to 5.

1. A population map shows

____ (*a*) which cities and countries are important in the world.

____ (*b*) how many people like to live in cities.

____ (*c*) how many people live in certain cities or areas of a country.

2. Which one of the following statements is true?

____ (*a*) Certain symbols always stand for the same population figures on all population maps.

____ (*b*) Population symbols are usually not explained.

____ (*c*) It is a good idea to check the key to see what the symbols on a population map represent.

3. Caracas, Venezuela, has a population of 3 million. Which one of the following represents the population of Caracas?

____ (*a*) ■ Under 1 million

____ (*b*) ▲ 1 million to 5 million

____ (*c*) • Over 5 million

4. Which one of the following statements is most likely to be true?

_____ (a) Most people do not care where they live.

_____ (b) Most people like to live in areas with steep mountains.

_____ (c) Most people like to live where they can earn a living.

5. If each dot on a population density map equals 200,000 people, what would be the population of a section that has four dots?

_____ (a) 400,000　　　_____ (b) 8,000,000　　　_____ (c) 800,000

B. True or False: If every part of the statement is true, write **T.**
If any part of the statement is false, write **F.**

_____ 1. The symbols representing population figures on a population map are usually explained in the key.

_____ 2. On a dot population density map, each dot stands for a city.

_____ 3. A population map shows why people live in certain areas of a country.

_____ 4. Patterns on different population maps always stand for the same population statistics.

_____ 5. A population density map can be used to show how many people live in a certain area or in an entire country.

C. Study the following population map of Japan.

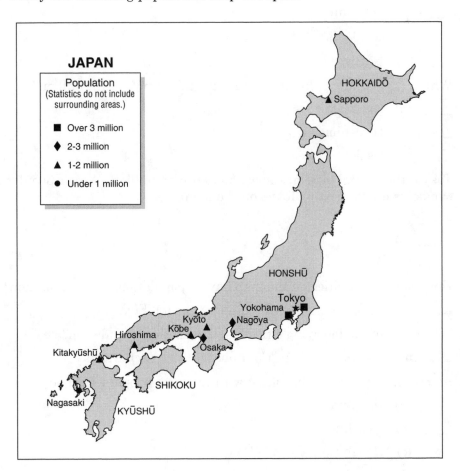

Place a check mark next to the correct answers to questions 1 to 10.

1. The map shows the population of

_____ (a) the entire country of Japan.

_____ (b) the major cities of Japan.

_____ (c) each island of Japan.

2. The symbol used to show a city with a population between 1 million and 2 million is

_____ (a) •

_____ (b) ▲

_____ (c) ■

3. The symbol • stands for a population of

_____ (a) under 1 million.

_____ (b) 1 million to 2 million.

_____ (c) over 2 million.

4. The city of Kyōto has a population

_____ (a) under 1 million.

_____ (b) between 1 and 2 million.

_____ (c) over 2 million.

5. One of the following cities has a population of 3,307,000. Which city is it?

_____ (a) Yokohama

_____ (b) Kitakyūshū

_____ (c) Nagōya

6. Which city has a population over 2 million, but not over 3 million?

_____ (a) Nagasaki

_____ (b) Hiroshima

_____ (c) Osaka

7. Tokyo, the capital city, has a population of 8 million. Which population symbol is drawn next to Tokyo on the map?

_____ (a) •

_____ (b) ▲

_____ (c) ■

8. How many other cities on the map have a population of over 2 million?

____ (a) Three   ____ (b) Four   ____ (c) Five

9. Which one of the following cities has the smallest population?

____ (a) Nagasaki   ____ (b) Kōbe   ____ (c) Osaka

10. According to the map, the island with the most people would be

_____ (a) Hokkaidō.

_____ (b) Kyūshū.

_____ (c) Honshū.

D. Study the following population map of South-West Asia/Africa.

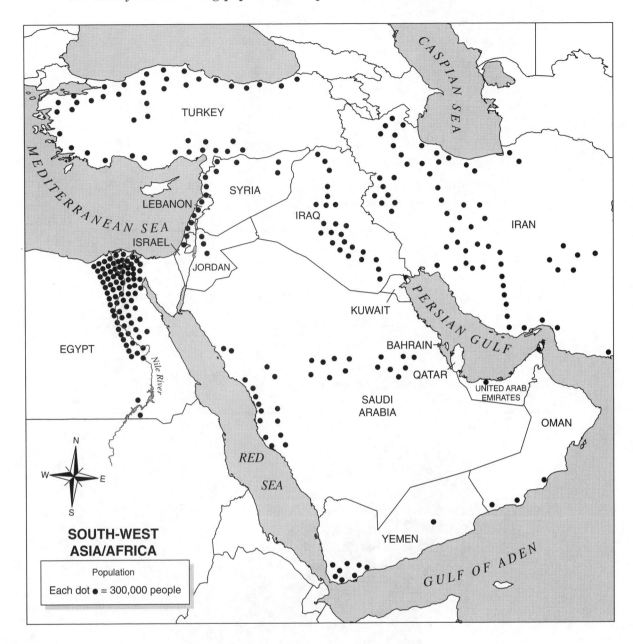

Place a check mark next to the correct answer to questions 1 to 4.

1. The map shows

____ (*a*) the population of major cities of South-West Asia/Africa.

____ (*b*) the population density of the countries of South-West Asia/Africa.

____ (*c*) important cities of South-West Asia/Africa.

2. Each dot • on this map stands for

____ (*a*) 200,000 people.

____ (*b*) 300,000 people.

____ (*c*) 500,000 people.

3. Which one of the following countries shows the greatest density of people?

_____ (a) Egypt

_____ (b) Saudi Arabia

_____ (c) Iran

4. In Saudi Arabia most of the people live in the

_____ (a) northern part of the country.

_____ (b) central part of the country.

_____ (c) southern part of the country.

5. Why do you think there are so many dots in Egypt along the Nile River? (Answer in one or two sentences.)

_____

_____

_____

_____

E. Study the following map of South Asia.

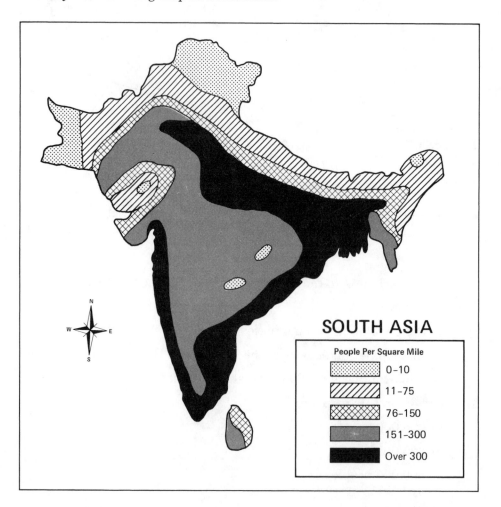

Place a check mark next to the correct answers to questions 1 to 5.

1. The map shows the

____ (a) boundary lines of different countries in South Asia.

____ (b) population of major cities in South Asia.

____ (c) population density of South Asia.

2. The population statistics on the map are shown by

____ (a) symbols.

____ (b) dots.

____ (c) patterns.

3. The pattern ▨▨▨ stands for

____ (a) 11 to 75 people per square mile.

____ (b) 76 to 150 people per square mile.

____ (c) 151 to 300 people per square mile.

4. The pattern ▉ stands for

____ (a) 76 to 150 people per square mile.

____ (b) 151 to 300 people per square mile.

____ (c) over 300 people per square mile.

5. A population of 200 people per square mile is shown on the map by the pattern

____ (a) ▤

____ (b) ▨

____ (c) ▉

F. Study the map of Africa on page 234.

Place a check mark next to the correct answers to questions 1 to 9.

1. The map shows the

____ (a) population density of Africa.

____ (b) population of the major cities of Africa.

____ (c) boundary lines of countries in Africa.

2. The population statistics on the map are shown by

____ (a) symbols.

____ (b) dots.

____ (c) patterns.

3. The meanings of the patterns on the map are

____ (a) explained in the index.

____ (b) explained in the key.

____ (c) not explained at all.

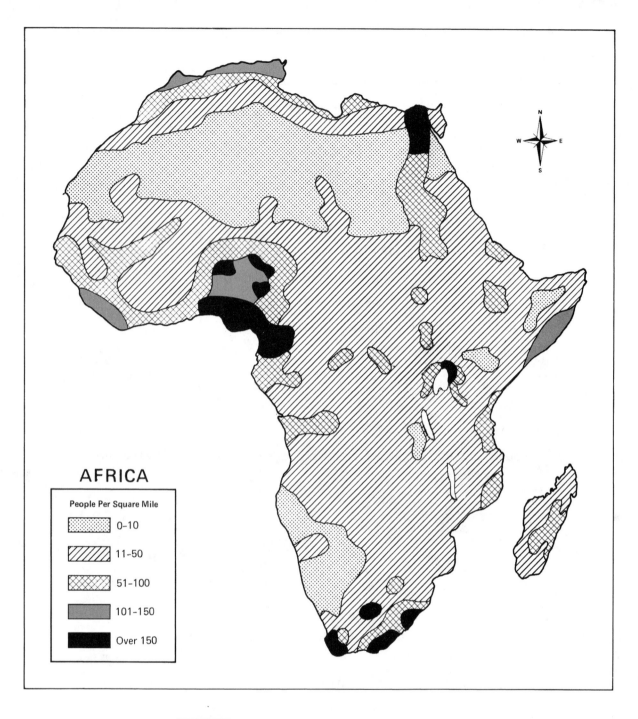

AFICA

Pople Per Square Mile

	0–10
	11–50
	51–100
	101–150
	Over 150

4. The pattern 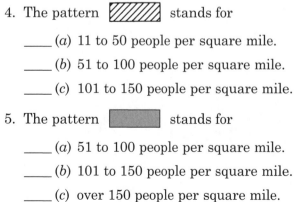 stands for

____ (a) 11 to 50 people per square mile.

____ (b) 51 to 100 people per square mile.

____ (c) 101 to 150 people per square mile.

5. The pattern ▨ stands for

____ (a) 51 to 100 people per square mile.

____ (b) 101 to 150 people per square mile.

____ (c) over 150 people per square mile.

6. A population of 200 people per square mile is shown on the map by the pattern

_____ (a) [dotted pattern]

_____ (b) [cross-hatch pattern]

_____ (c) [solid black pattern]

7. Which pattern on the map covers an area of Africa that is probably desert?

_____ (a) [dotted pattern]

_____ (b) [gray pattern]

_____ (c) [solid black pattern]

8. A large city is most likely to be located in an area with which pattern?

_____ (a) [dotted pattern]

_____ (b) [gray pattern]

_____ (c) [solid black pattern]

9. In which part of Africa do the fewest people live?

_____ (a) The north

_____ (b) The south

_____ (c) The east

10. In one or two sentences of your own words, answer the following question. "What does a population density map show?"

_____

_____

_____

_____

CHAPTER 29
Relief Maps

Most maps are printed on flat paper. But we know that the surface of the earth is not completely flat. Various types of geographical features make the earth's surface uneven. They include:

Mountains: landmasses much higher than nearby areas

Volcanoes: mountains with an opening in the top or side through which melted rock, steam, and ashes are forced out from inside the earth

Plateaus: high, flat landforms

Hills: high, rounded landforms, usually not as tall as mountains

Where there are no high landforms, the earth may be covered by *plains*—areas of low, flat land.

How can we show on paper what these landforms of different heights look like? One way is to show a side view, as in this drawing. —

Another way is to draw a map that shows the height, or altitude, of landforms. This type of map is called a *relief map.*

Where do we start measuring altitude? The height of land is very different in different parts of the world. Only the surface of the water of the oceans is the same height throughout most of the world. Therefore, the measurement of altitude starts on the surface of the oceans. This surface is called *sea level.*

A relief map uses different patterns or colors to show the altitude of landforms. The key on a relief map shows these patterns or colors and the altitudes they represent.

Below is a cross-section relief map. It shows the same drawing of landforms that you saw above. This time patterns have been added to show the altitudes of the landforms. The key next to the drawings gives the altitude of each of these patterns.

By using the key, you can see how high the landforms are.

Answer the following questions using the drawing below.

1. The pattern ⬛ stands for

_____ (a) 1,001 to 2,000 feet above sea level.

_____ (b) 2,001 to 5,000 feet above sea level.

_____ (c) 5,001 to 10,000 feet above sea level.

Which answer did you choose? The key shows that the pattern ⬛ stands for 1,001 to 2,000 feet above sea level. This means that every area on the drawing with this pattern has an altitude between 1,001 and 2,000 feet. Therefore, the answer to question 1 is (a).

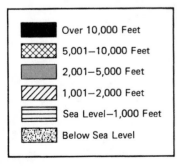

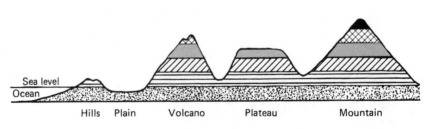

2. The top of the mountain in the drawing has an altitude

_____ (a) between 2,001 and 5,000 feet.

_____ (b) between 5,001 and 10,000 feet.

_____ (c) over 10,000 feet.

What was your answer? The pattern at the top of the mountain is ▬▬ . The key shows that any area with this pattern has an altitude of over 10,000 feet. Therefore, the answer to question 2 is (c).

In some areas of the world, dry land is actually located below sea level. The plain in the drawing is below sea level and is shown with the pattern ▨▨ . Higher land around the plain keeps it from being flooded by ocean water.

Most relief maps use a top view rather than a side view of an area. The maps you have studied in earlier chapters all use top views, as if you were looking down at an area. The most common top-view relief map looks like the following map of South America. Different patterns are used to show the altitudes of landforms. The key

Mount Aconcagua, +22,834

SOUTH AMERICA

Relief

Dark Brown	▬▬	Over 10,000 Feet
Light Brown	▨▨	5,001–10,000 Feet
Yellow	▨	2,001–5,000 Feet
Light Green	▨	1,001–2,000 Feet
Dark Green	☰	Sea Level–1,000 Feet

tells you what altitude each pattern represents. Some maps use colors in place of patterns. The colors used most often are written next to the patterns in the key.

Answer the following questions using the top-view relief map of South America on page 237.

1. The relief map shows

_____ (a) how many people live in South America.

_____ (b) the important cities of South America.

_____ (c) the altitudes of different landforms in South America.

Which answer did you choose? The key shows that different patterns on the map stand for the different altitudes of landforms in South America. Therefore, the answer to question 1 is (c).

2. The measurement of altitude starts at

_____ (a) the bottom of the landform.

_____ (b) sea level.

_____ (c) the top of the landform.

Which answer did you choose? The key shows that the measurement of altitude starts at sea level. Therefore, the answer to question 2 is (b).

3. The pattern [   ] stands for an altitude

_____ (a) between 2,001 and 5,000 feet above sea level.

_____ (b) between 5,001 and 10,000 feet above sea level.

_____ (c) over 10,000 feet above sea level.

Which answer did you choose? The pattern [   ] on the key stands for an altitude between 2,001 and 5,000 feet. Therefore, the answer to question 3 is (a).

4. Mount Aconcagua, shown on the map of South America, has an altitude of

_____ (a) 10,000 feet.

_____ (b) 16,880 feet.

_____ (c) 22,834 feet.

Which answer did you choose? Very high mountains are usually shown on a map with their exact altitudes written near them. Find Mount Aconcagua on the map. The name and height of the mountain are shown like this: $\underset{+22,834}{\textit{Mount Aconcagua,}}$. This means that Mount Aconcagua is 22,834 feet above sea level. Therefore, the answer to question 4 is (c).

5. Most of South America is

_____ (a) mountainous.

_____ (b) desert.

_____ (c) flat with some hills.

Which answer did you choose? The patterns used the most on the map are [////] and [≡]. These patterns represent land that has an altitude of less than 2,000 feet. This land is most likely to be flat with some hills. Therefore, the answer to question 5 is (c).

6. Explain in your own words why this statement is false: "Green on a relief map always stands for trees and grass." (Answer in one or two sentences.)

_____

_____

_____

_____

_____

_____

What did you write? Most students believe that the green on a relief map stands for trees and grass. But this is not true. Green is the most commonly used color for land that is at a low altitude. The key on this map of South America tells you that light green and dark green stand for altitudes between sea level and 2,000 feet. So green usually stands for low altitude and *not* for trees and grass. If this idea was part of your answer, you wrote a good answer to question 6.

7. Why do you think few people live in areas shown on the map with the pattern ▮▮ ? (Answer in three or four sentences.)

_____

_____

_____

_____

_____

_____

_____

_____

What answer did you write? The key shows that the pattern ▮▮ stands for areas with an altitude of over 10,000 feet. These areas are almost certainly mountainous. High mountain areas generally have a cold climate and are not good for growing crops. So, few people would want to live in mountainous areas. If your answer contains some of these ideas, you wrote a good answer to question 7.

The relief maps in the exercises that follow do not all look alike. The keys will help you to understand these maps.

USING WHAT YOU HAVE LEARNED

A. Place a check mark next to the correct answers to questions 1 to 9.

1. A relief map shows

____ (a) how many people live in a country.

____ (b) why people live on high landforms.

____ (c) the altitude of landforms.

2. Which one of the following is NOT a high landform?

____ (a) Plain

____ (b) Mountain

____ (c) Plateau

3. The measuring of altitude starts

____ (a) at the foot of a mountain.

____ (b) at sea level.

____ (c) below sea level.

4. Different altitudes on a relief map are

      _____ (a) always shown by colors.

      _____ (b) shown by patterns or colors that are explained in the key.

      _____ (c) shown by patterns but are not explained in the key.

5. A landform 4,500 feet above sea level would be shown on a relief map by the pattern

      _____ (a)   ▤   0 to 1,000 feet.

      _____ (b)   ▨   1,001 to 2,000 feet.

      _____ (c)   ▦   2,001 to 5,000 feet.

6. Green on a relief map usually stands for

      _____ (a) land at low altitudes.

      _____ (b) trees and grass.

      _____ (c) mountainous land.

7. Brown on a relief map usually stands for

      _____ (a) land below sea level.

      _____ (b) deserts.

      _____ (c) mountainous land.

8. The phrase "below sea level" means

      _____ (a) underneath the sea.

      _____ (b) lower than the surface of the oceans.

      _____ (c) below the level of any body of water.

9. A plateau is

      _____ (a) a high, flat landform.

      _____ (b) low, flat land.

      _____ (c) a volcano.

10. Explain in two or three sentences why a relief map would be helpful to the pilot of a small airplane.

_____

_____

_____

_____

_____

_____

_____

B. Study the following map of South Asia.

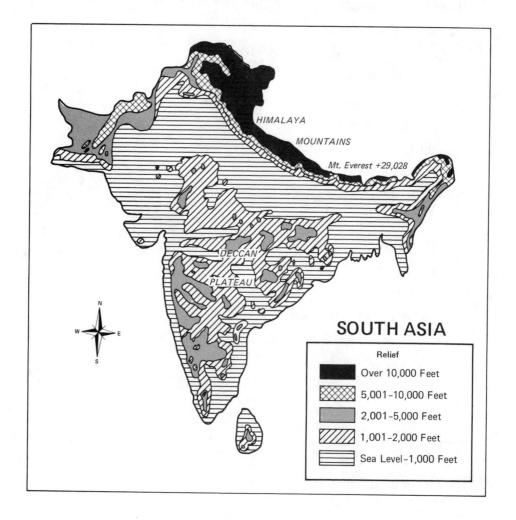

Place a check mark next to the correct answer to questions 1 to 10.

1. The relief map shows

   _____ (*a*) how many people live in South Asia.

   _____ (*b*) the altitudes of landforms in South Asia.

   _____ (*c*) the boundaries of countries in South Asia.

2. The altitudes on the map are shown by

   _____ (*a*) symbols.

   _____ (*b*) boxes.

   _____ (*c*) patterns.

3. The key on the map explains

   _____ (*a*) the difficult words on the map.

   _____ (*b*) the meanings of the patterns on the map.

   _____ (*c*) how to use an index.

4. The pattern ▬ stands for an altitude

_____ (a) under 1,000 feet.

_____ (b) between 2,001 and 5,000 feet.

_____ (c) over 10,000 feet.

5. The altitude of a landform on the map is measured from

_____ (a) the bottom of the landform.

_____ (b) the top of the landform.

_____ (c) sea level.

6. The center of South Asia is a vast

_____ (a) mountain range.

_____ (b) plain.

_____ (c) plateau.

7. The Himalaya Mountains at the top of the map have an altitude

_____ (a) less than 1,000 feet.

_____ (b) between 5,001 and 10,000 feet.

_____ (c) over 10,000 feet.

8. Mount Everest in the Himalaya Mountains has an altitude of

_____ (a) 10,000 feet.

_____ (b) 22,300 feet.

_____ (c) 29,028 feet.

9. The lowest areas in South Asia are

_____ (a) mostly in the north.

_____ (b) mainly in the south.

_____ (c) only in the east.

10. The highest areas in South Asia are

_____ (a) in the south.

_____ (b) in the north.

_____ (c) on the island.

C. Study the relief map of Russia on page 243.

Place a check mark next to the correct answers to questions 1 to 6.

1. The relief map of Russia shows

____ (a) heights of landforms.

____ (b) major seaports.

____ (c) population.

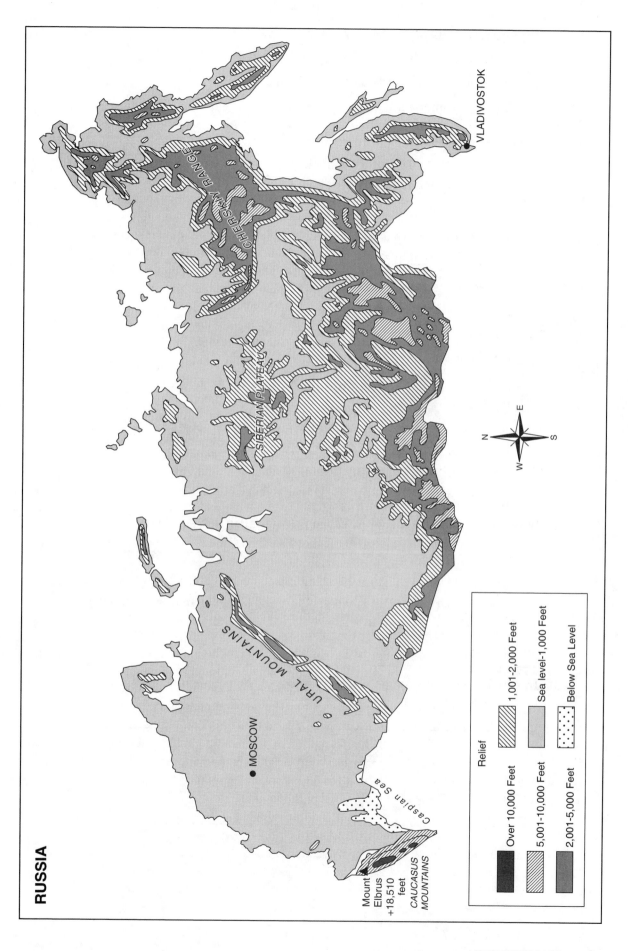

RUSSIA

VLADIVOSTOK

CHERSKY RANGE

SIBERIAN PLATEAU

URAL MOUNTAINS

MOSCOW

Caspian Sea

Mount
Elbrus
+18,510
feet
CAUCASUS
MOUNTAINS

N E
W S

Relief

Over 10,000 Feet		1,001-2,000 Feet
5,001-10,000 Feet		Sea level-1,000 Feet
2,001-5,000 Feet		Below Sea Level

2. The patterns used on the map

____ (*a*) are put on the map to make the country look interesting.

____ (*b*) represent the altitude of landforms.

____ (*c*) show important sightseeing areas.

3. The pattern  stands for an altitude

____ (*a*) between 2,001 and 5,000 feet.

____ (*b*) between 5,001 and 10,000 feet.

____ (*c*) over 10,000 feet.

4. Most of the western areas on the map are

____ (*a*) 5,001 to 10,000 feet.

____ (*b*) below sea level.

____ (*c*) sea level to 1,000 feet.

5. The mountain range nearest the Caspian Sea is the

____ (*a*) Caucasus.

____ (*b*) Ural.

____ (*c*) Cherskiy.

6. On the map, there is an area of land below sea level located

____ (*a*) on the Siberian Plateau.

____ (*b*) next to the Caspian Sea.

____ (*c*) all along the northern coast.

7. What is the altitude of Mount Elbrus? (Answer in one sentence.)

____

____

8. What is the altitude of the Siberian Plateau? (Answer in one sentence.)

____

____

9. In which area of Russia do you think most of the people live? Why? (Answer in two or three sentences.)

____

____

____

____

____

____

10. How does the map on page 243 show that it must have been difficult to build the Trans-Siberian Railroad between Moscow and Vladivostok? (Answer in one or two sentences.)

_____

_____

_____

_____

_____

CHAPTER 30
Rainfall and Climate Maps

Rainfall

Rain is a major source of water for humans, animals, and plants. It influences the way people dress and the kinds of houses they live in. Rain also affects the production of food and the kinds of work people do.

Some areas of the world have almost no rain all year long. Other areas have rain almost every day of the year. In many countries, the amount of rainfall differs from one area of the country to another.

Maps can be drawn to show how much rain a country receives over a period of time. They are called *rainfall maps*.

Look at the rainfall map of Israel on page 247.

This map shows the average amount of rain different areas of Israel receive during a year. By using the key, you can see how much rain each area receives. One large area of the country receives 0 to 10 inches of rain a year. The pattern [ ] covers this area. Areas receiving 11 to 20 inches of rain a year have this pattern [ ] . Another area of the country receives 21 to 40 inches of rain and is shown by the pattern [ ] .

Answer the following questions using the rainfall map of Israel.

1. The rainfall map shows that

_____ (a) Israel receives no rain at all.

_____ (b) Israel receives the same amount of rain in every area of the country.

_____ (c) not every area of Israel receives the same amount of rain in a year.

Which answer did you choose? The key shows that Israel receives three different amounts of rainfall in a year. This map uses patterns to show the different areas of Israel where three different amounts of rain fall. Therefore, the answer to question 1 is (c).

2. The rain on this rainfall map is given in

_____ (a) inches.

_____ (b) feet.

_____ (c) buckets.

Which answer did you choose? At the top of the key you can see the words "(in inches)." This means that the rainfall on the map is given in inches. Therefore, the answer to question 2 is (a).

_____ 3. True or False: The area of Israel that receives the least amount of rain in a year is southern Israel.

What was your answer? The key shows that the area with the pattern [ ] receives the least amount of rainfall (0 to 10 inches) per year. On the map, the area with this pattern covers the southern part of Israel. Therefore, the answer to question 3 is True.

Sometimes a rainfall map is called a *precipitation map*. Precipitation means water that falls as rain or snow. It is just as important to measure snowfall as it is to measure rainfall. (About 10 to 12 inches of snow—melted—are equal to one inch of rain.) On a precipitation map, the inches of precipitation may stand for snow or rain or both.

Climate

A map can also show *climates* in different areas of the world. Climate is the kind of weather each area of the world has over a long period of time. Weather is different from climate because it is the day-to-day changes in temperature, wind movements, and precipitation. Climate is the result of these changes over many years.

Different areas of the world have different climates. The following are some of the main reasons for these differences:

1. *Latitude.* A country located in the low latitudes usually has a warm climate. One located in the high latitudes usually

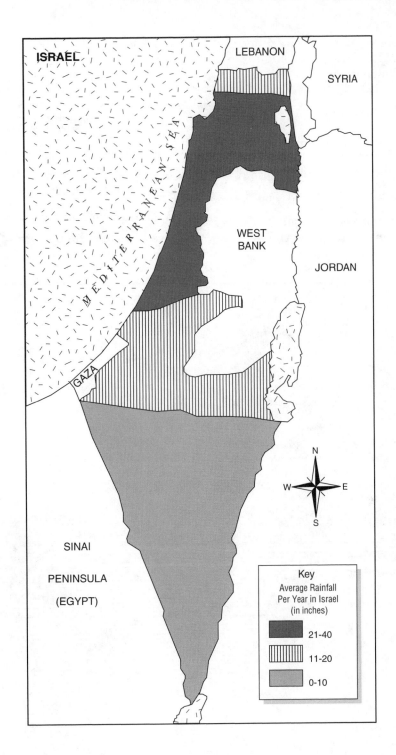

has a cold climate. Countries in the middle latitudes usually have a mild climate.

2. *Elevation,* or altitude (height above sea level). Land at a high elevation has colder temperatures than land at a low elevation.

3. *Landforms.* High landforms, such as mountains, block the movement of wind and clouds carrying precipitation. As a result, the region on the side of a mountain facing the wind may get all the rain or snow and have a wet climate. The region on the other side of the mountain may have a dry climate.

4. *Ocean breezes and ocean currents.* Such movements bring cooler temperatures in the summer and warmer temperatures in the winter. These help create a mild climate in an area.

A map that shows climates in different areas of the world is called a *climate map*. Look at the following map of Africa and study its key.

1. The map shows

_____ (*a*) how much rain Africa receives.

_____ (*b*) the different climates of Africa.

_____ (*c*) that all of Africa is a desert.

Which answer did you choose? The key shows that different patterns on the map stand for different climates. Because the map shows the different climates in Africa, the answer to question 1 is (*b*).

2. Which kind of climate is represented by the pattern ■■■ ?

_____ (*a*) Dry

_____ (*b*) Mild

_____ (*c*) Mountain

Which answer did you choose? The key shows you that the pattern ■■■ stands

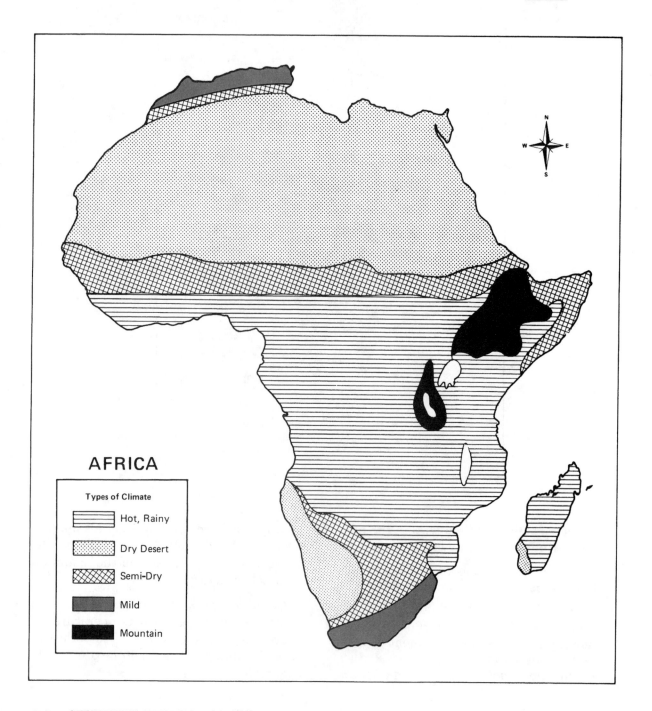

AFRICA

Types of Climate

Hot, Rainy

Dry Desert

Semi-Dry

Mild

Mountain

for a mountain climate. Therefore, the answer to question 2 is (*c*).

Mountain climate has this name because it is the climate found around mountain areas. At the bottom, or foot, of a mountain, the climate is usually warm enough for food to grow. But as you go higher up a mountain, the climate becomes colder, making it more difficult to grow food.

3. Why do you think few people live in the climate area with the pattern [▦] ?

   (Answer in two or three sentences.)

   _____

   _____

   _____

   _____

   _____

   _____

   _____

   _____

   _____

What did you write? The map does not give you the answer to question 3. But sometimes you can use information on the map to help you learn something that is not on the map. The key shows that the area on the map with the pattern [▦] has a dry desert climate. Since water is needed to grow food, it is difficult to live in the dryness of the desert. Most likely, few people live in an area with this kind of climate. If these ideas were contained in your answer, you wrote a good answer to question 3.

By studying rainfall and climate maps, you can see how areas of the world are affected by different weather conditions and climates. Rain, heat, cold, and wind are important weather conditions. They influence what you wear, what you do, and sometimes how you feel. Climate in an area affects the kinds of crops that can be grown and how buildings are heated and cooled. Both weather and climate have a great influence on our daily lives.

Being able to understand and use rainfall and climate maps is an important Social Studies skill. The following exercises will give you practice in using these two important kinds of maps.

USING WHAT YOU HAVE LEARNED

A. True or False: If every part of the statement is true, write **T.**
If any part of the statement is false, write **F.**

_____ 1. Climate is the weather for a certain area over a long period of time.

_____ 2. If you say it rained on Monday and was sunny on Tuesday, you are talking about the climate.

_____ 3. If you say it is hot in Florida in the summer, you are talking about climate.

_____ 4. A rainfall map shows how much rain a country or area of land receives over a long period of time.

_____ 5. A climate map shows how people are affected by different climates.

_____ 6. Rainfall and climate have no effect on the kind of food a country grows.

_____ 7. Precipitation means any water that falls, including rain and snow.

_____ 8. In this chapter, precipitation on the rainfall maps is usually given in feet.

_____ 9. One inch of rain is equal to 10 to 12 inches of snow.

_____ 10. Rainfall and climate are always the same all over a country.

B. List and explain four reasons why different areas of the world have different climates.

_____

_____

_____

_____

_____

_____

_____

_____

_____

_____

_____

C. Study the following map of North Africa.

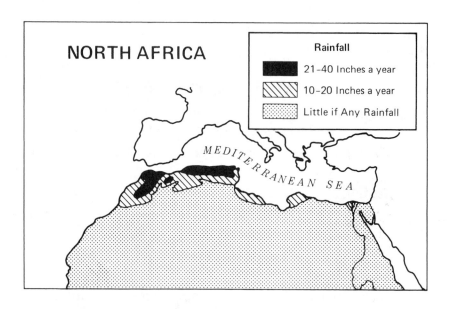

Place a check mark next to the correct answers to questions 1 to 5.

1. The map shows

_____ (*a*) the population of North Africa.

_____ (*b*) the altitudes of landforms in North Africa.

_____ (*c*) how much rain different areas of North Africa receive during the year.

2. The rainfall on the map is measured in

____ (a) inches.   ____ (b) feet.   ____ (c) temperature.

3. The pattern 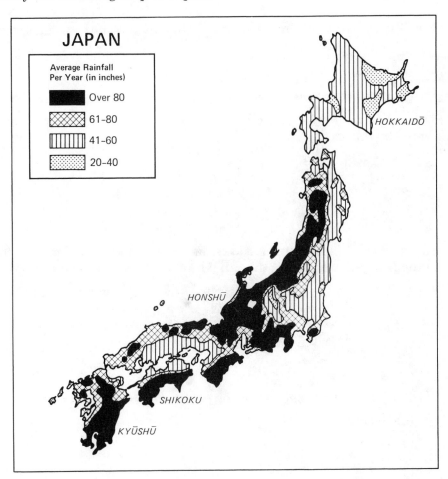 stands for

____ (a) little if any rainfall.

____ (b) rainfall between 10 and 20 inches a year.

____ (c) rainfall between 21 and 40 inches a year.

4. An area of North Africa receiving a rainfall of 25 inches a year is shown by this shading or pattern:

____ (a) ■

____ (b) ▨

____ (c) ▦

5. The best way to describe the land in the areas of North Africa covered by the pattern ▦ is to say it is

____ (a) desert.

____ (b) good land for growing crops.

____ (c) covered with mountains.

D. Study the following map of Japan.

Place a check mark next to the correct answers to questions 1 to 8.

1. The map shows

____ (a) how many people live in Japan.

____ (b) the altitudes of landforms in Japan.

____ (c) how much rain different areas of Japan generally receive during a year.

2. The pattern ⦀⦀⦀⦀ stands for rainfall

____ (a) between 20 and 40 inches a year.

____ (b) between 41 and 60 inches a year.

____ (c) between 61 and 80 inches a year.

3. An area of Japan receiving 90 inches of rain a year would be shown on the map by the pattern

____ (a) ▥

____ (b) ▨

____ (c) ▦

4. Which island in Japan has the least rainfall in a year?

____ (a) Hokkaidō

____ (b) Honshū

____ (c) Kyūshū

5. How much of the precipitation that falls in Japan is in the form of snow?

____ (a) 10%

____ (b) 50%

____ (c) Impossible to tell from the information given.

6. Plants that need a lot of water would most likely be grown in an area covered by this pattern

____ (a) ▥

____ (b) ▦

____ (c) ▨

Look at the map on page 229 that shows the population of some cities in Japan. Using the population map and the rainfall map, answer these questions:

7. Which of these cities generally receives the least amount of rainfall in a year?

____ (a) Kyōto

____ (b) Sapporo

____ (c) Nagasaki

8. Which of these cities generally receives the most rainfall in a year?

____ (a) Sapporo

____ (b) Kōbe

____ (c) Kitakyūshū

9. Look at the rainfall map. What does it tell you about when most of the precipitation falls in Japan? (Answer in one or two sentences.)

_____

_____

_____

_____

10. Why do you think it is important to know how much rainfall parts of Japan receive during a year? (Answer in one or two sentences.)

_____

_____

_____

_____

E. Study the following map of China.

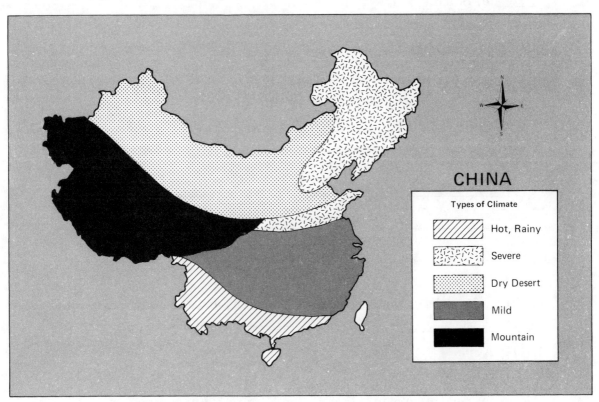

CHINA

Types of Climate

Hot, Rainy

Severe

Dry Desert

Mild

Mountain

Place a check mark next to the correct answers to questions 1 to 5.

1. The map shows

_____ (*a*) how much rainfall China receives each year.

_____ (*b*) the altitudes of landforms in China.

_____ (*c*) the different climates of China.

2. The different kinds of climates are

   ____ (a) explained in the key.

   ____ (b) explained in the photographs.

   ____ (c) not explained at all.

3. The climate on the map shown by the pattern ▒ is

   ____ (a) hot and rainy.

   ____ (b) dry desert.

   ____ (c) mild.

4. Severe (cold winters and hot summers) climate is shown on the map by the pattern

   ____ (a) ▨

   ____ (b) ▨

   ____ (c) ■

5. Which one of the following climates changes as the altitude changes?

   ____ (a) Severe

   ____ (b) Mild

   ____ (c) Mountain

6. Why do you think that most people in China live in the climate area shown like this ▨ ? (Answer in two or three sentences.)

   _____

   _____

   _____

   _____

   _____

F. Study the maps of South America on pages 255 and 256.

Place a check mark next to the correct answers to questions 1 to 10.

1. Map A is a

   ____ (a) climate map.

   ____ (b) population map.

   ____ (c) political map.

2. Map B is a

   ____ (a) climate map.

   ____ (b) population map.

   ____ (c) political map.

MAP A

3. Which map shows the boundary lines and capital cities of the countries of South America?

_____ (*a*) Map A

_____ (*b*) Map B

_____ (*c*) Both Map A and Map B

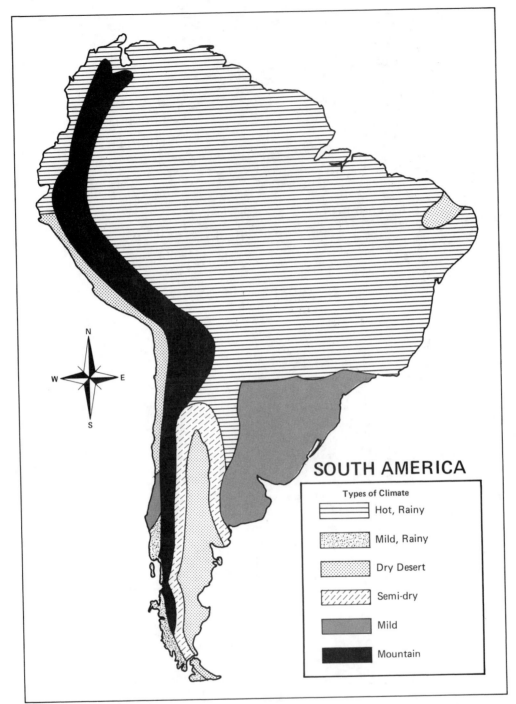

MAP B

4. Use Map A and Map B to determine which one of the following countries has a mostly mild climate.

____ (a) Brazil

____ (b) Venezuela

____ (c) Uruguay

5. Which one of the following countries has a dry desert climate?

_____ (a) Bolivia

_____ (b) Argentina

_____ (c) Uruguay

6. Brazil has a mostly

_____ (a) hot, rainy climate.

_____ (b) mild, rainy climate.

_____ (c) dry desert climate.

7. Which type of climate is NOT found in Chile?

_____ (a) Mountain

_____ (b) Mild, rainy

_____ (c) Hot, rainy

8. Which three capital cities are in a hot, rainy climate?

_____ (a) Santiago, Buenos Aires, La Paz

_____ (b) Brasília, Caracas, Georgetown

_____ (c) Bogotá, Lima, Asunción

9. Which of these climates does Peru have?

_____ (a) Mountain, dry desert, and hot, rainy

_____ (b) Mild, semi-dry, and hot, rainy

_____ (c) Mild and mountain

10. Most of South America tends to have a

_____ (a) dry desert climate.

_____ (b) hot, rainy climate.

_____ (c) mountain climate.

CHAPTER 31
Vegetation, Land Use, and Product Maps

As you have learned, rainfall and climate have a lot to do with the way land is used. An area with plenty of rain can be good for growing valuable crops. But an area that does not have much rain will have little vegetation (natural plant life, such as flowers, grass, and trees) and may also be poor for growing crops.

Cold, heat, wind, and other climate conditions also affect the plant life in a country. These climate conditions play a part in deciding what kinds of crops can be grown. For example, there is little plant life near the South Pole. No crops are grown there because of the extremely cold climate and the snow and ice that cover the land.

Maps can be drawn to show what types of vegetation are found in a country. Maps can also show what the land is used for and what products (things made or grown) are found in an area.

Natural Vegetation Maps

The map on page 259 shows plant life found in Russia. This kind of map is called a *natural vegetation map* because it shows plants that grow naturally and not those set out by people. By studying the map and its key, you will see that different areas have different kinds of natural vegetation.

1. The natural vegetation map shows

_____ (a) what crops are grown by people.

_____ (b) where different kinds of natural plant life can be found.

_____ (c) what food is most popular in Russia.

Which answer did you choose? Natural vegetation means plant life grown by nature and not by people. The plant life differs from area to area, depending on altitude, rainfall, and other climate conditions. Natural vegetation maps show where different kinds of plant life grow in a country or region. On the map, large areas of land are covered by patterns that stand for different kinds of natural plant life found in Russia. Therefore, the answer to question 1 is (b).

_____ 2. True or False: Most of Russia has a natural vegetation of grassland.

What was your answer? The key explains the patterns used on the map to represent different kinds of vegetation. The pattern covering the largest area of Russia is ▨. It stands for forests and not for grassland. Therefore, most of Russia has a natural vegetation of forests. The answer to question 2 is False.

By studying a natural vegetation map, you can see how a country might make use of its land. Land that has a natural vegetation of trees could be used for forestry (growing and caring for trees). Grassland with enough rainfall could be used for growing crops. Grassland that does not receive much rainfall might be used for grazing (feeding grass to) animals. Sometimes land that has many mountains or lacks enough rainfall to be used to grow anything might be an area where useful minerals are found.

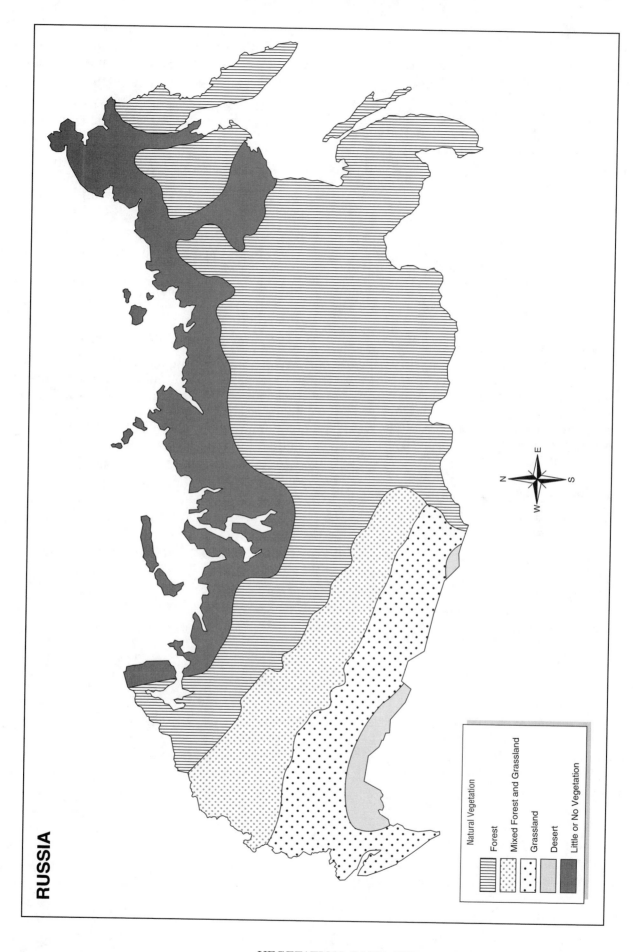

RUSSIA

Natural Vegetation

	Forest
	Mixed Forest and Grassland
	Grassland
	Desert
	Little or No Vegetation

Land Use Maps

Maps can be drawn to show how people make use of the land they live on. These maps are called *land use maps.* Look at the land use map of Russia on page 261.

Notice that this map is different from the natural vegetation map of the same area of the world, which shows plant life grown by nature. A land use map shows how people use the land.

1. This land use map shows

    _____ (a) natural vegetation.

    _____ (b) how large areas of land are used by people.

    _____ (c) the kinds of machines used on farms.

Which answer did you choose? The four patterns on the land use map of Russia are explained in the key. These patterns stand for farming, grazing, forestry, and little-used land. They show how large areas of land are used by people. Therefore, the answer to question 1 is (b).

Look at both the natural vegetation and land use maps of Russia to answer the following questions.

2. An area of Russia appears on the natural vegetation map as having desert vegetation. This same area on the land use map is used for

    _____ (a) forestry.

    _____ (b) farming, some grazing.

    _____ (c) grazing, some farming.

Which answer did you choose? Find the pattern for desert vegetation in the key of the natural vegetation map. It is [gray box] . Then find the area on the natural vegetation map where this pattern appears. Now look at the same area on the land use map. The pattern on it is [gray box] . The key for the land use map shows that this pattern stands for land that is used for grazing and some farming. Therefore, the answer to question 2 is (c).

3. An area of Russia that is used mainly for farming appears on the natural vegetation map as

    _____ (a) grassland and forest.

    _____ (b) desert and forest.

    _____ (c) grassland and desert.

Which answer did you choose this time? Find a large area of land on the land use map that is used for farming. Now find the same area of land on the natural vegetation map. The area on the vegetation map is shared by two different kinds of vegetation. One kind of vegetation is grassland [dotted box] . The second is mixed forest and grassland [dotted box] . Therefore, the answer to question 3 is (a).

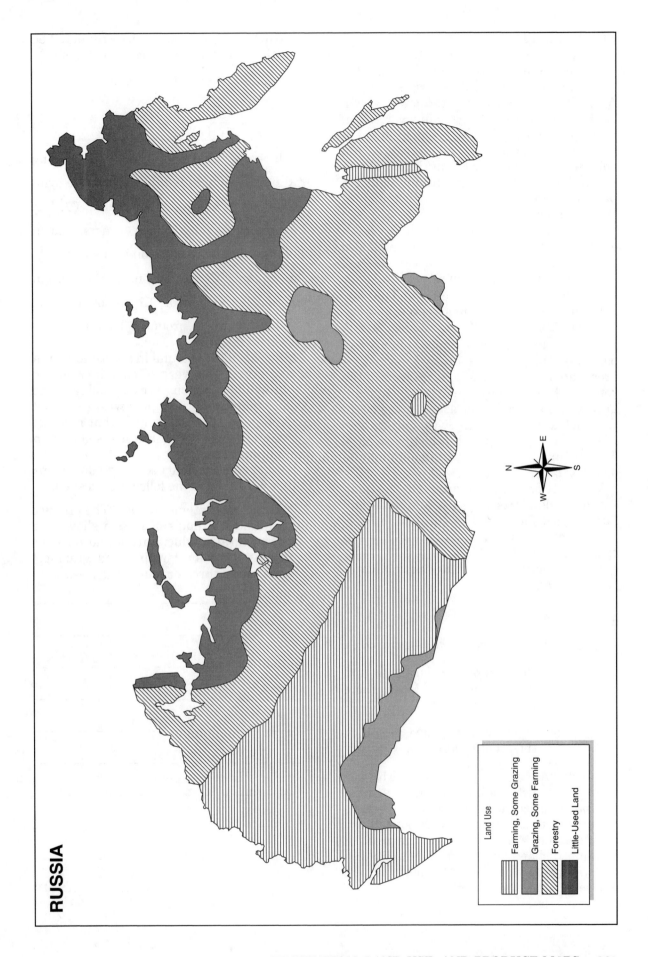

RUSSIA

Land Use

Farming, Some Grazing

Grazing, Some Farming

Forestry

Little-Used Land

Product Maps

A map can be drawn to show the agricultural and mineral products of a country. Agricultural products are the crops grown or the animals raised in a country. Mineral products are the valuable resources found in the earth, such as coal, oil, iron ore, and gold. A map that shows the agricultural and mineral products of a country is called a *product map*. Look at the product map of Russia on page 263.

This map shows where certain crops are grown and animals are raised. The map also shows where important minerals are located.

On the map, picture symbols stand for crops, animals, and minerals. The key explains what each symbol represents. For example, the symbol ⚘ stands for oats. A product map may have many pictures of oats, but this does not always mean that great amounts of oats are grown in the country. It may only mean that oats are grown in many different areas of the country. Each area of the country that grows oats is shown on the map with a picture of oats. The amount of oats grown in an area may be small or large.

The sections shaded gray on the map stand for industrial areas where mills and factories are found. Agricultural and mineral products are made into different goods in these mills and factories.

Use the product map of Russia to answer the following questions.

1. The map shows

    _____ (a) how much wheat is grown.

    _____ (b) the major agricultural and mineral products and where they are located.

    _____ (c) which products are grown in the greatest amount.

Which answer did you choose? The key shows that pictures on the map stand for the major agricultural and mineral products found in Russia. The map does not tell you which products are produced in the greatest amount. It shows only the different products and where they are located. Therefore, the answer to question 1 is (b).

2. Which symbol is NOT correctly matched with the mineral product it represents?

    _____ (a) 🜚 gold

    _____ (b) 🛢 coal

    _____ (c) ⚒ oil

Which answer did you choose? By looking at the key, you can see that 🜚 is the symbol for gold. The symbol for coal is 🛢. But the symbol for oil is not ⚒, as stated in choice (c). The symbol for oil in the key is ♟. The symbol ⚒ is the one for copper. In question 2, the symbol ⚒ is not correctly matched with its product. Therefore, the answer to question 2 is (c).

Minerals may be found in almost any area of a country. But very often minerals are found in mountainous areas. Compare the product map in this chapter with the relief map on page 243. You can see that much of the mineral wealth of Russia is found in areas of high altitude.

Look at both the land use and product maps of Russia to answer the following question.

3. Why is this statement true? "The product and land use maps of Russia show that agricultural products are found on land that is used for farming and grazing." (Answer in three or four sentences.)

    _____

    _____

    _____

    _____

    _____

    _____

    _____

    _____

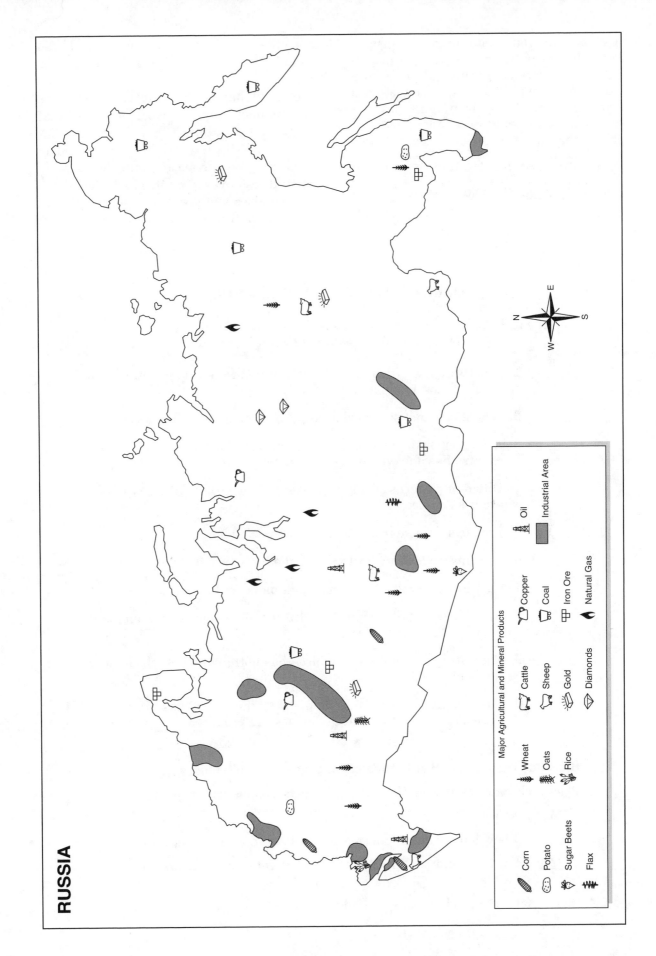

RUSSIA

Major Agricultural and Mineral Products

Corn
Potato
Sugar Beets
Flax

Wheat
Oats
Rice

Cattle
Sheep
Gold

Copper
Coal
Diamonds

Oil
Iron Ore
Natural Gas

Industrial Area

What did you write in your answer? Symbols are used on the product map to show the different agricultural products of Russia. On the product map, many of these symbols are in the western and southwestern areas of the country. The land use map shows that the western and southwestern areas are used for farming ▤ and grazing ▨ . It makes sense that the areas used for farming and grazing would have the most agricultural products. If you included these ideas, you wrote a good answer.

By studying natural vegetation, land use, and product maps, you can learn a great deal about a country. They show you what people may do for a living, what kind of trade may be carried on, and the types of natural resources a country has. The following exercises will give you more practice in using these three important kinds of maps.

USING WHAT YOU HAVE LEARNED

A. True or False: If every part of the statement is true, write **T.**
If any part of the statement is false, write **F.**

_____ 1. A natural vegetation map shows where different kinds of natural plant life are found in a country.

_____ 2. A land use map shows what kinds of food are grown in a country.

_____ 3. A product map shows what agricultural and mineral products a country has and where they are located in the country.

_____ 4. Different patterns on a land use map show how large areas of land are used by people.

_____ 5. Products are usually shown on a map by symbols.

_____ 6. Growing and caring for trees is called grazing.

_____ 7. Agricultural products are crops, animals, and minerals.

_____ 8. Rainfall, cold, heat, wind, and altitude have an influence on plant life and the growth of crops.

_____ 9. The natural vegetation of an area has nothing to do with the way the land is used.

_____ 10. The symbols on a product map show where products are grown, raised, or made, not what quantities are produced.

B. Study the maps of South America on pages 265 and 266.

Place a check mark next to the correct answers to questions 1 to 9.

1. Map A shows

____ (a) how much land in South America is used for farming.

____ (b) where different kinds of natural vegetation are found in South America.

____ (c) what products can be found in South America.

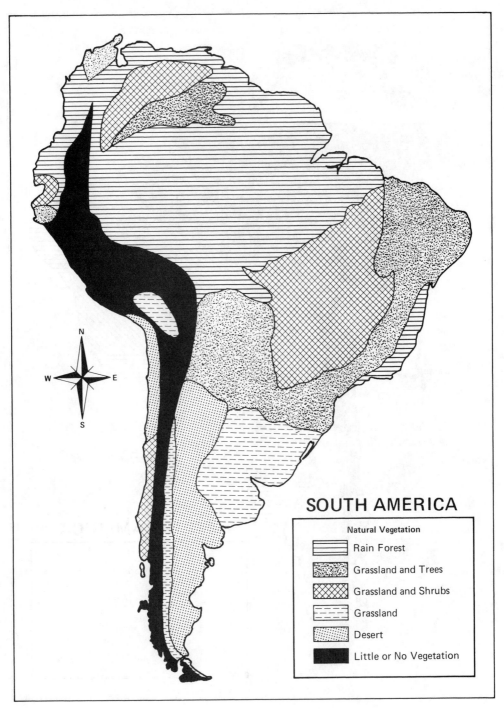

MAP A

2. Map B shows how

____ (*a*) much land in South America is covered by desert.

____ (*b*) much farming is done in South America.

____ (*c*) large areas of South America are used.

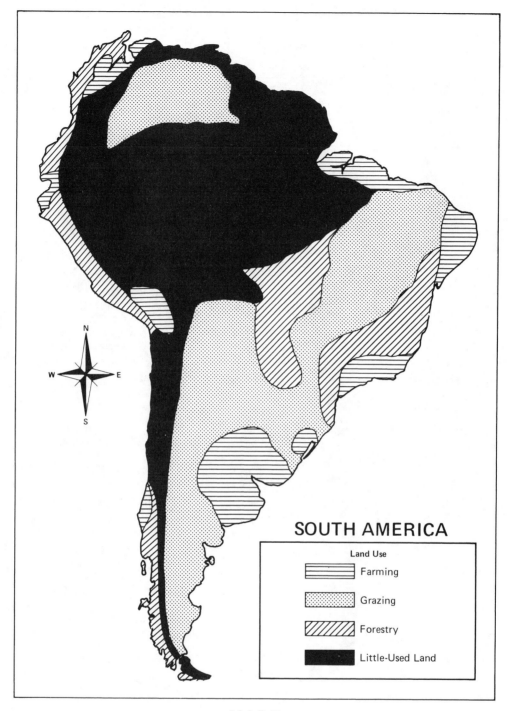

MAP B

3. The pattern on the natural vegetation map for grassland is

_____ (*a*) ▥

_____ (*b*) ▤

_____ (*c*) ▨

4. Most of the northern areas of South America have a natural vegetation of

_____ (*a*) rain forest.

_____ (*b*) grassland.

_____ (*c*) desert.

5. The pattern ▨ on the land use map stands for

_____ (*a*) forestry.

_____ (*b*) farming.

_____ (*c*) grazing.

6. Farming in South America is done

_____ (*a*) on land with various kinds of natural vegetation.

_____ (*b*) only on land that has a natural vegetation of grassland.

_____ (*c*) mostly on land that has a natural vegetation of grassland and shrubs.

7. Which one of the following statements is true?

_____ (*a*) Desert areas of South America have no vegetation.

_____ (*b*) Desert areas of South America are good for forestry.

_____ (*c*) Desert areas of South America are used for grazing animals.

8. Most of the land in South America is used for

_____ (*a*) forestry.

_____ (*b*) farming.

_____ (*c*) grazing or very little.

9. The areas on the natural vegetation map with the pattern ▨ are used mostly for

_____ (*a*) farming.

_____ (*b*) grazing.

_____ (*c*) forestry.

10. Explain in your own words the difference between a natural vegetation map and a land use map.

_____

_____

_____

_____

_____

_____

C. Study the following map of South Asia.

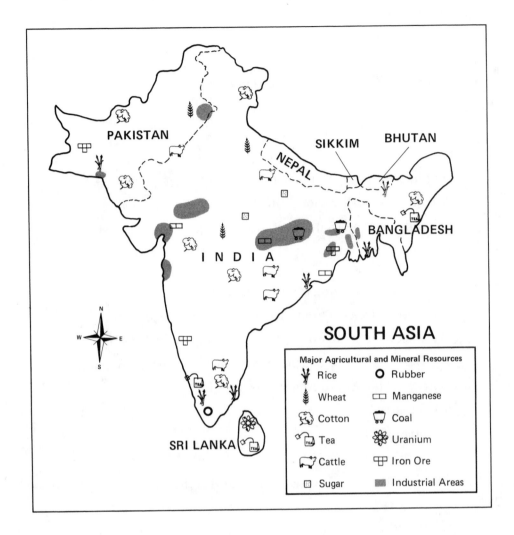

Place a check mark next to the correct answers to questions 1 to 9.

1. The map shows

____ (*a*) only the agricultural products of South Asia.

____ (*b*) only the mineral products of South Asia.

____ (*c*) the major agricultural and mineral products of South Asia.

____ (*d*) all of the agricultural and mineral products of South Asia.

2. Rubber is shown on the map by the symbol

____ (*a*) 🐑

____ (*b*) ⊞

____ (*c*) ●

____ (*d*) 🛒

3. Manganese is shown on the map by the symbol

____ (a) ⊡

____ (b) ⬕

____ (c) 🛒

____ (d) ✻

4. The symbol ▫ stands for

____ (a) cotton.

____ (b) sugar.

____ (c) coal.

____ (d) manganese.

5. Which one of the following symbols does NOT stand for an agricultural product?

____ (a) ⍦

____ (b) ⬝

____ (c) ⬝

____ (d) ⊞

6. Which mineral is mined in the island country of Sri Lanka?

____ (a) Coal

____ (b) Uranium

____ (c) Iron ore

____ (d) Manganese

7. The areas on the map colored ▩ are

____ (a) large farms.

____ (b) mines.

____ (c) industrial areas.

____ (d) seaports.

8. Which minerals can be found in the largest industrial area of India?

____ (a) Uranium, iron ore

____ (b) Coal, uranium

____ (c) Iron ore, manganese

____ (d) Coal, manganese

9 In India, rubber is produced mainly in the

____ (a) north.

____ (b) south.

____ (c) east.

____ (d) west.

10. India is more an agricultural country than an industrial country. How does the map show this to be true? (Answer in two or three sentences.)

_____

_____

_____

_____

_____

_____

D. Study the maps of China on pages 270 and 271.

Place a check mark next to the correct answers to questions 1 to 8.

1. Map A shows

_____ (*a*) where different kinds of natural plant life are found in China.

_____ (*b*) what crops are grown in China.

_____ (*c*) how large areas of China are used by people.

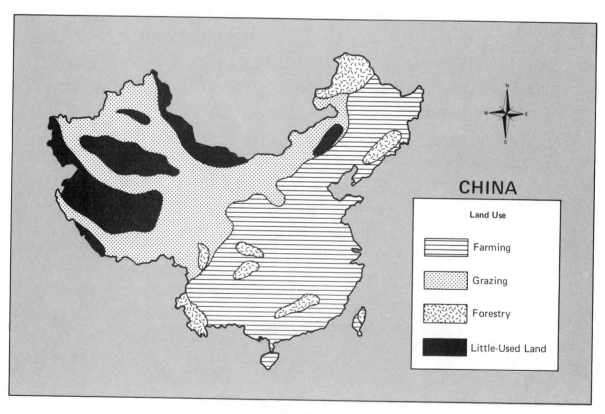

MAP A

2. Map B shows

    ____ (a) the major agricultural products of China and where they are found in the country.

    ____ (b) which agricultural products in China are found in the greatest quantity.

    ____ (c) the major agricultural and mineral products of China.

3. The area of China that is used mainly for farming is in the

    ____ (a) north.   ____ (b) east.   ____ (c) west.

4. Soybeans are shown on the product map by the symbol

    ____ (a)

    ____ (b)

    ____ (c)

5. The symbol 🌾 on the product map stands for

    ____ (a) rice.

    ____ (b) cotton.

    ____ (c) millet.

6. Forestry is carried out

    ____ (a) only in southern China.

    ____ (b) only in northern China.

    ____ (c) in many different areas of China.

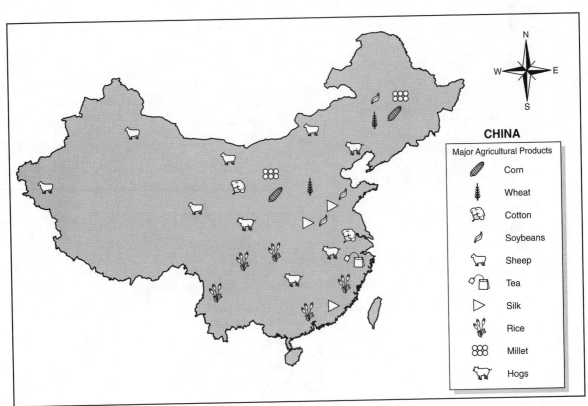

MAP B

7. There is only one picture representing tea on Map B. This means that

　　____ (a) the people in this area are the only Chinese who like to drink tea.

　　____ (b) the government allows tea to be grown in only this area.

　　____ (c) tea is grown mainly in this area of China.

8. Which statement is supported by the information on both maps?

　　____ (a) Some farming is done in the grazing areas of China.

　　____ (b) Silk is produced in the grazing areas of China.

　　____ (c) Hogs are raised mainly in the grazing areas of China.

9. Why are the following pattern and symbol found in the same area of China? ▨ 🐑 (Answer in two or three sentences.)

　　_____

　　_____

　　_____

　　_____

　　_____

10. How does the product map show that western China has relatively little farming? (Answer in one or two sentences.)

　　_____

　　_____

　　_____

　　_____

E. Study the maps of Africa on pages 273, 274, and 275.

Place a check mark next to the correct answers to questions 1 to 14.

1. Map A shows

　　____ (a) how many minerals are found in Africa.

　　____ (b) where different kinds of natural plant life are found in Africa.

　　____ (c) how much land in Africa is used for farming.

2. Map B shows

　　____ (a) where different kinds of natural vegetation are found in Africa.

　　____ (b) the important agricultural and mineral products of Africa.

　　____ (c) how large areas of land in Africa are used by people.

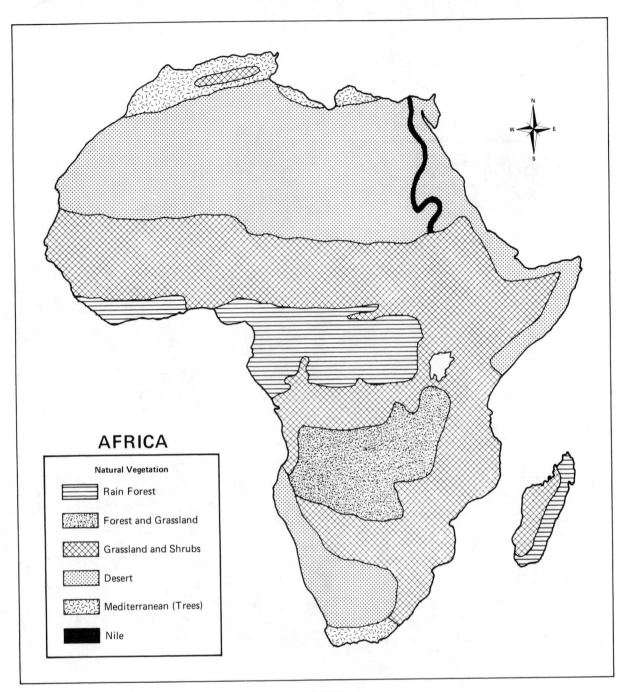

AFRICA

Natural Vegetation

	Rain Forest
	Forest and Grassland
	Grassland and Shrubs
	Desert
	Mediterranean (Trees)
	Nile

MAP A

3. Map C shows

_____ (*a*) the major agricultural and mineral products of Africa and where they are found.

_____ (*b*) how much coffee and cotton are grown in Africa.

_____ (*c*) that Africans work hard to grow many different kinds of crops.

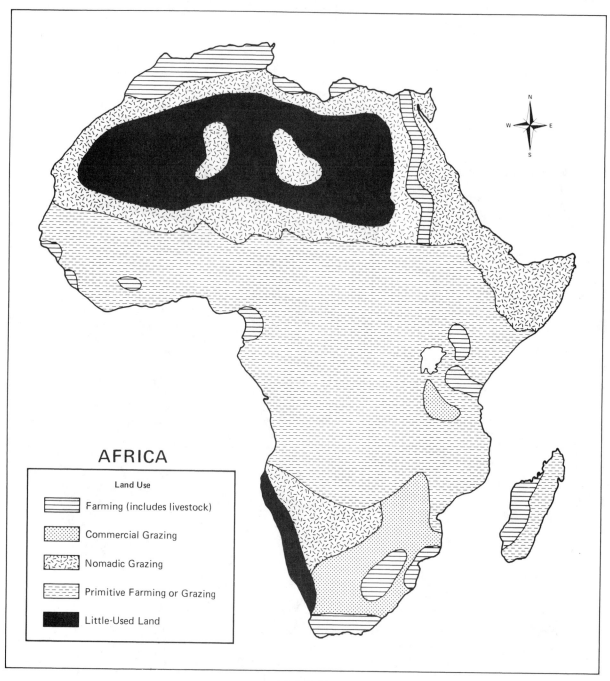

AFRICA

Land Use

	Farming (includes livestock)
	Commercial Grazing
	Nomadic Grazing
	Primitive Farming or Grazing
	Little-Used Land

MAP B

4. Most of northern Africa is covered with

_____ (a) grassland vegetation.

_____ (b) rain forest vegetation.

_____ (c) desert vegetation.

5. Rain forest vegetation is found in

_____ (a) northern Africa.

_____ (b) central Africa.

_____ (c) southern Africa.

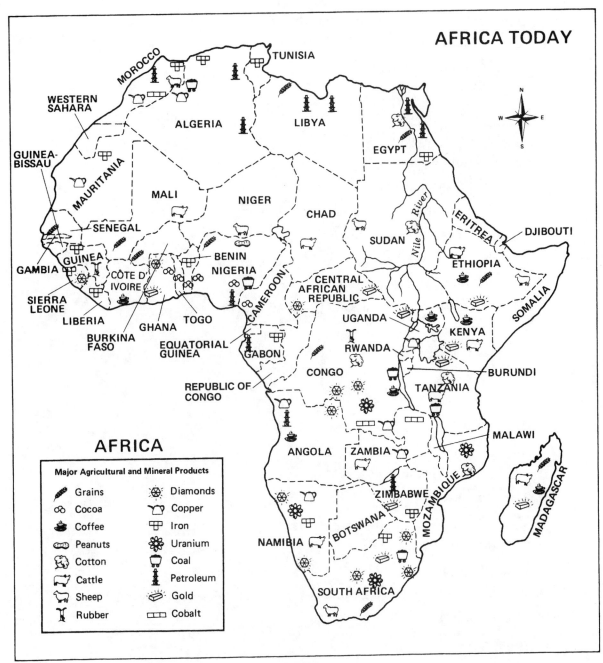

AFRICA TODAY

MOROCCO · TUNISIA · WESTERN SAHARA · ALGERIA · LIBYA · EGYPT · GUINEA-BISSAU · MAURITANIA · MALI · NIGER · CHAD · ERITREA · DJIBOUTI · SENEGAL · SUDAN · GAMBIA · GUINEA · BENIN · NIGERIA · ETHIOPIA · CÔTE D'IVOIRE · CAMEROON · CENTRAL AFRICAN REPUBLIC · SOMALIA · SIERRA LEONE · LIBERIA · GHANA · TOGO · UGANDA · KENYA · BURKINA FASO · EQUATORIAL GUINEA · GABON · RWANDA · REPUBLIC OF CONGO · CONGO · TANZANIA · BURUNDI · ANGOLA · ZAMBIA · MALAWI · MADAGASCAR · ZIMBABWE · MOZAMBIQUE · NAMIBIA · BOTSWANA · SOUTH AFRICA

Nile River

AFRICA

Major Agricultural and Mineral Products

- Grains
- Cocoa
- Coffee
- Peanuts
- Cotton
- Cattle
- Sheep
- Rubber
- Diamonds
- Copper
- Iron
- Uranium
- Coal
- Petroleum
- Gold
- Cobalt

MAP C

6. The area on the land use map with the pattern ▬ is shown on the natural vegetation map by the pattern

_____ (a) ▤

_____ (b) ▨

_____ (c) ▒

7. Most of the land in Africa is used for

_____ (a) commercial grazing.

_____ (b) nomadic grazing.

_____ (c) primitive farming or grazing.

8. The Nile River Valley is used mostly for

____ (*a*) farming.

____ (*b*) commercial grazing.

____ (*c*) nomadic grazing.

9. Which area of natural vegetation is NOT used for primitive farming?

____ (*a*) grassland and shrubs

____ (*b*) rain forest

____ (*c*) Mediterranean

10. Rubber comes from an area of Africa with

____ (*a*) grassland vegetation.

____ (*b*) desert vegetation.

____ (*c*) rain forest vegetation.

11. The land in the Nile River Valley is used to grow

____ (*a*) cotton.

____ (*b*) peanuts.

____ (*c*) cocoa.

12. Coffee is grown in

____ (*a*) Algeria.

____ (*b*) Nigeria.

____ (*c*) Côte d'Ivoire.

13. Uranium is found in

____ (*a*) Egypt.

____ (*b*) Namibia.

____ (*c*) Libya.

14. Which one of the following countries has mostly desert vegetation?

____ (*a*) Libya

____ (*b*) Congo

____ (*c*) Nigeria

15. How does the product map (Map C) show that South Africa must be a very rich country? (Answer in two or three sentences.)

_____

_____

_____

_____

_____

_____

F. Study the maps of mainland Southeast Asia on pages 277, 278, and 279.

F-1. Describe in your own words what each of the maps shows.

MAP A _____

_____

_____

_____

MAP B _____

_____

_____

_____

MAP C _____

_____

_____

_____

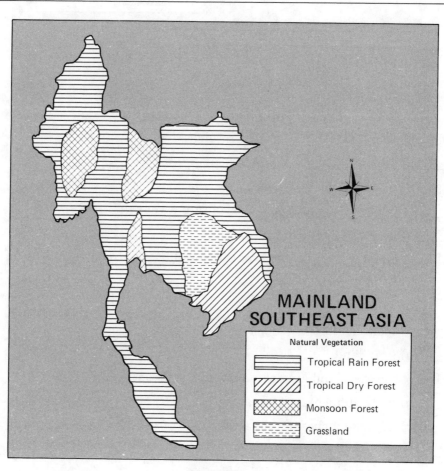

MAP A

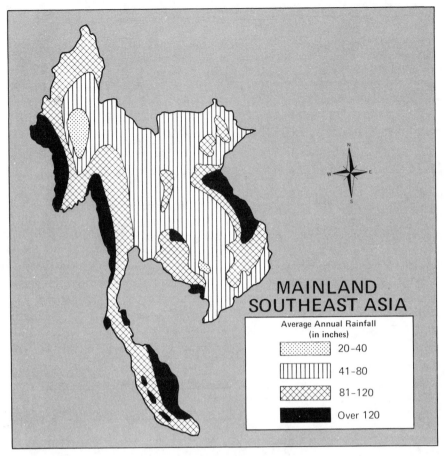

MAP B

F-2. Place a check mark next to the correct answers to questions 1 to 10.

1. Most of mainland Southeast Asia receives

_____ (*a*) under 40 inches of rain a year.

_____ (*b*) under 80 inches of rain a year.

_____ (*c*) between 41 and 120 inches of rain a year.

_____ (*d*) over 120 inches of rain a year.

2. Most of mainland Southeast Asia is covered by a natural vegetation of

_____ (*a*) tropical rain forest.

_____ (*b*) tropical dry forest.

_____ (*c*) monsoon forest.

_____ (*d*) grassland.

3. Most of the grassland area of mainland Southeast Asia receives

_____ (*a*) 20 to 40 inches of rain a year.

_____ (*b*) 41 to 80 inches of rain a year.

_____ (*c*) 81 to 120 inches of rain a year.

_____ (*d*) over 120 inches of rain a year.

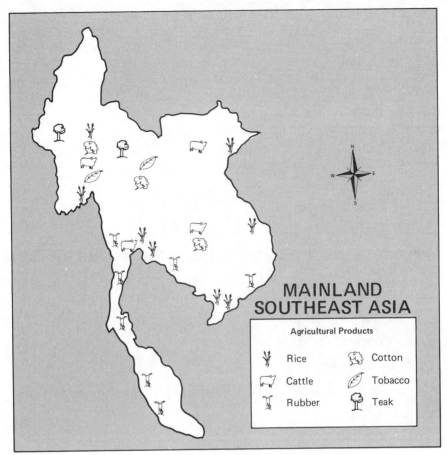

MAP C

4. Which one of the following symbols is NOT matched with its product?

____ (a) ¥ rice

____ (b) ⬭ tobacco

____ (c) 🐑 cotton

____ (d) ⛨ teak

5. The grassland area of mainland Southeast Asia is used

____ (a) to grow rice and tobacco.

____ (b) to produce rubber and teak.

____ (c) to grow cotton and to raise cattle.

____ (d) for hunting animals.

6. Most of the rubber is produced in areas with a yearly rainfall of

____ (a) under 20 inches.

____ (b) between 20 and 40 inches.

____ (c) between 41 and 80 inches.

____ (d) over 80 inches.

7. Which product is produced in eight different places?

_____ (a) Rice

_____ (b) Cotton

_____ (c) Tobacco

_____ (d) Rubber

8. Which products can be found in the tropical dry forest area?

_____ (a) Tobacco and cotton

_____ (b) Teak and cattle

_____ (c) Rice and rubber

_____ (d) Cotton and cattle

9. What is the main type of vegetation in the sections that have a rainfall over 120 inches?

_____ (a) Monsoon forest

_____ (b) Tropical rain forest

_____ (c) Tropical dry forest

_____ (d) Grassland

10. In mainland Southeast Asia, most of the rubber production is in the

_____ (a) north.

_____ (b) south.

_____ (c) east.

_____ (d) west.